Radical Transitions

Radical Transitions

The Survival and Revival
of Entrepreneurship in the GDR

Andreas Pickel

Westview Press

BOULDER • SAN FRANCISCO • OXFORD

Table 3.1 is reprinted from Anders Aslund, *Private Enterprise in Eastern Europe: The Non-Agricultural Private Sector in Poland and the GDR, 1945–83* (New York: St. Martin's Press, 1985). The permission of St. Martin's Press and Macmillan Ltd is gratefully acknowledged.

This Westview softcover edition is printed on acid-free paper and bound in library-quality, coated covers that carry the highest rating of the National Association of State Textbook Administrators, in consultation with the Association of American Publishers and the Book Manufacturers' Institute.

Published in 1992 in the United States of America by Westview Press, Inc., 5500 Central Avenue, Boulder, Colorado 80301-2847, and in the United Kingdom by Westview Press, 36 Lonsdale Road, Summertown, Oxford OX2 7EW

Library of Congress Cataloging-in-Publication Data
Pickel, Andreas.
  Radical transitions : the survival and revival of entrepreneurship
in the GDR / Andreas Pickel.
    p. cm.
  Includes bibliographical references and index.
  ISBN 0-8133-8354-4
  1. Germany (East)—Economic conditions. 2. Mixed economy—Germany
(East) 3. Entrepreneurship—Germany (East) I. Title.
HC290.78.P5 1992
338'.04'09431—dc20
                                                                91-34209
                                                                CIP

Printed and bound in the United States of America

The paper used in this publication meets the requirements
of the American National Standard for Permanence of Paper
for Printed Library Materials Z39.48-1984.

10   9   8   7   6   5   4   3   2   1

For my parents
and my teacher Fred Eidlin

Contents

Acknowledgments

This study would have been impossible without the assistance of many East Germans who helped me to establish contacts, collect information, and conduct interviews in the German Democratic Republic (GDR) in 1987 and 1988. At a time when East Germany was still under the rule of the Communist party (SED), and unofficial contacts with foreigners inquiring into matters of official policy were not without risk, private individuals and entrepreneurs, as well as representatives of various organizations and academic institutions, were most forthcoming in offering information, insights, and personal opinions on the subject of private enterprise and private-sector policy in the GDR. Special thanks are due to my friend Klaus Greupner from East Berlin, who helped me in numerous ways from the very beginning of my research. I am indebted to Professor Jörg Roesler and Irene Falconere (Academy of Sciences of the GDR), Professor Waltraud Falk (Humboldt-Universität), Eberhard Engel (East German Christian Democratic Party, [CDU]), Manfred Bogisch and Klaus-Dieter Müller (East German Liberal Democratic Party, [LDPD]), Eberhard Schwarz (formerly vice-chairman of the East Berlin Chamber of Handicraft), Werner Sommer (vice-chairman of the East Berlin Chamber of Trade and Commerce), and Vera Fleischer (editor of *Das Neue Handwerk,* East Berlin). I am especially grateful to the numerous private entrepreneurs whom I interviewed, in particular to Reinhard Meissner and his family from Coswig near Dresden, who in the course of my frequent visits have become dear friends.

In West Germany, I greatly benefited from the advice and encouragement of Professor Hartmut Zimmermann (Arbeitsbereich DDR-Forschung at the Free University of Berlin) and the access to materials provided by Maria Haendcke-Hoppe (Forschungsstelle für gesamtdeutsche wirtschaftliche und soziale Fragen). I would also like to thank Wolfgang Mleczkowski in West Berlin (former functionary of the East German Liberal Democratic Party), Siegfried Suckut (Arbeitsbereich Geschichte und Politik der DDR am Institut für Sozialwissenschaften der Universität Mannheim), and Katharina Belwe (Gesamtdeutsches Institut, Bonn) for their assistance in the early stages of my research.

This book is a revised and expanded version of my doctoral dissertation. I had the good fortune of receiving intellectual support, suggestions, and criticisms from two supervisors during all stages of my dissertation research and writing without being put in the awkward position of having to respond to two conflicting sets of expectations. I am therefore very much indebted to Professor Richard Cornell and Professor B. Michael Frolic (York University, Toronto) for making the work on my dissertation a constructive and enjoyable learning experience.

Andreas Pickel

Acronyms

BSB	Betrieb mit staatlicher Beteiligung (enterprise with state participation)
CC	Central Committee
CDU	Christlich-Demokratische Union (Christian Democratic Union)
CPSU	Communist Party of the Soviet Union
DBD	Demokratische Bauernpartei Deutschlands (Democratic Farmers' Party of Germany)
DWK	Deutsche Wirtschaftskommission (German Economic Commission)
ELG	Einkaufs-und Liefergenossenschaft (purchase and delivery cooperative)
EVG	Erzeugnis-und Versorgungsgruppen (product and supply groups)
FDGB	Freier Deutscher Gewerkschaftsbund (Free German Trade Union)
HO	Handelsorganisation ([state] trade organization)
GBl	Gesetzblatt (law gazette [of the GDR])
GHG	Großhandelsgesellschaft ([state] wholesale enterprise)
KIOSZ	Hungarian Association of Artisans
KPD	Kommunistische Partei Deutschlands (Communist Party of Germany)
KWV	Kommunale Wohnungsverwaltung (municipal housing administration)
LDPD	Liberal-Demokratische Partei Deutschlands (Liberal Democratic Party of Germany)
LPG	Landwirtschaftliche Produktionsgenossenschaft (agricultural cooperative/collective)
NDPD	National-Demokratische Partei Deutschlands (National Democratic Party of Germany)

PGH   Produktionsgenossenschaft des Handwerks (handicraft
        cooperative)

SED   Sozialistische Einheitspartei Deutschlands (Socialist Unity
        Party of Germany)

SMAD   Sowjetische Militäradministration in Deutschland (Soviet
        Military Administration in Germany)

SPD   Sozialdemokratische Partei Deutschlands (Social Democratic
        Party of Germany)

VKSK   Verband der Kleingärtner, Siedler und Kleintierzüchter
        (association of small-scale farmers, settlers, and small-animal
        breeders)

1

Introduction

Why do achievements differ so widely from aspirations? Because this is usually the case in social life. . . . Social life is not only a trial of strength between opposing groups: it is action within a more or less resilient or brittle framework of institutions and traditions, and it creates—apart from any conscious counteraction—many unforeseen reactions in this framework, some of them perhaps even unforeseeable.

—Karl Popper[1]

Scope and Explanatory Problems

This is a study of the private economy in the German Democratic Republic (GDR) from the end of World War II to early 1991. It examines the tension between Marxist-Leninist ideology—which demands the socialization of the privately owned means of production—and pragmatism—the policy makers' need to make compromises in the face of a variety of economic and political obstacles that stand in the way of realizing ambitious ideological goals. The analysis attempts to shed light on the general problem of the constraints and opportunities encountered by reformist policy-makers in bringing about a transition from an existing to a new socio-economic order. The historical and empirical subject-matter of this study is East Germany's private economy in the transition from a capitalist to a socialist society, its integration into socialism, and its development in the present transition towards a market economy.

The idea that the socialization of the means of production is a necessary and inevitable step in the transition to a socialist society has powerfully shaped the economic policies of Communist rulers. The assumption was that the elimination of private ownership was necessary in order to establish the political hegemony of the working class and its Party by depriving the propertied classes of their economic power base, and as a basic precondition for the rational and efficient management of society's economic affairs by abolishing the capitalist market with its incurable

1

anarchic and exploitative tendencies. The type of centrally planned economy developed in the Soviet Union under Stalin since the late 1920s became the model for economic restructuring in all Eastern European countries that fell under the military and political hegemony of the Soviet Union after World War II. The fact that Communist political power could not be effectively challenged after the imposition of one-party dictatorship explains why the fundamental remaking of economic ownership structures could be carried out in spite of its often horrendous social and economic consequences.

The present analysis of private-sector policy in the GDR begins with an intellectual problem that has rarely been noticed as such, and that has never been systematically examined. The GDR, until the advent of *perestroika* widely considered Moscow's staunchest ally under the rule of an ideologically orthodox Communist party (SED), has had a peculiar history with respect to its private economy. Unlike the other Soviet-bloc countries,[2] it preserved a mixed-ownership economy throughout the 1950s and 1960s. The present study will attempt to resolve this apparent inconsistency between ideology and reality in the GDR.

Poland, Hungary and the Soviet Union, which at various points during the 1980s began reintroducing forms of private enterprise, exacerbated the problems of corruption and illegality in their economies, as well as keeping private entrepreneurs in a state of existential insecurity. Contrary to the policy makers' intentions, the newly established private firms were rejected by the official socialist system. None of these problems were characteristic for the East German private sector during the same period. This poses the second explanatory problem. What accounts for the surprising legality, stability, and security in the GDR private economy of the 1980s?

With the rapid marketization of the East German economy in 1990 as a result of the monetary and economic union and the unification of Germany, apparently ideal conditions were created for the private sector. However, private investment fell far short of widely held expectations, the existing private economy is struggling to survive, and the state economy virtually collapsed. The spectre of permanent de-industrialization and catastrophic rates of unemployment is haunting the former GDR. This poses the third explanatory problem. What accounts for the fact that the rapid creation of very favourable political and economic conditions for the private sector has produced a profound social and economic crisis?

The Explanatory Framework

The framework for analysis that will be presented in this section is primarily addressed to the first two explanatory problems of this study which are posed by the survival and functioning of the GDR private economy under Communism. While this framework is developed in critical opposition to conceptions and assumptions about the nature of Communist regimes, its theoretical implications extend beyond the field of Communist studies. They apply to any attempts to reform society in a radical fashion, and thus to the present radical restructuring in East Germany and other post-Communist countries. The usefulness of this theoretical framework will therefore have to prove itself in its broader applicability to problems of radical reform, in particular to the third explanatory problem stated above which is posed by the failures of the current radical transition strategy in East Germany.

The explanatory framework will be introduced in the following fashion. I will begin by identifying assumptions about the nature of Communist regimes that let the GDR private economy appear as a surprising phenomenon, and suggest why these assumptions are unsatisfactory. Next, I will consider some potential solutions to the explanatory problems of this study that are based on different theoretical assumptions and show why they too must be considered inadequate. Finally, I will present an approach that can resolve the explanatory problems on the basis of an alternative set of theoretical assumptions.

Two basic assumptions concerning Soviet-type regimes are inadequate for an understanding of the history of the private sector in the GDR because they systematically misguide thinking about the relationship between ideology and policy in Communist regimes. The first of these assumptions is that the fundamental goal of Communist rulers to establish a centrally planned economy based on the national control of the means of production required the comprehensive nationalization of private productive property. The second, closely related assumption is that the dictatorial political power of Communist regimes has permitted them to realize this goal. I will refer to this as the "quasi-omnipotence of Communist rulers" thesis.[3]

These assumptions, to be sure, correspond to important aspects of economic and political reality. Guided and legitimized by the basic principles of Marxism-Leninism, Communist regimes everywhere have carried out nationalization based on their monopoly of political power. However, these assumptions are overly simplistic and therefore ultimately misleading. Nowhere have Communist regimes been able fully to eliminate private economic activity, nor have they always and uncompromisingly sought to do so.[4] There exists a rich variety of nationally and culturally specific forms of legal and illegal private economic activity in all Communist countries.[5] Each Communist regime has its own history of shaping, and being influenced by, its respective private sector. But only recently have these aspects become the subject of systematic analysis.[6]

The two assumptions identified above draw attention to unquestionably crucial aspects of these regimes—the ideological goal of the socialization of the means of production and the dictatorial political power at their disposal. At the same time, they let evidence to the contrary appear as marginal or due to temporary contingencies rather than as the outcome of *systemic obstacles* to political power.

The explanatory problem which is posed by the fact that an orthodox Communist party like the East German SED preserved a mixed economy for well over two decades after coming to power might be resolved by an "intuitive" approach. One could produce a historical-descriptive account of the evolution of the private sector in the GDR by drawing on a variety of explanatory models, and by stressing the unique and contingent aspects of the East German case. While such an "intuitive" and eclectic approach might produce a rich and illuminating explanation of the anomalous history of the GDR private economy, it would necessarily be of primarily historical rather than of more general theoretical interest. While one of the purposes of this study is to provide a historical reconstruction of the evolution of the private economy in the GDR, its theoretical goal is to explore the relationship between ideology and policy in more general terms. Unless our initial assumptions about this relationship are made explicit, such a historical reconstruction will by itself be of little theoretical significance.

Two theoretically interesting ways of resolving the explanatory problem are the following. First, the SED, it could be argued, like all Communist parties in power, maintained a facade of ideological orthodoxy[7] for purposes of legitimation, while its private-sector policies, like most other policies, were in fact shaped by pragmatic considerations, bureaucratic structures and attitudes, and the imperatives of modern industrial society. In other words, ideology played no significant role in policymaking for the private sector. This will be referred to as the "ultimate irrelevance of ideology" thesis.[8] Its solution of the problem, however, is unsatisfactory. One reason is that the SED repeatedly—and as late as 1972—carried out large-scale nationalization campaigns, so we would be faced with the new explanatory problem of why a Communist party with a pragmatic approach to the private sector persevered in its attempts to nationalize it.

A second solution that could be proposed is that, while the SED was indeed an ideologically orthodox Communist party, its leaders, like all Communist leaders, adopted a pragmatic approach whenever this appeared to be in the interest of preserving or strengthening the Party's (or their own) political power. This will be referred to as the "primacy of power politics" thesis.[9] At first glance, this solution is quite plausible. It is supported by the fact that in the late 1940s and early 1950s, both Soviet policy and the open border to West Germany imposed severe limitations on the SED's political power and in effect restrained its leaders' ideological ambitions. However, this solution is invalidated by the fact that when the SED had consolidated its political power in the early 1960s[10], it marked the beginning of the most prosperous and stable period for the East German private sector.

I have discussed four possible approaches of dealing with the explanatory problems of this study, and all four were found to be inadequate. Before presenting my alternative, the basic theoretical assumptions contained in each approach need to be stated explicitly to reveal the ultimate source of their inadequacy. The eclectic or "intuitive" approach makes no *a priori* assumptions about the relationship between ideology and policy, but prefers to draw on different, and possibly mutually inconsistent, models, depending on the individual events under analysis. The assumption underlying the "quasi-omnipotence of Communist regimes" thesis is that to the extent that Communist rulers are seriously committed to specific ideological goals such as comprehensive nationalization, their virtually unlimited political power will allow them to do so. The "ultimate irrelevance of ideology" thesis denies that ideology informs and guides policy, and therefore rejects ideology as a meaningful explanatory variable. The "primacy of power politics" thesis, while not categorically excluding the influence of ideology on policy, conceives ideology as an instrument in the struggle of elites and individuals for power.

The inadequacy of both the "quasi-omnipotence of Communist regimes" thesis and the "primacy of power politics" thesis stems from its close resemblance to what Karl Popper has described as the "conspiracy theory of society."

It is the view that an explanation of a social phenomenon consists in the discovery of the men or groups who are interested in the occurrence of this phenomenon (sometimes it is a hidden interest which has to be revealed), and who have planned and conspired to bring it about.[11]

The problem is not, as Popper points out, that conspiracies never occur. Nor is his contention—and this suggests where the weakness of the "ultimate irrelevance of ideology" thesis lies—that the conscious motives of actors play no significant role in social causation because "ultimately" only socio-economic structures or historical forces matter.

Of course, we act with certain aims in mind; but apart from these aims (which we may or may not really achieve) there are always certain unwanted consequences of our actions; and usually these unwanted consequences cannot be eliminated. To explain why they cannot be eliminated is the major task of social theory.[12]

Thus, the fact that the East German Communists did not carry out a comprehensive nationalization of the private economy need not be interpreted as evidence for the fact that they did not intend to do so—because considerations of political power prevented them from doing so, or because they had altogether abandoned the ideological goal. Rather, the survival of the GDR private economy may have been an *unwanted consequence* of the actions and policies of the Communist regime in its pursuit of this basic ideological goal. What does this imply for a theoretically more adequate approach to our explanatory problems? As Popper has further suggested:

> [It is] the *main task of the theoretical social sciences . . . to trace the unintended social repercussions of intentional human actions.*[13] [. . .] And it is, especially, the task of the social sciences to analyse in this way the existence and the functioning of *institutions* (such as police forces or insurance companies or schools or governments) and of social *collectives* (such as states or nations or classes or other social groups). . . . [T]he social theorist should recognize that the persistence of institutions and collectives creates a problem to be solved in terms of an analysis of individual social actions and their unintended (and often unwanted) social consequences, as well as their intended ones.[14]

The basic theoretical assumptions for the explanatory framework of the present study can now be formulated. (Assumptions 1–3 are consciously phrased in contradistinction to the basic assumptions of the approaches discussed above.)

1. Even to the extent that Communist rulers are committed to realizing specific ideological goals such as comprehensive nationalization, the fact that their political power is limited in principle by institutional and structural realities will not always allow them to do so, and will rarely allow them to carry out such measures in a planned fashion.
2. In many cases, ideology informs and guides policy. In principle, therefore, it is a meaningful explanatory variable.
3. For the same reason, it is inadequate to conceptualize ideological goals as merely instruments in the struggle of elites and individuals for power, for this would ignore the cognitive and programmatic functions of ideology for policymaking.
4. While ideological goals may inspire and shape policies, it is primarily their unintended consequences which explain the gap between desired results and actual outcomes.
5. Such unintended consequences of policies can be understood by examining their design and implementation in their specific political, economic, and institutional context.

6. The meaning of ideological goals may be adapted and revised, rather than being simply abandoned, in response to the unintended consequences of previous attempts to realize them.

The explanatory framework for the present study, presented schematically in Figure 1.1, can now be summarized. Crucial for an explanation of the unorthodox private-sector policy of the SED are a range of situational factors, as well as the intended and unintended consequences of private-sector policies. I distinguish five sets of situational factors:

1. external factors: the special German situation and Soviet policy;
2. economic factors: the existing economic structure of an advanced industrial region, as well as the specific economic objectives and problems of the time;
3. historical factors: legal and administrative traditions, entrepreneurial and artisanal traditions, public attitudes;
4. political factors: institutions such as small non-Communist parties, power struggles and leadership changes in the SED;
5. intended and unintended consequences: past private-sector policy successes and failures and their institutionalization (e.g. regulations, organizations, forms of economic and social integration, but also ideological reconceptualizations).

Situational factors shape the specific problem context within which the regime designs and implements its private-sector policy. The perception of what is desirable and feasible is filtered through existing ideological conceptions. Any policy has both intended and unintended consequences. They enter as new situational factors and in this way influence subsequent policy decisions. For example, unintended consequences of radical measures against the private economy, such as severe market imbalances or entrepreneurs leaving the country in large numbers, have a direct effect on political decision-makers and may lead them to reverse their measures. Most important, the intended and unintended consequences of preserving a private sector over time lead to its gradual institutionalization and integration into the larger socio-economic and political-ideological system. As an institutionalized and integrated subsystem, the private sector becomes valued for its economic contribution and looses its ideological "edge."

Summary of the Argument

The theoretical argument of the present study can now be summarized. I will begin with a restatement of the two main explanatory problems and

Figure 1.1   Schematic Representation of Explanatory Framework

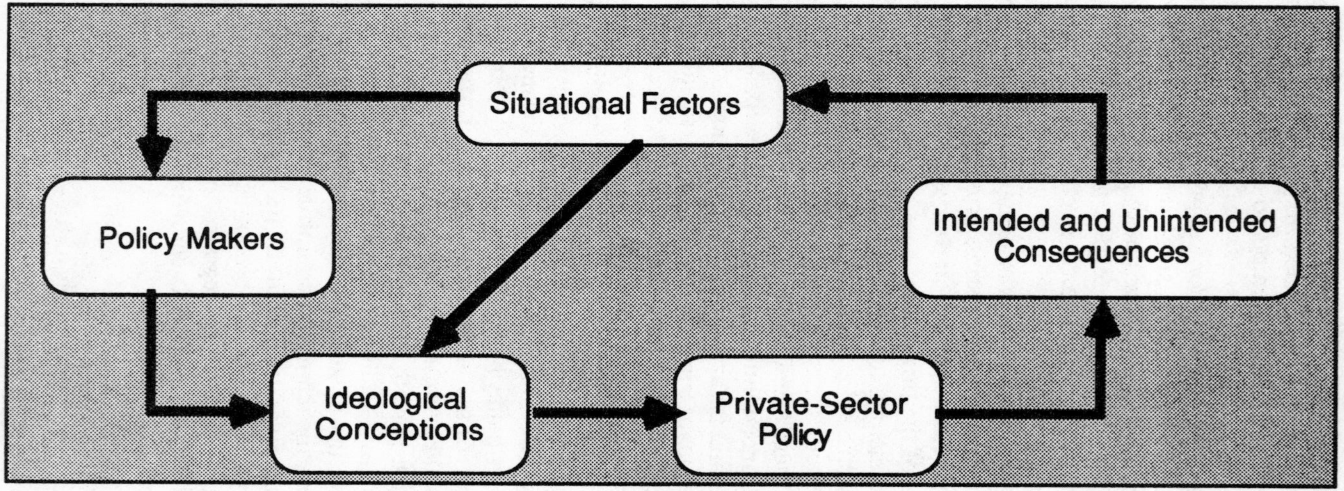

Source: Author

advance the central theses designed to resolve them. The present analysis of private-sector policy in the GDR takes as its point of departure an intellectual problem that has rarely been noticed and never been systematically explained. The GDR, until the advent of *perestroika* widely considered Moscow's staunchest ally under the rule of an ideologically orthodox Communist party (SED), has had a peculiar history with respect to its private economy. Unlike the other Soviet-bloc countries, it preserved a mixed-ownership economy throughout the 1950s and 1960s. The attempt to resolve this apparent inconsistency between ideology and reality in the GDR will take the form of a historical analysis. Its central thesis is that the emergence of a mixed ownership structure was an *unintended consequence* of what the Communists regarded as temporary compromises between their orthodox ideological goals and political and economic constraints. These compromises led to the gradual "organic" integration of the private sector into the socialist economy, and to its increasing ideological assimilation. This will be referred to as the *institutional integration thesis.*

Poland, Hungary, and the Soviet Union, which at various points during the 1980s began reintroducing forms of private enterprise, exacerbated the problems of corruption and illegality in their economies, as well as keeping private entrepreneurs in a state of existential insecurity. Contrary to the policy makers' intentions, the newly established private firms were rejected by the official socialist system. None of these problems were characteristic for the East German private sector during the same period. This poses the second explanatory problem. What accounts for the surprising legality, stability, and security in the GDR private economy of the 1980s? The attempt to account for the absence of private sector problems commonly encountered by other Communist countries in the 1980s follows an empirical analysis of the specific forms of economic, political, and social integration of the East German private sector into the socialist state. The surprising legality, stability, and security in the GDR's private economy, it will be argued, is a result of its historical evolution as an integral component of the official socialist system. This will be referred to as the *institutional continuity thesis.*

The theoretical argument can be summarized as follows. The unresolved status of Germany in the post-war years and the vulnerable position of the East German regime posed political obstacles to rapid nationalization, and forced the SED to be more sensitive than other Communist regimes to the social and economic consequences of fundamental restructuring. Rather than radically abolishing private ownership, administrative means and institutional forms of controlling the private economy evolved. The survival and gradual functional integration of private enterprise into the socialist economy was an *unintended consequence* of what SED leaders considered temporary, pragmatic compromises. Not until the 1960s did the SED ideologically recognize the resulting mixed ownership structure which had emerged as its own special model of socialism. Ideas had finally been adjusted to reality.

With the reassertion of ideological orthodoxy in the early 1970s, the size of the private economy was significantly reduced. What is of particular theoretical significance, however, is the stability, legality, and economic security in the remaining private sector in the GDR in the late 1970s and 1980s. This contrasts sharply with conditions in the recently revived private economies in other Soviet-bloc countries. The explanation proposed here is that unlike these countries, the GDR had an *institutional infrastructure* for the private economy that had evolved over three decades of Communist rule—entrepreneurial traditions and attitudes, a functioning regulatory framework, public administration and forms of integration into the state economy, limited forms of interest representation, and favourable public attitudes. In short, as a result of *institutional continuity,* an existing private sector was successfully integrated into its economic, social, and political environment.

The present analysis of private-sector policy in the GDR suggests that a gradualist strategy of economic transformation in many respects may be more beneficial than a forced wholesale introduction of a new economic order. The reason is that any new order, regardless of how efficiently it is presumed to function in principle, must be introduced into, and adapted to, an existing socio-economic formation—an institutional infrastructure, social traditions and attitudes, economic and cultural practices, and political interests. There is no clean canvas on which reformers could draw a new socio-economic order. Many of the disastrous consequences of the Stalinist model were a result of the way in which it was introduced—in a wholesale fashion with ruthless disregard for the existing socio-economic formation.

These considerations suggest why the radical transition strategy pursued in the unified Germany is producing a range of serious and unexpected problems. With the monetary and economic union between the FRG and the GDR in July 1990 and the unification of Germany in October of the same year, East Germany was set on a course of rapid and wholesale socio-economic transformation. By the spring of 1991, it had become evident that this radical transition strategy could not produce the quick successes that had been widely expected. Rather than launching the East German economy on a path of self-sustained development, instant marketization led to the virtual collapse of the state sector and skyrocketing rates of unemployment. Surprisingly, even the East German private sector failed to perform nearly as well as had been anticipated.

From the vantage point of the argument proposed here, these unintended consequences of rapid and wholesale change did not come entirely unexpected. Although the West German political and economic order functions exceedingly well in West Germany, its transplantation to East Germany clashed with the existing institutional infrastructure, social traditions and attitudes, and economic and cultural practices that have evolved over four decades of socialism. Of course, institutions and individuals can change, but adaptation takes time. The virtual collapse of the East German economy and the resulting enormous rates of unemployment, I will argue, are unintended consequences of a radical strategy of change. In their attempt to deal with these problems, today's policy-makers will find themselves forced to revert to a gradualist strategy of reform. While some of these consequences may have been avoidable had a less radical approach been followed from the start, they may now prove very difficult to reverse.

A Brief Note on the Concepts of
Ideology and Institution

The presentation of the explanatory framework and the summary of the theoretical argument are necessarily abstract. The following section of this chapter will add empirical and historical substance to these theoretical considerations. In order to avoid unnessecary confusion with respect to two central concepts of this study, a clarifying note on the way "ideology" and "institution" are understood should be inserted here.

As the reader will be aware, the *concept of ideology* has been employed in many different theoretical and political contexts, and it evokes a broad range of meanings and significance. While an ideology such as Marxism-Leninism may be understood as a comprehensive *Weltanschauung,* a system of political symbols for the legitimation of Communist regimes, or even a theoretical social or applied policy science, I am here interested in its more limited function as a theory of and program for social change. All I assume for the purposes of this study is that an ideology contains certain programmatic elements that may be more or less directly translatable into corresponding policies. Evidently, some such elements are patently diffuse and leave a large gap between programmatic statement and policy. A study of the relationship between Marxist-Leninist ideology and private-sector policy is in a relatively fortunate position since, as Barrington Moore has observed, the "transfer of the means of production to the community as a whole represents the closest congruence between prerevolutionary anticipations and post-revolutionary facts of any aspect of Bolshevik doctrine and behavior."[15]

The *concept of institution* is central to the theoretical argument of this study. It is my contention that the survival and stability of the East German private economy is a result of its largely unintended institutional integration into the economic, political, and social system of GDR socialism. The concept of institution is here taken to refer not only to private firms and to such organizations as Chambers of Handicraft, small political parties, and local administrative departments, all of which played an important role in this process of integration. It also includes *traditions*—business and administrative *practices,* such as high standards of professional ethics among private entrepreneurs, and an impersonal and efficient ("Prussian") approach on the part of civil servants, as well as public *attitudes* and widely shared *values.* Only some of the more important and most "visible" institutions can be systematically analyzed in the present study. However, it should be noted that the gradual process of reducing the scope of the private economy and of integrating it into the East German socialist system may have preserved many functioning institutions that had grown over a long period of time and that, if a wholesale strategy of nationalization had been followed, might have been completely lost—both for East German socialism and for East Germany's presently emerging post-communist socio-economic order.[16]

The GDR Private Sector as an Anomaly: The Historical and Empirical Context

The East German private sector has represented an anomaly in the comparative context of Communist regimes. The first anomaly is, most visibly, quantitative. While sweeping nationalizations reduced the private economies of Hungary, Czechoslovakia, and Poland (with the exception of its agricultural sector) to negligeable size and marginal existence by the early 1950s, private enterprise in the GDR continued to play a significant role until the early 1970s. At the end of 1971, the largest private enterprise in the GDR had 873 employees, and 38 out of a total of 2,976 private industrial firms employed more than 100 people.[17] With a workforce of over 1 million, the private and semi-private[18] economy accounted for 16 percent of the East German workforce.[19]

In 1972, about 10,000 private and semi-private enterprises with almost 480,000 employees were transformed into state-owned enterprises. The size of the East German private economy was reduced to more "normal" proportions. After a period of uncertainty and benign neglect, in 1976 the SED made a renewed commitment to the remaining private sector—approximately 85,000 handicraft firms and 40,000 retail trade firms. A policy of promoting the private sector was consistently maintained to the end of the Communist era in 1989. Less spectacular though nevertheless surprising is the fact that in 1980 the GDR (with 5.2 percent) still had a larger share of its non-agricultural workforce in the private sector than both Poland (4.9 percent) and Hungary (3 percent).[20] In the 1980s, developments in the private sectors of other Soviet-bloc economies became increasingly complex. Both Poland and Hungary adopted more favourable policies starting in the early 1980s, and the Soviet Union under Gorbachev launched its first comprehensive private sector reform program since the NEP in the 1920s.

With the rapid expansion of the private economy in Poland and the Soviet Union and the moderate growth in Hungary in the 1980s, the GDR no longer qualifies as a special case in purely quantitative terms. In fact, between 1976—the year the policy of promotion was adopted by the SED—and 1989, the size and structure of the private sector remained almost unchanged. What at first glance may appear as stagnation in the East German private economy turns out to be an impressive stability. For practically none of the problems that have plagued private-sector policy in Hungary,[21] Poland,[22] and the Soviet Union[23] played any significant role in the implementation of the GDR policy of promoting private economic initiative. This represents the second aspect of the anomaly.

Illegal practices and corruption in the process of securing supplies, licenses, or "favours" from local officials remained on a modest scale. The public hostility to private enterprise so prevalent in the Soviet Union was almost non-existent in the GDR. Further, there was virtually no ideologically-motivated resistance on the part of local officials responsible for the implementation of the policy. Finally, state enterprises did not show any significant resistance to the private sector. To be sure, private firms in the GDR were not without problems, chief among them inadequate material and technical supplies. In addition, licensing was for the most part handled restrictively by local organs. On the other hand, the practice of ascertaining the "objective" need for the services or products of applicants insured that those in possession of a license were practically guaranteed supplies sufficient to maintain a secure economic existence. This may be contrasted with the more liberal licensing provisions in Hungary, under which new entrants into the private artisanal sector preferred operating on a part-time basis because of considerable economic and political uncertainty. Under the even more extreme conditions in Poland and the Soviet Union, the operation of a private firm implied high legal and political risks due to the necessity to tap into illegal supply channels and to bribe local officials. In all these respects, the East German private economy in the 1980s remained an anomaly in the Soviet bloc.

It might be tempting to account for this anomalous situation of stability, legality, and security in the GDR private sector in terms of cultural factors. The Prussian legal and administrative tradition, the Protestant work ethic, and the German propensity to obey the powers that be are stereotypes that immediately spring to mind, though events of the fall of 1989 have deprived at least the latter cliche of some of its plausibility. While cultural factors such as these no doubt play some role, it would be utterly simplistic to suggest them as the main explanation for the situation in the East German private economy in the 1980s. Cultural factors exist, survive and change in the course of socio-economic and political development. Their influence and effect can only be gauged if placed in their social and institutional context.

For a wider conceptualization of the problem situation, let us recall the general considerations discussed earlier concerning the systemic obstacles faced by Communist regimes. I have suggested that even radical measures aimed at fundamentally remaking the existing order must be taken in the framework of existing socio-economic structures and institutions. The more sweeping the measures, the greater their likelihood for generating unintended consequences that may prove very costly in both economic and political terms. More or less consciously, the regime will work out compromise solutions with *existing* structures and institutions. We can now return to the comparative perspective to illustrate this argument.

In both Poland and the Soviet Union, the regimes adopted radical measures of private sector liberalization. In Poland, this was primarily a response to the highly unstable political conditions since the rise of Solidarity and the country's economic and institutional disintegration. Rapidly losing its legitimacy, the regime acted from a position of weakness and in an unsystematic fashion, having little control over the implementation of its policy at the local level. In the Soviet Union, the economic and institutional crisis was becoming equally severe, but the reformist leadership took the initiative before the delegitimation of Communist power had crippled its ability to take the lead. The main political opponents to private sector liberalization were to be found in the Party, particularly at the local level of implementation. In Hungary, neither the economic disintegration nor the loss of legitimacy were quite as far advanced as in Poland and the Soviet Union, respectively. However, the regime did not follow up on its rhetorical endorsement of the private sector with effective policies.

The situation for each regime differed not only with respect to the political and economic conditions under which private sector reform polices were shaped. More important, each regime was situated in a different institutional and ideological context. While political and economic conditions are paramount in accounting for the *genesis* of the various private-sector policies, the institutional and ideological context can explain their *results and consequences*. In Poland, there was little ideological resistance to a liberalization of private enterprise, but the institutional infrastructure and traditions[24] insured that the expansion of the private sector would further promote corruption and collusion between private entrepreneurs and local officials, creating great profit opportunities for both. In the Soviet Union, the private sector reforms came as an ideological shock. Appropriately designed for a functioning market economy, they encountered a barren institutional landscape that offered them little support and enormous opposition, sabotage, and persecution. In Hungary, the situation was least dramatic. Ideological resistance was relatively low, the liberalization measures unspectacular, and the existing institutional infrastructure sufficient to prevent a rapid and radical decline into illegality and corruption.

The main reasons for the stability, legality, and security characteristic for the East German private sector in the 1980s can now be identified. First, the SED did not act under enormous political and economic pressure in designing its private-sector policy. There was political stability and, compared to Poland, the Soviet Union, and Hungary, relative economic prosperity. Second, the institutional and social environment for the implementation of the policy was extremely favourable. The 1972 nationalization had eliminated only private and semi-private industry, but not private handicraft[25] and trade. While it created temporary uncertainty in the remaining private sector, the period until the SED's return to a positive commitment to private enterprise in 1976 was of short duration. It did not destroy the institutional infrastructure for the private economy that had evolved over three decades of Communist rule—a functioning regulatory framework, entrepreneurial traditions and attitudes, public administration, forms of integration into the state economy, the Chambers as organizational links between the state and the private sector, interest representation by the Bloc parties,[26] and public acceptance of private enterprise. In short, an existing private sector was successfully integrated into its economic, social, and political environment. My contention is that the stability, legality, and security in the East German private economy—which makes it into an anomalous case in the Eastern European context in the 1980s—is a result of its institutional continuity.

Ed Hewitt, in his study of economic reform under Gorbachev, has argued that:

> Any partial reform must be scrutinized . . . to reach a judgment on how well it will fit into the existing system, or, to put it another way, what the probability is that the old system will "reject" this "implant." Although not all partial reforms are doomed to fail, probably a good starting assumption is that partial reforms will create tensions that will lead Soviet leaders either to reverse the reforms or to introduce further reforms.[27]

The *institutional integration thesis* proposed here means that the partial reform of the GDR private sector in the 1970s and 1980s fit well into the existing system. The absence of the problems encountered in private sector reform in Poland, the Soviet Union, and Hungary—i.e., the stability, legality, and security in the GDR—is accounted for by the fact that the "implant" was not "rejected" by the system. The private sector already formed an integral part of the socialist economy. Aslund has suggested that the prospects for the successful implementation of the new private-sector policy in the Soviet Union depends on "how far economic, political and legal reform as a whole goes. Every link has to be in its place, if the social chain shall grow strong enough to carry cooperatives and individual enterprise."[28] GDR policy makers in the 1980s had a distinct advantage in that no significant economic, political, and legal reforms were necessary to support a positive private-sector policy. The social chain was already strong enough.

An account of the evolution of this favorable policy environment in the GDR is the subject of Chapters 2 and 3. Chapters 4–7 examine the structure of the East German private economy in the 1980s and its forms of economic, political, and social integration into society. Chapter 8 analyzes the "democratic awakening" of the institutions of the private sector in the fall of 1989 during and after the collapse of the Communist regime. Chapter 9 examines the implications of the radical transition to a new order for the East German private sector and explores the relevance of the theoretical argument informing this study for the problems produced by East Germany's second radical transition since the summer of 1990.

State of the Literature

The scholarly literature on the East German private economy is not extensive. Scholarly works in English are practically non-existent, the major exception being a comparative study of the East German and Polish private economies by Swedish economist Anders Aslund, which will be discussed in more detail below. Not surprisingly, most Western academic studies of the GDR have been produced by scholars from the Federal Republic. While there is a small number of articles and monographs on specific aspects or sectors of the private economy, most of which were written in the 1950s and 1960s, no comprehensive West German analysis of private-sector policy in the GDR has been published to date. The most consistent and detailed analyses since the mid-1960s, primarily of the private handicraft sector in the GDR, have been produced by Maria Haendcke-Hoppe and Karl C. Thalheim from the West Berlin *Forschungsstelle*.[29] The East German literature—both economic and historical—is considerable in size, including a significant number of doctoral dissertations. There is, however, also no comprehensive GDR study of private-sector policy from the late 1940s to the present.

The reason why practically no attention has been given to the East German private economy in the West is that it has hardly been noticed, and if it was noticed, it was considered a marginal and transitory phenomenon. Where it has been analyzed, the perspective employed has usually been strongly shaped by normative presuppositions according to which any nationalization and/or restrictive regulation of private enterprise appeared as an injustice inflicted upon the private economy by Communist dictators. Such a perspective, particularly from a West German point of view, is intellectually plausible as well as politically understandable. The SED regime has never had nearly the degree of legitimacy as that enjoyed by the democratic regime in the Federal Republic. I do not wish to take issue with the normative orientation as such, nor does my identifying the existence of these normative premises imply that it makes such a perspective less "scientific."

What I propose is simply that such an approach is necessarily one-sided, shedding light on some important phenomena at the expense of other aspects which may prove equally, or even more, fruitful for an understanding of the functioning of the regime.[30] The perspective adopted in the present study of Marxist-Leninist ideology and private-sector policy in the GDR is almost diametrically opposed to the traditional view. My assumption is that comprehensive nationalization of the privately-owned means of production is the "normal" course followed by Communist regimes. Given their explicit goals and the extent of political power at their disposal, the puzzling phenomenon in need of explanation is not that they embark on nationalization. Rather, it is the survival and functional integration of what is ideologically considered a remnant of the old order and a "foreign" element under socialism.

This may also account for the fact that the GDR literature on the private economy is fairly extensive. The mere existence of private enterprise poses an intellectual and a political problem for the regime and its ideological defenders because it seems to conflict fundamentally with its goals and the conception of the new socialist order. Three general approaches to the problem used by GDR analysts and ideologues may be distinguished, corresponding to political exigencies at the time of writing: the historical, the offensive, and the defensive approaches. *First,* the historical approach, prevalent mainly since the mid-1970s, is more analytical and less ideological than the other two approaches. Written after the 1972 nationalization, the private economy no longer constituted a Soviet-bloc anomaly and, *qua* history, could be examined in a more detached fashion. While some studies hardly go beyond celebrating the

SED's private-sector policy as a creative and politically astute choice on the part of its leaders, there are also some very incisive and insightful analyses available.[31] *Second,* the offensive approach is dominant in periods of, or immediately following, a major nationalization campaign. There is little work following this approach in the 1952–1953 ideological offensive, mainly because its measures had to be reversed almost as quickly as they were taken. It was most important in the 1958–1960 period when the GDR regime under the leadership of Walter Ulbricht pursued an ambitious program of catching up with the East on the nationalization front and with the West in economic prosperity.[32] There is no scholarly literature proposing the nationalization of the private and semi-private industry preceding the 1972 campaign itself. This indicates that there was no ideological or theoretical debate preparing the ground, suggesting that the decision taken by the new leadership under Erich Honecker is best understood as a political coup rather than an economic reform. Finally, *third,* the defensive approach was the most prevalent from the late 1940s to the late 1960s. During this time, the GDR had to defend its deviant course of tolerating a significant private sector and convince itself that it was nevertheless as socialist as its allies.[33] Often engaging in rather tedious exegesis of the classics to prove the legitimacy of its own approach to socialism, during the 1960s the "mixed" socialism of the GDR was discussed with increasing self-confidence, climaxing in SED leader Ulbricht's claim that the GDR rather than the Soviet Union offered the best model for highly industrialized countries.

The first comprehensive study of the GDR private economy came in 1985 with Swedish economist Anders Aslund's *Private Enterprise in Eastern Europe.*[34] In addition to the GDR, Aslund examines the Polish private economy, providing an extremely useful and insightful comparative analysis. Aslund stresses the important economic function of private enterprise in centrally-planned economies which runs counter to the ideological imperative of the socialization of the means of production.

> We face an inherent contradiction of a Soviet-type economy between the inability of the socialised sector to perform essential economic activities and the communist intention to abolish private ownership of the means of production. If the private sector falls below a certain size, determined by the functioning of the rest of the economy, a virtually deterministic process starts. The smaller the private sector becomes, the worse the market balances grow, and the more corrupted the economy.[35]

Aslund argues that "the inherent interests of the public sector cause a fall in the private sector until it has become so small that it is legally degenerate. Before that, no force has proved strong enough to resist the aspiration of the public sector in the long term."[36] Only the GDR might have escaped this decay because of a strong central power, good management and the fact that the nationalization process was gradually carried out over three decades. Despite the SED's policy reversal of 1976, Aslund considered the GDR private economy in the early 1980s to be "on the verge of corruption, with mild but widespread illegal practices."[37]

When the private economy has become fully corrupted, there is a qualitative change in private-sector policy that Aslund has presented in the form of a cyclical four-stage model. In the first stage after a clampdown on the private sector, serious market imbalances emerge and allow black marketeers to reap large profits. As a result, the government loosens regulations in the hope that better opportunities for legal private economic activity will reduce the black market. In the second stage, market balances improve under more liberal conditions, private production increases, leading to a growth in profits, greater recourse to illegal supplies, and labour migration from the state to the private sector. The third stage is characterized by a negative response from officials and the public to excessive earnings and illegality, and calls for restrictions from the state sector and party apparatus long before markets have been balanced. In the fourth stage, restrictive regulations are implemented and market balances once again deteriorate. Aslund suggests that the "mechanics of the policy cycle are entirely economic."

Of great significance, moreover, is Aslund's contention that "the Marxist doctrine of the abolition of private ownership of the means of production is not a necessary condition for the cycle."[38] The two central non-economic preconditions are the unacceptability of high incomes and of massive shortages. The main limitation on the applicability of this model to the GDR, according to Aslund, is that market imbalances and corruption there were never as severe as in Poland.[39] "Until at least 1972, the private and semi-private economy in the GDR were [sic] sufficiently large and well-distributed to provide a tolerable market balance. . . . Consequently, the economy has not been fully corrupted. . . . This has allowed GDR rulers . . . great liberty from economic compulsion, so *the fate of the private sector could be decided politically.*"[40]

Aslund's argument suggests what is a crucial point for the present study of ideology and private-sector policy in the GDR. Most Eastern European countries quickly reached a state of economic corruption in the wake of comprehensive nationalization in the immediate years following the coming to power of Communist regimes. Subsequently, the ideological imperative of the abolition of the private means of production dwindled to insignificance as Communist regimes were trying to deal with the dilemma posed by market imbalances, severe shortages, and illegal practices, on the one hand, and popular and bureaucratic resistance to the institutionalization of profitable private enterprise, on the other. For reasons to be explored in detail in Chapters 2 and 3, the East German Communists pursued a course of gradual nationalization extending over three decades, thus sparing the country of the worst unintended consequences of eliminating the private economy. As Aslund has proposed, this gave the GDR regime considerably more leeway to bring to bear political considerations in its private-sector policy. It means that in contrast to the other Soviet-bloc regimes that had largely fulfilled the ideological imperative of nationalization and subsequently had to struggle with its economically disastrous unintended consequences, the SED remained confronted with two political tasks. First, it had to develop ideological justifications for its "deviant" course. Second, it had to integrate institutionally the private sector and private entrepreneurs into the socialist economy and society.

A recognition of the centrality of these two political imperatives in GDR private-sector policy is indispensable for an understanding of the stability, legality, and security of the East German private economy in the late 1970s and 1980s. Contrary to Aslund, I will argue that there was no legal degeneration in the GDR private sector from 1976–1989. This was not primarily due to the unwavering support of the party and state apparatus for the private economy—though policy measures and their implementation during that period were quite consistent, leading to a recovery and modest expansion of the private sector. The main reason for its stability and legality are to be found in the existing institutional mechanisms for the integration of the private sector that had evolved during the three decades of "deviant" private-sector policy. I am referring not only to economic integration—regular and stable access to supplies, price controls, institutionalized state/private sector cooperation—but also to ideological, political, and social integration. Ideologically, private handicraft and trade had long held the official status of alliance partners of the working class. Politically, the Bloc parties and Chambers acted—albeit in a limited capacity—as interest representatives of the private sector. Socially, though often envied, private entrepreneurs were widely regarded as hard-working and respectable citizens.

Aslund's explanatory model has recently been rejected on the grounds that Polish private-sector policy in the 1980s has undermined its validity. Jacek Rostowski concludes that since there has been a more or less continuous liberalization and rapid expansion of private enterprise in Poland throughout the 1980s, "Aslund's law of the cyclical development of the private sector around a very low level clearly no longer holds in Poland."[41] The same might be concluded from the recent Soviet experience. This criticism is unjustified, however, to the extent that Aslund specified as one of the initial conditions for his "law" "an unchanging ideological outlook"[42] and explicitly stated in his general conclusions that "a legally degenerate private sector is most likely to remain so, fluctuating with the policy at a low level, *as long as the political and economic system remains*."[43] Both Poland in the 1980s and the Soviet Union in the late 1980s have certainly undergone momentous changes in ideological outlook and in their political systems. The same cannot be said for the GDR until the fall of 1989. Nevertheless, throughout the late 1970s and 1980s a gradual change in ideological perceptions of small-scale private enterprise can be detected, particularly as reflected in the work of economists and social scientists.[44] The increasingly conservative leadership under Honecker proved incapable of undertaking systematic and far-reaching private sector reform. This underlines once more the fact that stability, legality, and security in the East German private economy were above all the result of institutional continuity rather than of political design.

Notes

1. K.R. Popper, *The Open Society and Its Enemies,* Vol. 2, 5th ed., rev. (Princeton: Princeton University Press, 1966), p. 95.

2. There is one notable exception. In Poland, the agricultural sector remained largely in private ownership. Nevertheless, the GDR is a special case in preserving a mixed ownership structure in manufacturing, handicraft, and trade sectors.

3. These assumptions are implicit in approaches following the totalitarian model.

4. On the Soviet Union, see especially Stephen F. Cohen, *Bukharin and the Bolshevik Revolution* (New York: Knopf, 1973) and, by the same author, *Rethinking the Soviet Experience Politics and History since 1917* (New York: Oxford University Press, 1985).

5. See section 4 of the Bibliography which lists the literature analyzing both the official and unofficial private sectors in Soviet-type economies. Most of these studies date from the latter half of the 1980s, indicating that this aspect of Communist societies has only very recently been discovered as a worthwile object of study.

6. In addition to the relatively recent literature on the second economy referred to in note 5, see also Karl-Eugen Wädekin, *Agrarian Policies in Communist Europe* (The Hague/London: Allanheld, Osmun, 1982).

7. Thus, as Alexander Gerschenkron, "Review" of Part I: Realism and Utopia in Russian Economic Thought, in E.J. Simmons, *Continuity and Change in Russian and Soviet Thought* (New York: Russel and Russell, 1967), p. 106, has put it: "Basic tenets of Marxian ideology suffered a radical revision. One may refer alone to such pillars of the Marxian edifice as the view on the role of great men in history, the principle of internationalism, the marcescence of the state, and the idea of egalitarianism, and consider in that light the shameless idolization of Stalin, the excesses of Soviet Russian chauvinism, the hyperthrophy of the Soviet state, and the deliberate policy of a far-reaching income differentiation. [. . .] [I]t is tempting to suggest that in a very real sense the advent of the

Bolsheviks to power spelled the end of Marxian ideology in Russia." Much the same point has been made by the Swedish economist Anders Aslund, *Private Enterprise in Eastern Europe* (New York: St. Martin's Press, 1985), p. 222, with respect to private sector policy in most East-bloc countries once their private economies reached a state of legal degeneration. Aslund's work is one of the few systematic studies of the private sector under Communist regimes. His argument will be discussed further below in this chapter.

8. Such a solution would be favoured by the bureaucratic, the developmental, and the "industrial society" models which share an emphasis on structures and processes common to all modern industrial societies with large-scale bureaucracies.

9. This solution might be favoured by the defenders of a modified version of the totalitarian model. See, for example, C.J. Friedrich, "Totalitarianism: Recent Trends," *Problems of Communism* (May–June 1968). It would be consistent with an elite approach to the study of Communist regimes. See, for example, G. Breslauer, "The Nature of Soviet Politics and the Gorbachev Leadership," in A. Dallin and C. Rice, eds., *The Gorbachev Era* (Stanford, Cal.: Stanford Alumni Assoc., 1986).

10. In 1961, the SED, with the support of the Soviet Union, had largely "solved" its intra-German problem by building the wall.

11. Popper, *Open Society,* Vol. 2, p. 94.

12. Karl R. Popper, *Conjectures and Refutations* (New York: Harper & Row, 1968), p. 124.

13. *Ibid.,* p. 342.

14. *Ibid.,* p. 125.

15. *Soviet Politics: The Dilemma of Power* (New York: Harper & Row, 1965), pp. 411–412.

16. See on this aspect of continuity as an important barrier to wholesale social and economic restructuring, Karl. R. Popper, "Towards a Rational Theory of Tradition," in his *Conjectures and Refutations,* pp. 120–135.

17. Anders Aslund, *Private Enterprise,* p. 178.

18. "Semi-private economy" refers to privately operated industrial enterprises in which the state holds shares, as well as to private retail firms that operate under a commission contract with a state enterprise. See especially Chapter 3 and Chapter 4.

19. *Statistisches Jahrbuch 1972,* pp. 53, 55. Not including employment in private agriculture which was insignificant.

20. Anders Aslund, "Private Enterprise in Poland, the GDR and Hungary," *Bidrag till Öststatsforskningen,* Vol. 11, No. 1 (1983), 26.

21. On developments in the Hungarian private sector in the 1980s, see, for example, I.R. Gabor and T.D. Horvath, "Failure and Retreat in the Hungarian Private Small-Scale Industry (Data for a revision of government policy towards the small industry in the eighties)," *Acta Oeconomica,* Vol. 38, Nos. 1–2 (1987), 149. G.J. Kovacs, "Job-Creating Capacity of the Private Sector in Hungary Between 1981–1985," *Acta Oeconomica,* Vol. 37, No. 3–4 (1986), 341–354. T. Laky, "Small Enterprises in Hungary—Myth and Reality," *Acta Oeconomica,* Vol.

32, Nos. 1-2 (1984), 39-63. K. Okolicsanyi, "HSWP Economic Committee Proposes Selling Off State-Owned Enterprises and Land," *Radio Free Europe Research,* Vol. 14, No. 22 (2 June 1989), 31-36. See also the literature listed in Section 4 of the bibliography.

22. On developments in the Polish private sector in the 1980s, see J. Rostowski, "The Decay of Socialism and the Growth of Private Enterprise in Poland," *Soviet Studies,* Vol. XLI, No. 2 (April 1989), 194-214. Roman Stefanowski, "Problems with the Privatization of Industry," *Radio Free Europe Research,* Vol. 14, No. 37 (15 September 1989), 25-26. For developments in the early 1980s, see Aslund, *Private Enterprise.* See also the literature listed in Section 4 of the bibliography.

23. For developments in the Soviet private sector in the late 1980s, see A. Aslund, *Gorbachev's Struggle for Economic Reform* (Ithaca, N.Y.: Cornell University Press, 1989), esp. Chapter 6. M. Belkindas, "Privatization of the Soviet Economy under Gorbachev II: 1. The Campaign Against Unearned Income; 2. The Development of Private Cooperatives," *Berkeley-Duke Occasional Papers on the Second Economy in the USSR,* Paper No. 14 (April 1989). S. Pomorski, "Privatization of the Soviet Economy under Gorbachev I: Notes on the 1986 Law on Individual Enterprise," *Berkeley-Duke Occasional Papers on the Second Economy in the USSR,* Paper No. 13 (October 1988).

24. "The reason for the speculative character of Polish entrepreneurs is to be found in the Stalinist period. Ever since, they have been offered such conditions that they cannot manage without committing major economic crimes, making them liable to several years imprisonment. The key problem has always been supplies. Because of discrimination and general scarcity, hardly any Polish entrepreneur can subsist without acquiring illegal supplies and paying bribes." Aslund, "Private Enterprise in Poland," 28.

25. The handicraft sector in the GDR includes a large variety of occupations, such as car mechanics, plumbers, butchers, bakers, and electricians. For a systematic description of the composition of this and other sectors of the East German private economy in the 1980s, see Chapter 4.

26. See Chapter 7.

27. E.A. Hewitt, *Reforming the Soviet Economy. Equality versus Efficiency* (Washington, D.C.: The Brookings Institution, 1988), p. 18.

28. Aslund, *Gorbachev's Struggle,* p. 176.

29. The full name of the research institute is *Forschungsstelle für gesamtdeutsche wirtschaftliche und soziale Fragen* (Research Institute for All-German Economic and Social Issues), which is funded by the government of the FRG.

30. The single most important figure in bringing about a paradigmatic reorientation in West German GDR studies away from the "totalitarian model" in the late 1960s and 1970s was sociologist Peter C. Ludz (see Bibliography, "West German Sources," for references to some of his works). An earlier, very rich study of the dynamics of the SED regime was E. Richert, *Macht ohne Mandat. Der Staatsapparat in der sowjetischen Besatzungszone Deutschlands* (Power without mandate. The state apparatus in the Soviet zone of occupation in Germany) (2nd ed. rev. Opladen: Westdeutscher Verlag, 1963).

31. In my view the best and the most prolific writer on this aspect of GDR economic history is Professor Jörg Roesler, head of the section for the Economic

History of the Socialist Countries at the GDR Academy of Sciences in East Berlin. A list of his relevant works is cited in the bibliography.

32. See, for example, Klaus Steinitz, "Probleme der sozialistischen Umgestaltung des Handwerks in der DDR" (Problems in the socialist restructuring of the handicraft sector in the GDR), *Wirtschaftswissenschaften*, Vol. 7, No. 8 (1959), 1121–1139.

33. See especially *Politische Ökonomie des Sozialismus und ihre Anwendung in der DDR* (Political Economy of Socialism and its Application in the GDR; Foreword by W. Ulbricht) (Berlin: Dietz Verlag, 1969).

34. Aslund, *Private Enterprise*.

35. *Ibid.*, p. 219.

36. *Ibid.*, p. 220.

37. *Ibid.*, p. 219.

38. *Ibid.*, p. 222.

39. Aslund offers the following explanation: "The slower speed of GDR socialisation has contributed to maintain balances and legal standards for a much longer time. As its administrative capacity was not so badly overstrained in the initial stage, the socialised sector could be better organised than in Poland. These effects linger on, and the GDR still requires a smaller private sector than Poland for the same economic functioning." *Ibid.*, pp. 222–223.

40. *Ibid.*, p. 222; emphasis added.

41. Rostowski, "The Decay of Socialism," 199.

42. Aslund, *Private Enterprise*, p. 222.

43. *Ibid.*, p. 223; emphasis added.

44. See especially Chapter 7.

2

Mixed Economy by Default:
Private-Sector Policy, 1945–1955

In the initial post-war years, the single most important determining force behind political and economic developments in the territory of the future GDR was the German policy of the Soviet Union as the occupying power. The division of Germany into two separate states in 1949 was the result of a gradual change in conceptions and strategies concerning Germany on the part of the Western allies and the Soviet Union as relations between the allied powers deteriorated in the immediate post-war period. The present chapter provides an account of the crucial first ten years after the war in the East German private economy. While during this period, the Communist regimes in other Eastern European countries implemented comprehensive nationalization policies and imposed the Stalinist economic model, the GDR retained a mixed ownership structure. The main causes are not be found in fundamentally different East German ideological conceptions of how to bring about a transition to socialism. Rather, Soviet policy and the unresolved German situation confronted the East German regime with specific political and economic problems that favoured and even necessitated a pragmatic approach towards the private sector. The theoretical argument advanced in this chapter is that as an *unintended consequence* of unsuccessful, more comprehensive nationalization policies attempted in this period and the subsequent political compromises the Communists were forced to make, there was a *gradual institutional integration* of the private sector into the emerging socialist economy and planning system.

Already during the war, a whole range of models for a post-war Germany had been developed—apparently including the option of an immediate transfer of the Soviet system to the Soviet zone of occupation under the direction of the German Communist Party (KPD).[1] Yet, as Alexander Fischer has suggested:

It can be assumed that Soviet policy toward Germany at the end of the war was directed at neither a division of Germany nor its subjugation and sovietization. Rather, the Soviet side maintained the objective of economic exploitation in the framework of allied reparation policy and sought a platform for a common occupation policy in Germany that would be feasible in the short-term.[2]

Soviet policy towards Germany was shaped by a number of larger issues—relations with the United States, the Soviet Union's interest in consolidating its new sphere of influence in Eastern Europe, and its interest in extracting reparations from the German economy. All of these factors made it advisable not to prejudge developments in Germany as a whole by a policy of extensive nationalization in the Soviet zone of occupation. Soviet policy was decisive for shaping the strategy and tactics of the German Communists.

The Emerging Political Framework

In addition to KPD and the Social Democrats (SPD), which merged into the SED in 1946, two other political parties—the Christian Democratic Union (CDU) and the Liberal Democratic Party (LDPD)—made public their political programmes in June and early July of 1945. In order to be granted official status as political parties, the Soviet Military Administration in Germany (SMAD) had stipulated that all four parties had to incorporate themselves into the "Anti-Fascist Democratic Bloc," a national front organization officially constituted on 14 July 1945. The programmatic principles of the Democratic Bloc were general and uncontroversial, so that in this respect it was probably based on a genuine consensus of political forces.[3] The two Marxist parties had no (KPD) or no systematic (SPD) program for immediate nationalization. The Communists even advocated the "unrestricted development of free commerce and of private entrepreneurial initiative on the basis of private ownership,"[4] the two "bourgeois" parties, CDU and LDPD, called for the nationalization of key industries, the punishment of responsible Nazis, and the redistribution of large land holdings.[5]

The general strategy of the KPD/SED and the Soviet Union in those post-war years had the following basic objectives: (1) Winning over, or at least organizationally binding, all active non-communist groups, and thus controlling them; (2) ensuring close cooperation with SMAD after the transfer of civil administration to German institutions; (3) popularizing crucial measures by sharing responsibility with all political forces, thus giving added legitimacy to the political-administrative decisions of SMAD and preventing explicit criticism;[6] (4) establishing a model for political developments in the other zones of occupation; and (5) creating an organizational form through which to bring about a transformation in the structure of the "bourgeois" parties.[7]

The political activity of the Democratic Bloc was severely circumscribed by the existing power structures. The Bloc's main organ, the Central United Front Committee, had no legislative or controlling power vis-à-vis the decisions of SMAD. It thus had no opportunity to shape the establishment of the social and political order. "It could only participate in decisions that were submitted by the occupying power, and only within a power structure in which the KPD (and later the SED) occupied key positions."[8] The Communists were clearly the dominant players in the Democratic Bloc. Both CDU and LDPD largely failed to take the initiative in the Bloc or to clarify their own political goals. The CDU, for instance, characteristically put up adamant resistance only on individual issues, such as rejecting expropriation without compensation.[9]

The local and *Land* level elections of 1946 seemed to signal a turning point in the distribution of political power within the Bloc. On zonal average, the two "bourgeois" parties combined had gained slightly more votes than the SED, and in some *Land* assemblies had even won a majority of seats. Yet the political power of these representative bodies was very limited, both by the SED-dominated Bloc committees and the Soviet administration.[10] The momentum the SED may have lost, in any case symbolically, during those elections was quickly regained as the division of Germany further deepened and the zones were increasingly integrated into the two opposing international power spheres. In the "anti-imperialist" struggle, the SED laid claim to a leading role as the most consistent "anti-fascist" force.

A fairly explicit statement of the SED's goals at this time can be found in a 1947 political-ideological analysis of Bloc policy in the party's theoretical organ *Einheit*.[11] Its author, Rudolf Appelt, argued that while the political order created by Bloc policy is "more democratic and progressive than bourgeois-parliamentary democracy," it is not a socialist order. Rather than constituting an obstacle to future socialist development, however, it created the necessary favourable preconditions. The working class was therefore not abandoning socialism, but, given the current situation in Germany in which socialism was not on the agenda, it was the only correct and revolutionary policy. The "Anti-Fascist Democratic Bloc" was both a political front of parties with different programmes, and a social bloc encompassing different strata of society. Because the working class is large in numbers, highly organized, and united, Appelt argued, it constituted the decisive power centre in the Bloc.

Anton Ackermann, member of the Central Secretariat of the SED's Central Committee since 1946, was the official proponent of the thesis of a special German road to socialism.[12] Ackermann, quoting Lenin, argued that only the general principles of the Russian Revolution had applicability, and that the speed of socialist transformation had to depend on the specific conditions of each country. He expressed the hope that Germany's special road to socialism could be completed without further bloodshed.[13] One year later, in September 1947, Ackermann addressed the question of what this special road might imply for the private sector.[14] He made it clear that neither the land reform nor the nationalization of banks, trusts, and other large enterprises in the Soviet zone of occupation should be considered as socialization. The new "anti-fascist democratic order" offered protection for small-scale private farmers, producers, and proprietors who had suffered under the rule of monopoly capital and Junkers, as well as imposing controls on larger capitalist enterprises.

> It does not mean a transition to socialism, not even its partial or gradual realization, but it takes us directly to the threshold leading to socialism, creating incomparably more favourable conditions for the final victory of the socialist workers' movement than could ever exist even under the "freest" conditions of the most liberal bourgeois-democratic republic . . . this *possibility* will become a *reality* only if at the level of Germany as a whole the forces of imperialist counterrevolution will be defeated and everywhere in Germany the same new road is followed as in that part of Germany which has set the example of establishing the new democratic order.[15]

These statements indicate an attempt on the part of the SED in 1947 to reconcile two conflicting political goals. On the one hand, it was necessary not to foreclose the option of a united Germany—in which the party hoped to play a strong role—by nationalizing private industry, and this was certainly in keeping with Soviet objectives of the time. On the other hand, it was necessary to provide an ideological justification of the "anti-fascist democratic order" as a progressive step which did not create obstacles for a future socialist order. In both Poland and Hungary, where the larger issues shaping Soviet policy in Germany were not so relevant, extensive nationalization of industrial enterprises had already been carried out in 1946.[16]

In order to realize its ideological claim to the leading role, the SED sought to secure its dominance by incorporating the mass organizations (which it controlled) into the Bloc, a proposal that predictably led to conflicts with the two other Bloc parties. The SED's strategy coincided with growing East-West conflicts and the resulting initiatives on the part of the Soviet Union to integrate its own zone of occupation more closely into its own sphere by reforming the political and economic structure of East Germany along the Soviet model. A quasi-government, the *Deutsche*

Wirtschaftskommission (German Economic Commission; DWK), was established by SMAD in June of 1947 without consultation with the Bloc, and on 12 February 1948 was given legislative powers.[17] The exclusion of Yugoslavia from the Cominform in June 1948 marks the beginning of the SED's move to become "a party of a new type," a Leninist cadre party claiming political leadership for society as a whole. As a response to the dangers of "Titoism," the SED proclaimed an intensification of the class struggle and renounced the thesis of the special German road to socialism.[18] Propelled by the Yugoslav "deviation", the SED thus joined the other Soviet satellites in embracing the model of the People's Democracy oriented toward the Soviet model.[19]

In 1948 the role of the CDU and LDPD, who acted as the political representatives of the private sector, was further undermined. In April and May, on the initiative of SMAD and the SED, two new political parties were established, the Democratic Farmers Union (DBD) and the National Democratic Party (NDPD), ostensibly for the purpose of strengthening control over the Democratic Bloc by including two parties that could be counted on as reliable allies of the SED. The NDPD, whose major constitutency was to be rank-and-file NSDAP members and sympathisers as well as former *Wehrmacht* members, and the DBD, which was to represent farmers and farm workers, both cut into the traditional constituencies of CDU and LDPD. Any effective opposition to SED policy by the two "bourgeois" parties was further hampered by the fact that in the tense atmosphere of the cold war, strong political disagreement on any issue could easily be interpreted as a lack of political loyalty toward the Democratic Bloc. They could no longer count on the tolerance of the military administration that they had enjoyed when the Soviets were still more responsive to intra-German considerations. This amounted to the *de facto* control of the SED over the personnel policy of all Bloc parties.[20]

Private-Sector Policy, 1945–1948

Four political-administrative decisions of great economic significance were taken by SMAD in 1945 without consulting the parties composing the Bloc. The decrees of 23 July and 27 July 1945 led to the closing down of banks and the establishment of a central administration for the Soviet zone. Decrees 124 and 126 of October 1945 sequestered a large number of primarily industrial enterprises owned by the state or Nazi activists, without however at this time spelling out their eventual transformation into state-owned enterprises.

The first fundamental decision affecting the basic structure of ownership in the Soviet zone concerned the issue of land reform. A positive resolution was adopted by the Bloc's Central United Front Committee despite the opposition of the CDU regarding the question of compensation.[21] Probably as a result of this conflict, SMAD and the KPD chose a different approach to obtaining democratic legitimation for the second fundamental economic reform. A referendum on the "Surrender of Enterprises of War and Nazi Criminals to the People" had been prepared by SMAD and the KPD early in 1946. It was to be held on 30 June of the same year in Saxony, a *Land* whose population could be expected to respond positively to the proposed measure. The referendum was approved by an overwhelming majority and subsequently served to legitimate similar nationalization measures in the other *Länder* without submitting them to a popular vote.[22]

From 1946–1949, private industrial firms, which accounted for at least one-third of industrial production,[23] were subject to a preliminary form of production planning (*Produktionsauflagen*). Individual firms received production targets specifying the quantity and basic structure of production derived from quarterly plans issued by the economic administrations of the *Länder*. Moreover, they were subject to price and wage regulations. A smaller number of private firms of lesser economic significance were exempt from production planning. Widespread shortages of supplies made it difficult for private firms to meet their targets. There were various ways in which private firms could and did circumvent targets and violate regulations.[24] Private entrepreneurs put up the most persistent and successful resistance against the new system in the area of taxation. A major reason for their "tax strike" was the tax legislation, which indiscriminately applied to private enterprises of all sizes, passed by the Allied Control Council in 1945/46 increasing income tax by 35 percent and corporate tax between 17 and 20 percent. The private sector had good allies in the finance and tax administrations, which were opposed to the new political authorities and which tolerated and reportedly even encouraged violations.[25]

The SED and the economic administrations at the *Land* level, which since early 1947 had been responsible for this initial approach to planning, attempted to coordinate and extend the planning system in the Soviet zone of occupation. The German Economic Commission (DWK; established in June 1947) could have implemented the already existing more ambitious designs for economic planning. The decisive opposition came from the Soviet military administration, which considered it premature to introduce fundamental innovations in the rudimentary planning system that it had established.[26] Widespread discontent with the planning system among private entrepreneurs led to attempts to set up new employers associations and a rise in economic crimes. It added up to what a GDR analyst has described as an "increasingly reserved attitude towards the anti-fascist democratic order."[27] The response of the SED in 1948 and early 1949, particularly of its middle ranks who perceived the problems in the private sector as an intensifying class struggle, was to carry out further nationalizations and to use the powerful weapon of material allocations to drive private firms out of business.[28]

Why Compromise? The Private-Sector Reforms of 1949/50

The period of "intensifying class struggle" in 1948/49 coincided with the transformation of the SED into a Leninist cadre party and the heating up of the cold war with the imposition of the Berlin blockade. Beginning in early 1949 under these conditions, the revision of the SED's private-sector policy might have been expected to result in further large-scale nationalizations of private industry. The Party had abandoned its strategic orientation of a special German road to socialism and pledged to follow the Soviet model; private entrepreneurs had increasingly demonstrated their lack of loyalty to the "anti-fascist democratic order"; the growing division of Germany diminished the prospects of a united Germany for which this order might have served as a model; and Czechoslovakia, another highly industrialized country, in 1948 had followed Hungary and Poland in undertaking sweeping nationalizations of private industry.[29] If the SED had in fact followed a course of large-scale nationalization in 1949, these would figure among the major factors accounting for such a policy. But actual events took a different course.

In early 1949, private firms accounted for 31.5 percent of gross industrial production. Most of these firms were of small or medium size and primarily in light industry and food processing, while key industries such as mining and heavy industry were state-owned or under Soviet control. As a result, the private industrial sector was extremely dependent on the state for supplies. The SED felt in possession of the commanding heights of industry. At the same time, however, the strong position of the private economy in the consumer goods and export sectors could not be disregarded. The SED had neither the manpower nor the expertise to replace private entrepreneurs in these industries. Nationalization would have required managerial resources and investment capital which were in short supply and had to be directed towards other industrial sectors.[30] The economic arguments in favour of preserving a private economy in industry thus carried considerable weight, particularly in light of its political implications. Even a temporary decline in consumer goods production would have weakened the political legitimacy of the new regime. The nationalization of "non-monopolistic" private industry would have met with the strong opposition of the CDU and LDPD at a time when the SED had not yet officially established its hegemonic role.

The fact that a more pragmatic approach was chosen should not be misinterpreted as an indication of the ultimate irrelevance of ideological factors and the primacy of economics. In ideological terms, it was only the relatively subordinate position of the private sector in industrial production that made its preservation for the time being an acceptable alternative. In other words, had the private industrial sector been perceived as posing a political challenge to the dominance of the SED and to the survival of the new order, it may well have been nationalized in spite of its economic costs.[31] This argument is supported by the fact that a different, i.e., more "dogmatic," approach was soon to be adopted by the SED towards private wholesale and retail trade, which in 1948/49 were still the dominant force in the "sphere of circulation."

The extreme shortages of the post-war period quickly led to the emergence of an extensive black market. Initially, popular Commissions for Trade and Supply were formed in an attempt to fight speculation and profiteering. In January 1946, the Chamber of Industry and Trade was established, with equal representation from the state administration, the trade unions, and the private economy. It formed the link between the administrative organs and the private trade sector, attempting to assure in particular that price and rationing regulations were followed. From 1945–1948, retail and wholesale trade were almost completely in private hands. Only a small cooperative sector in the form of consumer cooperatives had emerged. Until 1948 it accounted for the bulk of trade in agricultural products, but in 1948 it realized barely 20 percent of total retail turnover.[32] In November 1948 a state-owned retail organization was set up, the *Staatliche Handelsorganisation* (HO), though the immediate aim of this measure was practical rather than ideological. The HO retail shops' purpose was to undercut the black market by offering rationed goods at high prices, though below the price level of the black market.[33] For the organization, direction and control (but *not* operation) of wholesale trade, trade offices (*Handelskontoren*) had been established in 1946, and their administrative capacity and scope was enhanced by the setting up of a central trade association, the *Deutsche Handelsgesellschaft*. The actual operation of wholesale trade remained in the hands of private firms.[34]

The SED was soon to turn its attention also to the private handicraft sector, which in 1949 represented over 300,000 firms with just under 1 million employees. While the average employment per enterprise in the handicraft sector in 1948 was only 3.2 persons,[35] there was a substantial number of large firms. These had a strong influence on the handicraft purchase and delivery cooperatives (ELG) and the Chambers of Handicraft, which for political reasons the SED sought to limit.[36]

In the first half of 1949, the SED instituted a series of economic reforms aimed at controlling and taking advantage of the private sector without undertaking any further nationalizations. Strictly economic considerations no doubt played a crucial role in the adoption of a pragmatic approach towards the private sector. At the same time, the SED was able to justify this violation of socialist principles with reference to its political alliance with private entrepreneurs. The alliance policy, which could be legitimized with quotations from Marx, Lenin, and even Stalin,[37] thus unwittingly served an important cognitive purpose in expanding the ideological horizons of SED policy makers with respect to alternative routes to socialism. It laid a foundation for an approach to private-sector policy that, albeit not without interruptions, could be followed in the decades to come as a viable alternative to radical nationalization, when and if the SED considered it an opportune course. While in the official GDR literature the alliance policy has been widely described and defended as a creative and successful choice by the SED in the service of higher political goals dictated by the country's special conditions—the class struggle against West German monopolists and imperialism and the fight for German unity—it was a choice strongly suggested by political circumstances.

A recent analysis of the "increased class struggle in the area of economic policy in the GDR immediately after its foundation"[38] has drawn attention to the significant resistance and opposition the SED had to contend with from the private sector. This points to the fact that although the private sector created a host of ideological, political, and even economic problems, the SED simply did not yet feel strong enough politically to attempt a more determined move towards socialism. Further extensive nationalizations in 1949 would have required abandoning the alliance policy, thus formally ending the period of the "anti-fascist democratic order," and suppressing and/or driving out large numbers of citizens. It would have ended the cooperation with the Bloc parties which provided a minimum of democratic legitimacy for the new state. It would have further weakened the position of the Soviet Union in that a destablilized East Germany would have been a liability in the cold war. Support for this argument can be adduced with the benefit of hindsight. When three years later, after further consolidating its internal political position and effectively coopting the Bloc parties, the SED did embark on an extensive nationalization programme, the regime came dangerously close to the point of political collapse. These events will be discussed below after a brief outline of the reform package for the private sector adopted in 1949.

The SED's main objective for the industrial sector was to increase further the share in production of state enterprises, while trying to link the economic activities of private industrial firms to the plan and to limit private capital accumulation. This was to be achieved through a regulating system based on contracts, as well as fiscal incentives and restrictions (prices, taxes, credit, and wages). The contract system required private industrial firms to submit production offers to state contract offices (*Vertragskontore*) which, if approved, entitled them to supplies. On the basis of targets derived from the plan, the contract offices determined the product range, quality, and quantity of production. As the enterprises supplying raw materials and other supplies were for the most part state-owned, private firms were forced to enter into contracts. Investments and loans for private industry had to be approved. Prices were regulated, subject to annual review, and gross profits were fixed at about 7-8 percent. Wages in private industry were set 10-20 percent below the level of comparable state enterprises in order to attract labour to the state sector.[39]

The contract system had to be relaxed three months after its introduction because of its negative effects on private production. Private firms were now allowed to produce and receive supplies to some extent also outside official contracts.[40] Private firms in wholesale trade, where previously there had been no state enterprises at all but only a central administrative agency, were hardest hit by the 1949 reforms. A state wholesale enterprise, the *Deutsche Handelszentrale,* with branches in all *Länder* was set up in the summer of 1949.[41] Private wholesale firms were prohibited from selling products from or to state enterprises. By the end of the year, the state sector already accounted for 52 percent of total wholesale turnover[42] and by 1951 had increased its share to 86 percent.[43]

As to the retail sector, SED Secretary Walter Ulbricht had announced at the First Party Conference in January 1949, which laid down the basic principles of the new private-sector policy, that there was to be competition between private, cooperative, and state retail shops. The state retail trade enterprise (HO) quickly expanded its operations in 1949 and was able to squeeze out a large number of private shops in an already overcrowded market mainly as a result of receiving preferential deliveries. The private sector's share of retail trade turnover fell from 82 percent in 1948 to 44 percent in 1951.[44]

The handicraft sector was dealt with last in the private sector reform program. In early 1950, it was redefined to include only "primitive commodity producers," i.e., firms with a maximum of 10 employees. Larger handicraft enterprises were classified as "private capitalist producers" and moved from the jurisdiction of the Chamber of Handicraft to that of the Chamber of Industry and Trade. Like private industrial firms, private handicraft firms were indirectly incorporated into the plan through the contract system, although they were also allowed to establish contracts directly with state enterprises. A Handicraft Act passed in August 1950 included a range of stimulating measures covering prices, taxes, credit, and social insurance. It provided special incentives for private handicraft firms to work directly for the supply of the population, particularly in repairs and services.[45]

With its 1949/50 reforms, the SED had established a regulatory framework for the private sector which signified a compromise between the party's ideological aspirations and the political and economic constraints of the time. It had collected initial experiences with economic planning and the indirect steering and control of the private economy. These reforms were probably most significant not so much with respect to what they changed, but rather with respect to what they preserved. It is the *unintended consequences* of this first major compromise in fact and, at least in part, in ideological principle, with the idea and the reality of a private economy that would determine the future opportunities of this otherwise orthodox Marxist-Leninist party. The preservation of entrepreneurial skills and practices and the creation of intermediary organizations (especially the Chambers) was a consequence of the SED's more piecemeal approach to economic reform at a time when Poland, Hungary, and Czechoslovakia had already taken much larger steps towards the Soviet economic model. It would be wrong to suggest that this far-from-voluntary caution with respect to economic restructuring had been the result of a lasting ideological learning process. Rather, what I wish to propose is simply that the practical reaffirmation of the alliance policy with other classes remained an ideological option in the GDR's inventory of Marxism-Leninism, an option that could be legitimately invoked whenever policies of greater ideological purity seemed inopportune or had failed.

Toward a New Socialist Offensive, 1950–1952

The SED's pragmatic approach to the private sector manifested in the reform measures of 1949/50 contrasted with a growing dogmatic approach on the political front. The Party carried out extensive purges within its own ranks and in the leaderships of the Bloc parties CDU and LDPD. As a result, the Bloc parties' memberships dropped significantly. Between 1949 and 1951, the membership of the CDU was reduced from 212,000 to 170,000, that of the LDPD declined from 198,000 to 155,000.[46] For the general elections held in October 1950, the SED had succeeded in coercing the Bloc parties into giving their consent to unity slates. With the consolidation of the SED as a Stalinist cardre party, the transition to socialism had moved to the top of the political agenda.

Between 1950–1952, the Soviet Union intensified its efforts ostensibly aimed at working out a Four-Power Agreement on the German question. The Soviet interest in reunification was primarily motivated by its desire to have a neutral West Germany, or in any case delaying and perhaps even derailing the further integration of the Federal Republic into the Western military alliance. While the SED during this period stepped up its German reunification rhetoric,[47] it is highly unlikely that the leadership at this point was sincerely interested in such a development. For there could be little doubt that the free elections, on which the Western powers insisted as a precondition for initiating any reunification process, would deprive the Communists of their dominant political position. In March 1952, Stalin proposed to the former allies a peace treaty containing an explicit linkage between German unification and neutrality and, despite the Western powers' rejection of the crucial condition of neutrality, urged the beginning of negotiations in May. The Soviets' reunification overtures found an indirect, though unequivocal, response in the Germany treaty signed by the United States, Britain, France, and the Federal Republic in May 1952, expressing Bonn's renewed commitment to political and military integration with the West.[48]

Whether with the approval or against the wishes of the Soviet Union,[49] at its IInd Party Conference in July 1952 the SED resolved to move quickly towards the construction of socialism. The Party wanted to push ahead with its own integration into the Soviet bloc. While in itself the political situation just described favoured the SED's decision to abandon its compromise course, there were sufficient problems with its private-sector policy to provide further justification for a more dogmatic approach. Despite high growth rates in the private industrial sector in 1951 and 1952, the regulatory system for private firms met with increasing criticism, not least because entrepreneurs had found loopholes which allowed them to evade a number of the restrictions that had been imposed on them. For example, the anticipated migration of workers from the private sector to state enterprises as a result of the lower wage rates established in private industry did not materialize to any significant extent because private firms were able to provide special incentives and benefits to their workers. The relaxed contract system proved to give private industry more leeway for "unplanned" production than had been expected. Tax evasions continued, facilitated by the services of private accountants and a complicated tax system. In 1952 tax arrears of private industrial firms had reached 14.3 percent of their total tax payments due for that year. Until the IInd Party Conference, the SED leadership had refrained from tightening regulations in order not to affect the production of consumer goods by private industrial firms.[50]

In November 1952, the Central Committee of the SED gave the signal to tighten existing regulations, as it turned out not in an effort to adjust the system, but rather as the major instrument in a socialist offensive against private industry. Taxes were increased, outstanding debts, both tax arrears and loans, were to be repaid immediately, and all production was now to require approval by the state contract offices.[51] Private farmers and artisans were pressured, and often simply coerced, by local administrations to join cooperatives.[52] Supplies were cut for private retail firms, and many shops whose owners were forced to close down were taken over by the state retail organization (HO).[53] Tax rates for private handicraft firms were increased to a level that, according to calculations of the Ministry of Finance, would force them all into bankruptcy by the end of 1953.[54] All who were self-employed were excluded from the general state health and social insurance plan, and were offered much more expensive coverage under a new program. All private entrepreneurs and their families, except for children under 15 years, were deprived of their food ration cards, which compelled them to make purchases at much higher prices.[55] As a result, many private firms went bankrupt, many owners were arrested for violating the tough new rules, and farmers and private entrepreneurs left the country in large numbers.[56] Bankrupt or abandoned firms were placed under the trusteeship of local administrative organs which had neither the manpower nor the skill to maintain past levels of production.[57] In March 1953, the Chambers of Industry and Trade were dissolved and their functions transferred to state organs and enterprises.[58]

The economic results of the campaign, which was called off in June 1953 after only six months, were profound. Only 96.7 percent of the national economic plan for the first quarter of 1953 was fulfilled, less than 90 percent in the food industry. Total tax revenue from the private sector in 1953 fell by 20 percent despite the drastic increases in tax rates.[59] The economic difficulties faced by the SED in 1953 were compounded by lack of funds for ambitious investment plans in heavy industry and socialist incentive schemes for newly formed farming cooperatives. No provisions had been made in the existing 1951-55 five-year plan for financing the socialist initiatives decided by the IInd Party Conference.[60]

The SED's headlong rush into socialism may have been inspired by the fact that at the CPSU's XIXth Party Congress in October 1952, the GDR was for the first time counted among the "European People's Democracies".[61] With the support of the Soviet Union and its allies, the SED may have felt strong enough to attempt to close the developmental gap separating the ownership structure in its economy from that of the other Soviet-bloc countries. While resentment and resistance in the private sector grew, and the downturn in supply started to affect consumers, the first decisive opposition to the socialist offensive came from the Soviet Union within weeks after Stalin's death in March 1953. With a view to Soviet policy towards the West, the SED was advised to lower its socialist ambitions and not to count on financial support from the Soviet Union in trying to deal with its economic crisis. The new Soviet leaders proposed that the SED adopt an economic policy along emerging Soviet lines, giving priority to the consumer goods sector over heavy industry. In May, the SED sharply increased work norms for state industry in a last effort to save its policy of rapid socialist construction. Unexpectedly for the lead-

ership, this measure promptly led to unrest among the affected workers
and short strikes. The new Soviet High Commissioner in Germany,
Vladimir S. Semyonov, appointed in late May, demanded an immediate
and radical change in economic policy, and on 11 June 1953 the SED
Politburo announced a reversal of all measures affecting the private sector,
as well as the suspension of its ambitious investment policy. The work
norms, however, were not mentioned.[62]

The resulting large-scale strikes and mass demonstrations of 16 and 17
June 1953 took place almost a week after the declaration of the New
Course in private-sector policy, and therefore cannot be counted among
the factors contributing to its adoption. The workers' unrest in June 1953
was nevertheless significant for the SED's future approach to economic
policy. It was a "shock lesson" for the Party that the economic costs of
rapid socialist construction could cause such strong resentment and resistance in the working class that the SED's political survival might be put
at risk. As Staritz has suggested, in the years since 1953, at least up to the
1980s, the SED has demonstrated greater sensitivity and tactical skill than
in the preceding years.[63] The socialist offensive of 1952/53 is a clear
indication that the ideological ambitions of the SED did not distinguish it
from other Soviet-bloc Communist parties in that period. The SED did,
however, have the distinct advantage of being able to return to an
institutional framework and ideological position which in the course of
six months had been damaged and misused, but not irretrievably lost.

Return to Pragmatism

The New Course announced on 9 June 1953 brought a comprehensive
liberalization in private-sector policy. Bankruptcy proceedings were halted,
collection of tax arrears was stopped, and past tax evasions were no longer
prosecuted.[64] New regulations on pricing now allowed private industrial
firms to lower prices if this enabled them to increase their sales, as well
as permitted them to retain additional profits thus realized. Limits on
loans were abolished and more favourable conditions for credits established. The trade unions were instructed to encourage members employed
by private firms to do their best in assisting private employers to fulfil
their economic tasks,[65] rather than pursuing the class struggle strategy
recommended to private sector workers by the SED in the late 1940s and
early 1950s.[66]

On the whole, the "(n)ew legal provisions for state control of private
industry not only reestablished the status quo of 1951/52, but in several
respects went even further towards creating more leeway for private
initiative."[67] The Chamber of Industry and Trade was re-established with
district and county branches and assumed the functions of the state

contract offices.[68] As Aslund suggests, since "the Chambers lacked the necessary competence, capacity, and malice, they delegated the steering of the private sector to the market."[69] The policy reversal found further institutional expression in the establishment of a State Secretariat for Local Economy, the first central state organ responsible for the private economy.[70]

The results of the New Course were as immediate and profound as those of the preceding socialist offensive. During its first two months, 347 nationalized firms were reprivatized, 2,805 liquidated enterprises resumed operations, and 4,450 new firms were established. Private sector employment increased, and its total share of net production increased by one percent to 33 percent.[71] Private industrial firms raised their output by 9.8 percent in 1954 and 5.3 percent in 1955. During the entire first five-year plan period from 1951–1955, however, the share of private firms in gross industrial production had decreased from 22.4 to 13.7 percent, their number had declined by 4,000 to 13,800, and their workforce had dropped by about one-fifth.[72] The number of private handicraft firms in the same period had been reduced from 284.500 to 248,200,[73] but the sector's growth rate of 70.8 percent was astounding. Private incomes of their owners had increased by a phenomenal 123 percent[74] due in large part to the extremely favourable handicraft tax law of 1950.[75] Private retail trade, which in 1950 still accounted for 52 percent of total retail turnover, by 1955 was reduced to 32 percent. Nevertheless, 72.5 percent of all retail outlets were still under private ownership.[76]

Although on the whole the state sector was progressively increasing its share in all sectors of the economy and the private sector was performing well, the new private-sector policy was soon the cause of growing dissatisfaction within the SED. Many problems that had given rise to the socialist offensive of 1952/53 resurfaced under the more liberal policy from 1953–1955. The general charges of "anarchic tendencies" caused in the economy by private entrepreneurs taking advantage of the new opportunities and excessive profits appeared again. The central dilemma faced by policy makers was that when restrictive regulations were adopted to counteract the "anarchic and speculative excesses," there was a great risk of reducing private economic activity with its undesired consequences of a decline in production, particularly of mass consumer goods, and a weakening of economically important firms.[77]

The liberalization of price regulations, which allowed private producers to undercut prices in the state sector, was an incentive for private firms to concentrate on the production of more profitable goods and led to shortages in less profitable product lines.[78] The private textile industry even managed to take export shares from its competitors in state industry.[79] Private firms often were able to attract labour from the state sector.

The situation was precarious in the construction industry where, due to more favourable price regulations and low rates of taxation, private handicraft firms had a significant cost advantage over state construction enterprises. The result was that between 1952 and 1955 the state construction sector lost over 5 percent of its market share to private handicraft firms.[80] There were indications of growing concentration in private industry, and despite the general limit of 10 employees, over 4,500 private handicraft firms exceeded the limit by the end of 1955, some considerably.[81]

Compared to the problems the SED had with its private-sector policy in 1952 when it decided to embark on a socialist offensive, the ideological implications of the new policy were even more disquieting. In 1952 the attack on the private sector signalled only the beginning of what was to be a transition period. By 1954/55, socialist construction was to have been already well under way, thus the problems appeared all the more serious. Given the advances in nationalization made by the fraternal Communist parties, the SED's pragmatism looked—at any rate to more dogmatic minds—increasingly like political indecisiveness, incompetence, and failure. In 1954/55, however, private-sector policy was only one aspect of the New Course which rejected the primacy of heavy industry and represented an admission that the Stalinist model of the planned economy was seriously deficient. The criticisms of the existing planning system, which were shared by leading economic functionaries and theoreticians, foreshadowed the economic debates of 1957. In 1954/55, however, Ulbricht effectively opposed such critical views. At the meeting of the Central Committee in June 1955 he declared that, "[i]t was never our intention to choose such a course and we shall never choose it."[82]

The adaptations of, and structural innovations in, the system regulating the private economy that were prepared in 1955 and implemented since 1956 represent a creative further development of the private-sector policy of the New Course. It would be inadequate to characterize this simply as a pragmatic approach. Pragmatic, indeed, was the reversal of the socialist offensive in June 1953, as it was a response to an economic crisis and Soviet influence. To this extent, Ulbricht was correct in claiming that the SED leadership had not really chosen to embark on a new course. But the 1950–1955 period had demonstrated at least three things. First, that it was not possible to liquidate the private sector without incurring great and potentially intolerable economic and political costs. Second, that the private sector did not represent a political threat to the SED. Third, that an institutional and ideological framework had emerged that made a more gradualist approach in the transition period conceivable.

The ideological motivation to move ahead in the building of socialism was not only unbroken at an official or rhetorical level, it was also operative in the conception of the new private-sector policy after 1955. It was not simply a middle way between excessive regulation and excessive freedom of the private economy, a kind of aimless incrementalism, that the SED now pursued. Rather, it was an attempt to find a solution in principle to the alleged problems of private enterprise—such as slow technological change and adverse effects on worker motivation resulting in low labour productivity—a solution that would not entail the economic and political costs of all-out nationalization. The point may be obvious once it is stated: The opportunity for choosing such a course which is both a response to existing economic conditions *and* a response to ideological imperatives is possible only if two conditions are met. First, that there is a functioning institutional infrastructure integrating the private sector into the state economy and subordinating it to the socialist state apparatus. And second, that there are elements in the existing ideology that make the justification of such an approach politically legitimate.

By 1955, the initially tactical alliance policy of the SED had become established as an integral element of the party's official ideology. As the account presented in this chapter has shown, this was clearly an *unintended consequence* of a series of measures taken in response to economic and political constraints, rather than the result of a conscious design for a special German road to socialism. On the contrary, the SED had made several attempts at much more far-reaching nationalization of private firms, but those policies had failed. The successful policies turned out to be those that regulated the private sector, integrated it into the state economy, and gradually reduced its size. At the level of official ideology, this piecemeal approach could be justified in terms of the alliance policy— the anti-imperialist front uniting all classes in the GDR against West German monopoly capital. At the level of operative ideology, the SED had learned, by trial and error, the crucial lesson that ambitious socialist offensives are economically costly and politically risky. At the level of economic administration, valuable experience had been gained concerning the regulation of the private sector. In institutional terms, a variety of intermediary organizations—the Bloc parties, the Chambers—existed for the mobilization, representation and control of the private sector. At the same time, the SED remained strongly committed to completing the full transition to socialism. Yet, the opportunities created by the unintended ideological and institutional results of the late 1940s and early 1950s now permitted a new way of looking at the time required and the means to be employed for realizing this goal.

Notes

Starting in this chapter, I have marked the names of West German authors with an asterisk (*) to distinguish them from GDR sources.

1. H. Weber*, *Geschichte der DDR* (München: dtv, 1985), p. 49. Prof. Weber is one of the leading West German historians on the GDR.
2. A. Fischer*, *Der Weg nach Pankow. Zur Gründungsgeschichte der DDR* (The Road to Pankow. On the history of the foundation of the GDR) (München 1980), p. 15; quoted in Weber, *op.cit*, p. 50.
3. S. Suckut*, *Blockpolitik in der SBZ/DDR 1945–1949* (Bloc policy in the Soviet Zone of Occupation/GDR 1945–1949) (Cologne: Verlag Wissenschaft und Politik, 1986), pp. 17–18.
4. Quoted in H. Weber*, "Geschichte der SED" (History of the SED), in I. Spittmann, ed. *Die SED in Geschichte und Gegenwart* (Cologne: Verlag Wissenschaft und Politik, 1987), p. 7.
5. Suckut, *Blockpolitik*, p. 15.
6. E. Krippendorff*, *Die Liberal-Demokratische Partei Deutschlands in der Sowjetischen Besatzungszone 1945/48* (The Liberal Democratic Party of Germany in the Soviet Zone of Occupation) (Düsseldorf: Droste Verlag, 1961), p. 84.
7. Suckut, *Blockpolitik*, pp. 20–23.
8. *Ibid.*, p. 45.
9. *Ibid.*, pp. 25–27.
10. *Ibid.*, pp. 30–31.
11. R. Appelt, "Wesen und Ziele der Blockpolitik" (Character and goals of Bloc Policy), *Einheit*, 9 (1947), 825ff.
12. A. Ackermann, "Gibt es einen besonderen deutschen Weg zum Sozialismus?" (Is there a special German road to socialism?), *Einheit*, 1 (1946), 22–32.
13. *Ibid.*, 31–32.
14. A. Ackermann, "Produktions-und Eigentumsverhältnisse in der sowjetischen Besatzungszone Deutschlands" (Relations of production and of ownership in the Soviet Zone of Occupation), *Einheit*, 2, 9 (1947), 844–857.
15. *Ibid.*, 856–57.
16. J. Roesler, "Die Rolle der Planung und Leitung bei der Umgestaltung der privaten Industrie und des Handwerks in der Übergangsperiode" (The role of planning and administration in the restructuring of private industry and handicraft in the transition period), *Jahrbuch für Wirtschaftsgeschichte*, II (1972), 216.
17. Bundesminister für Innerdeutsche Beziehungen*, ed. *DDR-Handbuch*, 3rd rev. ed. (Cologne: Verlag Wissenschaft und Politik, 1985), Vol. 1, p. 276.
18. "Chronik", in I. Spittmann*, ed. *Die SED in Geschichte und Gegenwart* (SED in the Past and Present) (Cologne: Verlag Wissenschaft und Politik, 1987), pp. 211–12.
19. D. Staritz*, *Geschichte der DDR 1949–1985* (History of the GDR 1949–1985) (Frankfurt: Suhrkamp, 1985), p. 20. Staritz, together with H. Weber, is one of West Germany's leading experts on the history of the GDR.
20. Suckut, *Blockpolitik*, p. 37.

21. When the CDU's agreement could not be secured after adoption of the resolution—the Committee's decisions required unanimity—the two chairmen of the party were simply ousted. See *ibid.,* p. 25.

22. Weber, *Geschichte der DDR,* p. 115.

23. No statistics are published on the ownership structure of industrial enterprises between 1945 and 1948. In early 1949, private industrial firms accounted for 31.5 percent of gross industrial output (see next section).

24. W. Mühlfriedel, "Die Entwicklung der privatkapitalistischen Industrie im Prozeß der antifaschistisch-demokratischen Umgestaltung" (The development of private capitalist industry in the process of anti-fascist-democratic restructuring), *Jahrbuch für Wirtschaftsgeschichte,* 3 (1984).

25. *Ibid.*

26. W. Mühlfriedel, "Die Wirtschaftsplanung in der sowjetischen Besatzungszone von den Anfängen bis zur Bildung der Deutschen Wirtschaftskommission" (Economic planning in the Soviet Zone of Occupation from the beginnings to the formation of the German Economic Commission), *Jahrbuch für Wirtschaftsgeschichte,* 2 (1985), 28–29.

27. Mühlfriedel, "Private capitalist industry".

28. Personal information from Prof. Jörg Roesler, who pointed out that this nationalization drive is little known since it was not an officially declared as policy.

29. Roesler, "Die Rolle der Planung," 216.

30. *Ibid.,* 216–17.

31. The relative loyalty and willingness to cooperate with the state on the part of East German entrepreneurs compared to the "obstruction" practiced by their counterparts in Czechoslovakia and Poland is also stressed by J. Roesler, "Inhalt und Methodologie des Vergleichs der Herausbildung und Entwicklung sozialistischer Planwirtschaft in allen sozialistischen Ländern" (Content and methodology in the comparison of the emergence and development of the socialist planned economy in all socialist countries), in *Inhaltliche und methodologische Problem einer vergleichenden Wirtschaftsgeschichte des Sozialismus* (East Berlin: Humboldt-Universität, 1978), pp. 128–139.

32. A. Dorner and O. Rennert, "Zur Entwicklung des Binnenhandels während der antifaschistisch-demokratischen Umwälzung auf dem Gebiet der heutigen DDR" (On the development of domestic trade during the anti-fascist-democratic revolution on the territory of the present-day GDR), *Jahrbuch für Wirtschaftsgeschichte,* 2 (1977), 22.

33. *Ibid.,* 25.

34. *Ibid.,* 23.

35. Aslund, *Private Enterprise,* p. 251.

36. S. Wietstruk, *Entwicklung des Arbeiter-und Bauernstaates der DDR 1949–1961* (Development of the workers' and farmers' state of the GDR 1949–1961) (Berlin: Staatsverlag, 1987), pp. 128–29.

37. Stalin was invoked in an introductory quotation of an article on the role of the private sector in the Soviet zone of occupation. See, for example, W. Stoph, "Die Rolle der Privatindustrie in der Ostzone" (The role of private industry in the Eastern zone), *Einheit,* 4, 3 (1949), 243. For a historical-theoretical account of

alliance policy (*Bündnispolitik*), see H. Buske, W. Gahrig, J. Haschker et al. *Bündnispolitik im Sozialimus* (Alliance policy under socialism) (Berlin: Dietz Verlag, pp. 9—28; for a briefer statement, see *Kleines politisches Wörterbuch*, 6th ed. (Berlin: Dietz Verlag, 1986), pp. 151-152.

38. R. Schultze, "Der verschärfte Klassenkampf auf wirtschaftspolitischem Gebiet in der DDR unmittelbar nach ihrer Gründung" (The increased class struggle in the area of economic policy in the GDR immediately after its foundation), *Jahrbuch für Wirtschaftsgeschichte*, 2 (1977), 45-63.

39. This section is based primarily on J. Roesler, "Strategies and their realisation involving private industrial capital in the socialist construction of the GDR between 1949 and 1959," *Economic Quarterly* (Hochschule für Ökonomie, East-Berlin), No. 4 (1988), 34-45 and Wietstruk, *Entwicklung des Arbeiter-und Bauernstaates*. On the contract system, see also Roesler, "Die Rolle der Planung" and Mühlfriedel, "Die Entwicklung der privatkapitalistischen Industrie".

40. Aslund, *Private Enterprise*, p. 126.

41. Dorner/Rennert, "Zur Entwicklung des Binnenhandels," 24.

42. *Ibid.*

43. Aslund, *Private Enterprise*, p. 126.

44. *Ibid.*, p. 127.

45. Wietstruk, *Entwicklung des Arbeiter-und Bauernstaates*, pp. 128-129.

46. Staritz, *Geschichte der DDR*, pp. 61-63.

47. See in this context G. Zieger, *Die Haltung von SED und DDR zur Einheit Deutschlands 1949-1987* (The position of the SED and the GDR on the unity of Germany 1949-1987) (Köln: Verlag Wissenschaft und Politik, 1988), pp. 21-42.

48. This paragraph is based on Staritz, *Die Geschichte der DDR*, pp. 66, 72-73; Zieger, *Haltung von SED und DDR*, pp. 47-50.

49. B. Meissner, *Rußland, die Westmächte und Deutschland. Die sowjetische Deutschlandpolitik 1943-1953* (Russia, the world powers and Germany. Soviet policy towards Germany 1943-1953) (Hamburg: Nölke, 1953) suggests that the Soviets gave Ulbricht, who represented the SED's radical wing, the go ahead for full nationalization. Staritz, *Geschichte der DDR*, pp. 75-76, cites indications to the effect that the fundamental decisions of the IInd Party Conference angered the Soviets.

50. This paragraph is based on Roesler, "Strategies", 37-38.

51. *Ibid.*, 38.

52. Staritz, *Geschichte der DDR*, p. 81.

53. H. Schlenk*, *Der Binnenhandel der DDR* (Domestic Trade of the GDR) (Cologne: Verlag Wissenschaft und Politik, 1970), pp. 29-30.

54. Aslund, *Private Enterprise*, p. 140.

55. Staritz, *Geschichte der DDR*, p. 79.

56. The number of people leaving for the West increased from 22,000 in December 1952 to 58,000 in March 1953. *Ibid.*, p. 81.

57. Roesler, "Strategies", 38-39.

58. Schlenk, *Binnenhandel der DDR*, pp. 32-33.

59. Aslund, *Private Enterprise*, p. 140.

60. Staritz, *Geschichte der DDR*, pp. 78-79.

61. *Ibid.,* p. 81.

62. This paragraph is largely based on Weber, *Geschichte der DDR,* pp. 232–236, and Staritz, *Geschichte der DDR,* pp. 79–84.

63. *Ibid.*

64. Roesler, "Strategies," 39.

65. W. Mussler, *Der kapitalistische Sektor der Industrie als Problem der Übergangsperiode zum Sozialismus in der Deutschen Demokratischen Republik* (The capitalist sector of industry as a problem of the transitional period to socialism in the German Democratic Republic) (Berlin: Verlag Die Wirtschaft, 1959), pp. 76–77.

66. See on this class struggle position especially Stoph, "Die Rolle der Privatindustrie," 244.

67. Roesler, "Strategies," 39.

68. Mussler, *Der kapitalistische Sektor,* pp. 70–71.

69. Aslund, *Private Enterprise,* p. 141.

70. Mussler, *Der kapitalistische Sektor,* p. 71.

71. Aslund, *Private Enterprise,* p. 146.

72. Roesler, "Die Rolle der Planung und Leitung," 220.

73. Aslund, *Private Enterprise,* p. 251.

74. Roesler, "Die Rolle der Planung und Leitung," 220–221.

75. See above.

76. W. Heinrichs, "Zur Einbeziehung des privaten Einzelhandels in den sozialistischen Aufbau der DDR" (On the incorporation of private retail trade into socialist construction in the GDR), *Wirtschaftswissenschaft,* 5, 6 (1957), 835.

77. W. Mussler, "Die privatkapitalistische Industrie und die ökonomische Politik der Arbeiter-und Bauernmacht" (Private capitalist industry and the economic policy of the workers-and-farmers power), *Einheit,* Vol. 11, 5 (1956), 532.

78. *Ibid.,* 532–33; Mussler, *Der kapitalistische Sektor,* pp. 82–86.

79. *Ibid.,* p. 89.

80. *Ibid.,* pp. 90–91.

81. Aslund, *Private Enterprise,* p. 148.

82. W. Ulbricht at the XXIVth Plenum of the Central Committee of the SED, 1 June 1955, which marked the end of the New Course; quoted in M. McCauley, *Marxism-Leninism in the German Democratic Republic* (London: Macmillan, 1979), p. 93.

3

Piecemeal Social Engineering:
Private-Sector Policy, 1956–1976

The building of the Berlin Wall in August 1961 is generally considered a turning point in the history of the GDR.[1] From that time on both rulers and ruled were forced to live with each other. East Germans learned to accept the fact that they were ruled by a Communist party that they could not vote out of office. But since acceptance out of necessity is a precarious foundation for legitimacy, the SED in its turn learned to try harder and act more flexibly to produce results that would give more substance to this foundation. The second part of the historical analysis of private-sector policy in the GDR starts with the year 1956. The major reason is that, as the the concluding paragraphs of the preceding chapter have suggested, by the mid-1950s a piecemeal approach to socialist transformation had proved to be not only economically and politically advantageous for short-term tactical reasons, but also institutionally feasible and ideologically justifiable as a systematic strategy for the transition period. As already emphasized in Chapter 2, this more pragmatic approach to the private sector should not be confused with a tempering of socialist ambitions on the part of the SED. Rather, the institutional integration of the private sector into the socialist economy and its ideological justification, which had emerged as an unintended consequence of experiments in the late 1940s and early 1950s, had also unwittingly extended the SED's programmatic and policy repertoire in sharp contrast with conditions in other Soviet-bloc countries.[2]

My contention is that the SED did not differ from other Communist parties in the Eastern bloc with respect to its ideological ambitions, but rather with respect to the logic of the situation within which these ambitions had to be played out. During the period under consideration in the present chapter, two further major socialization drives occurred. The first from 1958 to 1960 led to the almost complete collectivization of private agriculture. The second in 1972 resulted in the nationalization of private and semi-private industrial firms and a large number of handicraft cooperatives. From the perspective adopted in this study, however, the interesting phenomenon in need of explanation is not the question why nationalizations occurred at all. Rather, the question is why a sizable private economy survived so long in spite of the ideological ambitions of the political rulers. According to the *institutional integration thesis* proposed in this study, the emergence of a mixed ownership structure can be explained as an *unintended consequence* of what the Communists regarded as temporary compromises between their orthodox ideological goals and political and economic constraints. These compromises led to the gradual "organic" integration of the private sector into the socialist economy, and to its increasing ideological assimilation.

Reforms for a Gradual Transformation of the Private Sector, 1956–1958

The far-reaching liberalization of private-sector policy in the wake of the 1952–53 socialist offensive confronted the SED with the same basic dilemma created by the 1949–50 liberal reforms—how to choose between further extending the state sector and fostering rapid economic growth. The economic benefits of a pragmatic private-sector policy entailed ideologically unacceptable costs. My argument that by 1955 the SED had learned a crucial lesson with respect to nationalization is corroborated by the fact that the private-sector policy adopted in early 1956 expressed a new, piecemeal approach for the transformation of private firms. It was conceived and worked out *before* the "thaw" in the Soviet Union following the XXth Party Congress of the CPSU also led to a fundamental re-evalution of, and far-ranging debate on, the political and economic strategies of the SED.

The most significant and innovative elements of the new approach to the private sector were a scheme for state participation in private industry, and a commission system for private retail trade. Both new organizational forms for private firms were designed to further integrate the private sector into the planning system. Ideologically, they were conceived as transition strategies that would allow private entrepreneurs gradually to change their firms into socialist enterprises and to evolve personally from bourgeois proprietors into socialist managers. These transitional forms of private ownership have, from a Western perspective, often been perceived—if they were perceived at all—as an ideological facade for the *de facto* nationalization of private firms.[3] As we will see in a moment, however, these schemes offered a number of genuine benefits to private owners, they were promoted through special financial incentives rather than simply being administratively foisted upon the private sector, and they did not fundamentally change the actual entrepreneurial role of the owner. Somewhat ironically, their ideological justification appears to have been as effective among many Western observers as it was in the GDR. For, according to the official view, the firms participating in these new schemes immediately became ideologically superior by changing their very essence from relics of capitalist society to dynamic elements of the emerging socialist society. At a more abstract level, these new forms of private ownership were seen to eliminate the fundamental contradiction between socialist state power and non-socialist relations of production. In more concrete terms, they were regarded as new instruments for restricting private accumulation and more effectively controlling private production.[4]

The first of these two new forms was the "enterprise with state participation" (*Betrieb mit staatlicher Beteiligung*, BSB), or semi-state enterprise (*halbstaatlicher Betrieb*), designed primarily for the private industrial sector. Private firms were transformed into limited partnerships (*Kommanditgesellschaften*) and the state became part-owner by contributing capital for which it was entitled to a corresponding share of profits. The state's liability was limited to the amount invested, whereas the private part-owner was the fully liable partner. While this mixed form of ownership was not really new—it had precursors under the Soviet Union's New Economic Policy and closely resembled the joint state/private enterprises briefly experimented with in China in 1955—it came into its own under the special conditions of the GDR.[5]

East German economic historian Jörg Roesler has summarized the economic rationale for state participation in the following way: "private enterprises whose modernization and expansion served the purpose of improving consumer goods production, export potential or auxiliaries to state enterprises, no longer received loans but instead [capital in the form of state participation]."[6] It was up to the private owner to submit an application to state authorities, and the first semi-state enterprises were formed in early 1956. Initially, private entrepreneurs were hesitant about taking such a step, and the Bloc parties made special efforts to persuade those who were Bloc party members to consider state participation.[7] In addition, special financial incentives were offered to induce private owners to enter into the new scheme. They included tax incentives, the opportunity to use "hidden reserves" legally for investment, and a management salary for the private part-owner in addition to his share in profits. State capital was used for expanding fixed assets, increasing working capital, and paying off debts to the state and private individuals.[8]

Based on interview material, Aslund has convincingly argued that "owner-directors remained firmly in charge of their enterprises, and that their acceptance of state participation meant no major change in their role."[9] While the state reserved to itself extensive rights, it made "minimal use of its rights to interfere in BSBs. . . ."[10] The state's capital share varied between 20 percent and 99.9 percent of the firm's assets. However, the "size of this share had no influence on the functioning of BSBs, but private partners felt safer the larger their shares were, since their position was conditioned by capital."[11] The ideological significance of state participation meant greater existential and political security for private part-owners, and thus constituted an added incentive to apply.

The number of applications had reached 4,000 by late 1958, and a growing number of applicants were now actually rejected. Grounds for rejection were both the economic health of the private firm and the state's interest in the firm's production profile.[12] Preference was given to large enterprises with a skilled workforce. Rejections rose from 10.9 percent of all applications in 1956 to 23.8 percent in 1957, reaching 36.4 percent by October 1958. BSBs accounted for 1.3 percent of all private enterprises in 1956, 4.4 percent in 1957, and 10.6 percent in 1958. The larger-than-average size of the converted firms is indicated by their share in private output which increased from 3 percent in 1956 to over 10 percent in 1957 and 29 percent in 1958.[13]

Petty commodity traders, unlike private industrial capitalists, had long been considered natural alliance partners of the working class. The time was considered ripe to include in the transition process private shops, which in 1955 still accounted for over two-thirds of all retail outlets.[14] It is more difficult to find any clear indication in the literature of the time whether there were economic reasons for introducing commission trade in addition to the ideological motives, which were taken for granted. The main reason mentioned was that private retailers possessed important skills and a good knowledge of the needs of their customers. Moreover, it was recognized that they were often more flexible than the retail outlets of state enterprises.[15] The transitional form introduced in 1956 for the private retail sector was commission trade (*Kommissionshandel*). It was said that while commission trade under monopoly capitalism served to exploit and eventually ruin small tradespeople by binding them closer to monopolistic trade enterprises, their closer integration into state trade organizations would be both economically beneficial as well as give private retailers a perspective for their future under socialism.[16]

A private retailer could apply for a commission contract with a state wholesale enterprise. He or she remained legally an independent entrepreneur and in possession of his or her business premises, which were leased from the state contract partner. The state enterprise was the owner of the goods offered by the retailer until sold, which meant that the risk shifted from the private tradesman to the state partner. The latter also assumed the responsibility for bookkeeping, thus reducing the administrative load of a commission retailer compared to that of a private retailer. Since the commission retailer had to make a security deposit amounting to one-third of his inventory, entering into a commission contract could immediately generate additional funds for the purchase of goods. Finally, because commission retailers were only subject to the maximum 20 percent tax on incomes from dependent employment, they could realize larger net incomes with a greater volume of supplies and a low marginal tax.[17] Private retailers were considerably less enthusiastic about the new scheme of state participation than their colleagues in private industry. By May 1957, only 206 commission contracts had been concluded.

Particularly strong resistance to intermediate forms of ownership existed in private handicraft. Since the SED's IInd Party Conference in July 1952, private artisans had been encouraged to form handicraft cooperatives (*Produktionsgenossenschaften des Handwerks*; PGH). By the end of the year, only 4 such cooperatives had been established, and in 1955 the number was still a very modest 85, accounting for only 0.3 percent of total handicraft turnover.[18] The so-called purchase and delivery cooperatives (*Einkaufs-und Liefergenossenschaften*; ELG), serving as wholesale organizations for the private handicraft sector since 1946, had developed into successful business operations, ignoring their political mission and becoming increasingly suspect ideologically for their "capitalist practices".[19]

It had become evident, particularly in the mobilization attempts by the Bloc parties, that the obstacles to the more rapid formation of handicraft cooperatives consisted not only in ideological reservations on the part of independent-minded private artisans, but also in the lack of adequate financial incentives. In 1956, therefore, a massive financial incentive scheme was implemented which exempted cooperatives from most taxes, offered special low-interest loans, and provided for other social benefits.[20] A new model statute for purchase and delivery cooperatives adopted in 1956 was to orient their activities closer to their original task of preparing private handicraft firms for the transition to socialist production.[21]

Significant progress in the collectivization of private agriculture proved to be even more difficult to the extent that joining an agricultural cooperative (*Landwirtschaftliche Produktionsgenossenschaft*; LPG) remained a private farmer's voluntary decision. By 1956, LPGs accounted for just over 23 percent of total agricultural land, reaching a share of 37 percent by the end of 1958.[22] The gains made between 1956 and 1958, however, were for the most part due to the administrative transformation of state farms into LPG. Private farmers, by contrast, remained unconvinced that joining a LPG would not substantially reduce their incomes, quite apart from losing their independence. A large number of LPGs were already heavily subsidized, and a material incentive program comparable to that devised for the handicraft sector would simply not have been financially feasible for the state.[23] Thus by 1958 when the new institutional forms and policies for the private sector in the transition period were in place, their success in winning over private entrepreneurs was mixed.

Toward the Second Socialist Offensive, 1958–1960

Since 1956, the general conditions for a pragmatic approach to implementing the new private-sector policies for the transition period had become rather favourable. At the GDR's top governmental organ, the Presidium of the Council of Ministers, the three ministers responsible for the major sectors of the economy—industry, agriculture, and consumption— received enhanced status by being appointed as deputy prime ministers. Under the leadership of the head of the planning commission, Bruno Leuschner, they formed an economic cabinet composed of pragmatic and professional economic specialists. This concentration of leading representatives of the economic leadership meant that the other members of the Presidium, including Ulbricht, were not involved in the questions of economic practice.[24] As Ernst Richert has pointed out, characteristic for the economic leadership's view in the latter part of the 1950s is a statement made by Erich Apel, head of the Economic Commission of the SED Politburo since 1958, that "socialist consciousness is measured in terms of productive output."[25]

The Soviet Union's renunciation of the doctrine of the intensifying internal class struggle and the renewed emphasis on specific national conditions in the transition to socialism after the XXth Party Congress of the CPSU[26] supported the SED's special approach to the private sector. In 1956 and 1957, anti-Stalinist sentiments in the GDR were rising rapidly within the SED and among East German intellectuals, being directed against the rule of apparatchiks and ultimately against Ulbricht and his followers. The workers, in contrast to 1953 and in contrast to mounting popular opposition in Hungary and Poland, remained passive. There was a liberalization of the debate in the Party and at the universities, with "revisionist" tendencies in economic theory on the rise.[27] Ulbricht strongly dismissed these reformist ideas at the Central Committee plenum in January 1957.[28] While on the whole the conception of a "third way" between capitalism and Soviet-style socialism remained diffuse, the most developed theoretical statement was worked out by a group around Wolfgang Harich, professor of philosophy and a leading party theoretician, during 1956 and early 1957. It included the demand for a new private-sector policy and the rejection of any forced collectivization. In March 1957, Harich and his associates were sentenced to long prison terms.[29]

Nevertheless, opposition to Ulbricht's hard course was also growing in the Politburo and the economic leadership. The opposition around Karl Schirdewan, member of the Politburo, demanded the continuation of de-

Stalinization and a slow-down in the speed of socialist transition. The anti-Ulbricht faction grew as long as Schirdewan appeared to have the tacit approval of Khrushchev as a possible successor to Ulbricht. Khrushchev's support for the opposition, however, ceased after the political crisis in Hungary, and Ulbricht quickly reasserted his authority. In February 1958, revisionist conceptions were rejected as a threat to the preservation of the SED's political power and their proponents were either demoted or had to renounce their "false" views.[30] The ground for a new ideological offensive had been prepared.

At the SED's fifth congress in July 1958, Ulbricht issued the programmatic declaration that the struggle for the victory of socialism in the GDR was to be intensified.[31] The so-called economic main task (*Ökonomische Hauptaufgabe*) was to catch up with West Germany in per-capita consumption by 1961.[32] While ruthlessly repressing inner-Party and intellectual opposition, the SED leadership attempted to create greater economic prosperity for the population, not least in order to reduce the outflow of citizens to the West. On this count the Party was moderately successful. From 1957 to 1959, consumer goods production grew significantly, the food rationing system was abolished in May 1958, and there was a considerable improvement in living standards.[33] This was also reflected in the declining number of people leaving the GDR. While in 1956, almost 280,000 East Germans had turned their backs on the GDR, their number declined to approx. 260,000 in 1957, 204,000 in 1958, and 144,000 in 1959.[34] The SED's piecemeal approach seemed to be paying off.

State participation was the most successful scheme for the private sector encountering the least resistance from private entrepreneurs. In 1958, two years after the scheme had been introduced, the number of semi-state enterprises (BSBs) was 1,541, and in 1961 it had reached 5,042. BSBs in 1961 accounted for 72.2 percent of gross output of the non-state industrial sector.[35] By 1960, 11,600 private retailers had entered into a commission contract (by comparison: 94,600 operated without commission contract) and 8,300 private restaurants were commission agents (10,100 still worked independently).[36] Despite the advantageous financial incentives and the political mobilization efforts by the Bloc parties, the private handicraft sector remained strongly opposed to the formation of cooperatives (PGH). In 1957, the year after the promotion measures had been passed, the number of newly founded PGHs was a mere 56 (up from 239 in 1956).[37] At the SED Central Committee meeting in October 1957, Ulbricht's demand that the transition process in handicraft be accelerated was defeated by the pragmatically-oriented economic leadership. Ulbricht was to gain the upper hand, however, when the Central Committee in February 1958 signalled the launching of a determined political and administrative campaign for the socialization of the handicraft sector.[38]

While some further incentives for the formation of PGHs were offered, new tax legislation in March 1958 was aimed at raising the disincentives for remaining a private artisan.[39] Intimidation as a form of "special incentive", however, apparently was also widespread.[40] In the second quarter of 1958 alone, 687 new PGHs were established, and another 979 in the third quarter. From the end of 1957 to the end of 1958, the number of PGHs had increased from 295 to 2,584, raising their share in total handicraft output from 1.4 percent to 12.9 percent.[41] However, very soon it became evident that the rapid transformation of private handicraft had negative economic consequences, particularly for the supply of consumer goods and services to the population, and new guidelines issued by the Council of Ministers in March 1959 subordinated the ideological goals of forming cooperatives to their anticipated economic benefits.[42]

The socialist offensive was carried out most ruthlessly in the agricultural sector. The Central Committee in December 1959 decided that private farmers required much more determined political "encouragement" to join agricultural cooperatives (LPG). Everywhere, SED county leaderships organized agitation groups composed of members from the whole range of political organizations to descend upon the countryside. Private farmers were systematically subjected to strong political and moral pressures.[43] Within three months, the number of LPGs almost doubled, and by the end of 1960 accounted for 84.2 percent of all farm land.[44] 15,000 private farmers fled to the West, leaving some 30,000 private farms in the GDR at the end of the campaign.[45] The "socialist offensive," however, had also spilled over into the retail and handicraft sectors of the private economy, as Erich Honecker acknowledged in the report of the Politburo to the Central Committee in July 1961:

> The discrimination against private retail shops in the provision of goods, the insufficient supply of private service handicraft with materials, the transformation of private restaurants into state (HO) restaurants, and the failure to issue licenses must end immediately.[46]

The overall impact of the 1958-60 socialist offensive on the private sector is reflected in Table 3.1.

199,000 East Germans fled the country in 1960 and by June 1961 another 103,000 had followed. Stricter border controls instituted in 1960, especially in Berlin, obviously could not slow the outflow of citizens. Already in 1960, the SED had started a propaganda campaign accusing the West of "trading in human beings" (*Menschenhandel*). From September 1960, the GDR restricted access for West Germans to East Berlin. The FRG government promptly retaliated by cancelling its trade agreement with the GDR as of the end of 1961.[47] The economic situation in the

Table 3.1   Reduction in Private Employment by Branch, 1958-1960

Employment at the end of each year
(1957 = 100)

Year	Total*	Industry	Handicraft**	Construction	Agriculture
1958	79.2	71.4	76.0	64.9	82.1
1959	65.0	48.8	66.8	45.1	68.3
1960	37.0	39.9	59.5	35.8	5.2

* Incl. commission trade   ** Excl. construction handicrafts
Source: Aslund, *Private Enterprise*, p. 165. © Anders Aslund, 1985.

GDR in 1960/61 quickly took on crisis proportions. The socialist offensive ground to a halt. Under the threat of serious destabilization on its Western flank, the Soviet-bloc countries in early August 1961 finally gave the GDR their support comprehensively to "secure its borders."[48] On 13 August 1961, the Berlin Wall went up.

The Emergence of the New Economic System

In 1959, the GDR had followed the CPSU in switching over to a seven-year plan in order to facilitate intra-CMEA coordination in the Soviet bloc's ambitious project of catching up with the West. Thus abandoning its current five year plan, the SED retroactively adopted the new plan for the period 1959–1965 in October 1959. The end of the plan period in 1965 was projected as the deadline for completing the construction of socialism.[49] At the same time, GDR planners began working on what became known as the "general perspective" (*Generalperspektive*), a long-range economic plan originally covering the period to 1975 and subsequently extended to 1980. Initiated by the Soviet Union in 1959, all CMEA member countries were by 1960 to have begun coordinating their economic development in one integrated "general perspective" for the 1960s and 1970s. Extrapolating the rates of decline in the private sector from 1958 to 1960, GDR planners took it for granted that private firms would soon completely disappear.[50]

The West German threat in 1960 to cut off a whole range of crucial exports to the GDR, however, led to a fundamental revision of the GDR's economic plans. Under the awkward motto "campaign for making [the country] free of disturbances" (*Aktion Störfreimachung*), many goals of the ongoing seven-year plan were postponed. The steep decline in economic growth after 1960 caused the SED to embark on a basic re-evaluation of its economic strategy. The preparation originally envisioned for the transition to communism sometime in the 1960s was gradually abandoned in favour of consolidating the results of the transition period to socialism. While the other Communist countries continued their work on the "general perspective," the SED in late 1961 initiated what became a lively and open debate among economists on future economic policy.[51]

The majority of East German economists considered the deteriorating economic performance since 1960 to be primarily the result of the country's inadequate economic system, rather than as a consequence of *Störfreimachung*. Two different solutions emerged in the debate. The first was a partial reform of the planning system, the second a radical reform of the "economic mechanism" giving priority to productivity and profitability over gross output. The proponents of the radical solution found unexpected support in the Soviet reform debate, where in September 1962 E.G. Libermann had advocated a similarly radical overhaul of the economic system.[52]

The Central Committee in October 1962 signalled the Party's choice for a radical reform for dealing with the country's acute economic problems. In December 1962, the Politburo coined the phrase "New Economic System" (*Neues Ökonomisches System*; NÖS) to symbolize the fundamental departure from the command system of planning and administration. The new policy in its basic outlines was officially adopted at the VIth Party Congress in January 1963. The "victory of socialist relations of production in all sectors of the economy"[53] was declared. At the Congress, the SED also adopted a new Party programme that reflected the ideological relaxation vis-à-vis the private sector.

> The social and economic possibilities for a restoration of capitalism are once and for all eliminated. The capitalist class has disappeared . . . . Thereby the system of exploitation of man by man is once and for all abolished . . . class antagonism almost completely overcome. Also the continued existence of small and medium-sized private enterprise cannot make any fundamental change to this fact, as these are closely linked to the socialist economy.[54]

Roesler has recently explained that in 1962 the dominant view among planners in the GDR on the future of the private sector was still shaped by their work on the "general perspective." Not only was it assumed that when the GDR entered the period of the transition to communism there would be little room for private economic initiative, but the further existence of private and semi-private firms was also considered economically and technically indefensible. The work of the planning commission on the "general perspective" and its implications for the private sector had become known among private entrepreneurs and were negatively affecting the performance of their firms.[55]

While the proponents of radical economic reform along the lines suggested by Libermann were defeated in the Soviet Union, Ulbricht and his followers, who had just pushed ahead with a sweeping ideological offensive after eliminating their more pragmatically-oriented opponents, showed themselves to be very flexible. After declaring the victory of socialist relations of production, the SED leadership not only proved capable of adopting a new economic reform strategy that went far beyond what the "pragmatists" had advocated in 1958. They also quickly moved to make peace with the remaining private sector by incorporating it— quite pragmatically—into the New Economic System. This ideological flexibility and political adaptability, however, was facilitated by the *institutional integration* of the private sector during the 1950s.

Once again, it should be emphasized that the argument proposed here is not that the ideological ambitions, in principle, of the East German communists had weakened. The 1958–1960 socialist offensive is clear evidence to the contrary. But the institutional forms for the transition to socialism of the private sector had proven more or less successful in winning the cooperation of private entrepreneurs—more so where independence and economic well-being were largely preserved as in semi-state enterprises and commission trade, less so where they had to be fundamentally compromised as in the handicraft (PGH) and agricultural cooperatives (LPG). On this basis, the SED ambitiously and ruthlessly pushed ahead in its socialist offensive until economic and political difficulties forced an end to the campaign. At that point, the only real success of the socialist offensive by its own standards was the far-reaching collectivization of agriculture. The rapid growth in the number of cooperatives (PGH) in the handicraft sector, particularly in 1958, had required a massive financial incentive program in addition to special "political" incentives, while in quantitative terms still leaving private firms in a dominant position.[56]

This alone would hardly have been enough to arrive at the programmatic conclusion that the transition to socialism had now been successfully completed.[57] This was a claim with great political significance, and its credibility derived almost wholly—i.e., with the exception of agriculture— from the regulatory framework and institutions that had evolved prior to the socialist offensive. In the 1950s they had found elaborate ideological justification and approval as a special *transitional* strategy for the GDR. The same arguments could now be employed to explain why a private sector of considerable size would be permitted to survive and thrive under the New Economic System.

Functional Socialism, 1962–1971

Already in March 1962, Ulbricht had made a general statement to the effect that the private sector would continue to play an important economic role in the GDR:

> For the managers of [semi-state, handicraft and other private] firms as well as for their employees, the transition from capitalism to socialism poses many complicated questions concerning scientific-technological progress, the organization of production, and economic problems which can only be solved *over an extended period of time in the interests of all sides.*[58]

The central goal of the New Economic System launched at the VIth Party Congress in January 1963 was to increase economic efficiency and overall performance. This was to be achieved through "economic levers" (*ökonomische Hebel*)—new steering and incentive mechanisms linking the objectives of central planners to the actions of enterprises and workers via profits and bonuses. Profit-making, rather than plan fulfillment, as the central criterion of economic success was to orient enterprises more effectively towards considerations of cost, pricing, turnover, and efficiency. Worker performance was to be stimulated through incentive wages, special bonuses, and additional holidays.[59] This paradigmatic shift from ideological motivation and political administration to economic-technical rationality in economic policy—much in the spirit of Apel's "socialist consciousness is measured in terms of productive output"—led to a reevaluation of the significance of ownership.

> The characteristic properties of our industry do not consist in the fact that there are large and small enterprises, advanced and backward ones, old and new ones, central and local, state and semi-state enterprises. Rather, it is necessary to distinguish between the various sectors of industry, i.e. machine-building, electrical engineering, metal products, and the many other industrial sectors.[60]

It was explicitly recognized that neither firm size nor the private sector's quantitative share alone were adequate criteria for gauging the economic importance of these firms. It was stressed that their specialization and their position in the economic system often made them functionally much more important than their size or quantitative share might suggest.[61] Moreover, it was pointed out that the GDR's experiences with the private economy demonstrated that private forms of ownership did not pose an insuperable obstacle to an economically-rational integration of such firms. Everything depended on properly stimulating their production in the

desired direction through price policy.[62] More serious problems were seen
to flow from the fragmentation of production in the private sector, but
this was to be dealt with through various forms of "socialist cooperation"
(*sozialistische Gemeinschaftsarbeit*).

Private-sector policy under the New Economic System thus integrated
private enterprises into a specialized and "cooperative" administrative
structure. An administrative reform carried out in 1962-63 abolished the
administrative division by ownership form. Regardless of ownership, all
industrial enterprises were now supervised by an economic council at the
district level (*Bezirkswirtschaftsrat*) through sectoral departments. And
service enterprises—state and non-state—were placed under the authority
of newly-established departments of "local service economy" (*Örtliche
Versorgungswirtschaft*) at the county and municipal levels.[63]

The main institutional form of "socialist cooperation" for the integration of private firms were so-called product groups (*Erzeugnisgruppen*).[64]
A product group is an association of a number of state enterprises, semi-
state enterprises, private industrial firms, and private and cooperative
handicraft firms in the same or related fields of production for the purpose
of coordinating the division of labour and the introduction of new technology. The strongest and most advanced enterprise (usually, though not
always, a state enterprise)[65] functioned as the "guiding enterprise" (*Leitbetrieb*). The work of the product group was coordinated by a product
group council elected by delegates from all participating firms. Membership for private firms was said to be voluntary, private entrepreneurs were
to be won over by treating them as equal partners and by demonstrating
to them the benefits they would be able to derive through participation.[66]

Aslund has suggested that product groups mainly distributed production between member firms, giving first choice to state enterprises. "Usually, this procedure did not run contrary to the interests of entrepreneurs.
BSBs [semi-state enterprises] frequently took up the production that
nationally-owned enterprises had dropped as unprofitable and generated
substantial profits, thanks to their higher efficiency."[67] Analogous associations for the service sector, "supply groups" (*Versorgungsgruppen*), were
increasingly established starting in 1965. While handicraft cooperatives
in the service sector were dissatisfied with the resulting division of labour,
private handicraft firms generally had a more positive attitude. The
disadvantage of being left with more unprofitable tasks, according to
Aslund, was outweighed for them by diminished state discrimination.[68]

There were no significant changes in private-sector policy during the
1960s, marking this as the longest period of stability for private firms in
the history of the GDR to that time. In industry, the combined share of
private and semi-state enterprises remained unchanged, accounting for
about 16 percent of gross output and 12 percent of the workforce, with

Table 3.2 Tax Contributions of the Private and Semi-Private Economy, 1962-1970

	1962	1963	1964	1965	1966	1967	1968	1969	1970
in billion Marks	3.1	3.4	3.6	4.1	4.7	4.7	8.1	9.0	9.9
share of total revenue in %	5.9	6.4	6.3	6.5	7.0	8.0	13.4	13.7	14.0

Source: G. Buettner, "Die historische Entwicklung des sozialistischen Staatshaushalts in der DDR," p. 210.

growth rates of 13.8 percent in the period 1961-65 and 29.6 percent between 1966-70.[69] The number of private retail shops decreased from 1962 to 1971 from about 80,000 to some 44,000, while the number of commission shops remained constant at 13,000. Their combined share of total sales points dropped from 52.3 percent to 44.8 percent.[70] The declining number of private firms in private handicraft and particularly in trade during this period was to a large extent due to "natural attrition", i.e. old age, death, or sickness.[71] The much steeper decline in the number of private retail shops (by almost half) compared to that of private handicraft firms (just over one quarter) suggests that the licensing practice for new entrepreneurs was more restrictive in private trade than in private handicraft.

The generally very good performance of the private and semi-private economy and its significant tax contribution[72] to the socialist state is reflected in Table 3.2. The large increase from 1967-68 in both absolute and relative terms is only in part accounted for by more rapid economic growth. An important factor was the industrial price reform and attendant changes in the tax system of 1967.[73] Thus, in addition to its economic functions, the private sector made a significant contribution to the state's tax revenues during the 1960s.

At the SED's VIIth Party Congress in 1967, "functional socialism" was reaffirmed and provided with an ideological rationale. The GDR was said to be on the road to the "developed social system of socialism" (*entwickeltes gesellschaftliches System des Sozialismus*; EgSS). Socialism was conceived as a "relatively independent societal formation", a separate stage of social development, in contradistinction to the other Soviet-bloc countries who proclaimed to be moving towards "developed socialist society", the first phase of communism. The core of the EgSS was the "Economic System of Socialism" (*Ökonomisches System des Sozialismus*;

ÖSS), which included the integrated private and semi-private economy. In its social aspect, the EgSS represented a "community of man" (*Menschengemeinschaft*) distinguished by an overriding harmony between different classes.[74]

The Economic System of Socialism found its comprehensive expression in a 900-page work entitled *The Political Economy of Socialism and its Application in the GDR,*[75] in which the ideological and institutional elements of the SED's economic policies, specifically also with respect to the private sector, were systematically assembled and theoretically and ideologically justified. It was stressed that the victory of the socialist relations of production in 1962 had established the preconditions for the integration of the private sector into the socialist economy and the possibility for its survival.[76] Private and semi-private firms no longer impeded the working of the "economic laws of socialism."[77] The majority of private *artisans, retailers, and entrepreneurs* have become socialistically labouring working people (*Werktätige*). The bourgeoisie has ceased to be its own independent class. The remnants of this class, the privately operating entrepreneurs, change their social status, they are above all intimately connected with the socialist economy and society. In this way one of the most important historical tasks of the transitional period has been solved.[78] The now-existing "identity of the fundamental interests of all classes and strata" was even viewed as a manifestation of the conditions envisioned by the *Communist Manifesto,* "an association in which the free development of each is the condition for the free development of all."[79] Under these conditions, the proper leadership of the Party and the socialist state would ensure that different interests, and even contradictions, would be recognized in time and, through a collective effort, resolved "without social conflicts and excessive and costly friction".[80] The political aspects of the SED's alliance policy were described, analyzed, and ideologically grounded at length in another official work, also published in 1969, entitled *Together Towards Socialism.*[81] Here, for example, the participation of members of the private sector in the GDR's political system was underscored, such as the work of over 5,000 deputies in the country's representative assemblies at all levels of government.[82]

The SED not only took considerable pride in its achievements. It also recommended its own approach to the private sector as a "creative further development of Lenin's ideas on state capitalism", which could serve as a relevant model for other industrialized countries.[83] Ulbricht's claims for a "model GDR" and his ideological reconceptualization of socialism as an independent societal formation like feudalism or capitalism, however, also carried clear implications for the existing socialist countries, including the Soviet Union. Increasingly self-confident, Ulbricht in effect criticized the other Communist parties for trying to jump a stage of social development—namely "his" socialism of the 1960s. Thus, at an international Engels symposium in East Berlin in 1970, he stated that his own party had had to learn that progress was more rapid if socialist ambitions were tempered by realism, adding: "Some may say: We have done this in a simpler way, we have carried it through in an administrative fashion.—It can be done like that too, but the results are accordingly."[84]

The institutional integration of the private sector, I have argued, provided the SED with a special opportunity to return to a more moderate and pragmatic approach whenever ambitious ideological initiatives had failed. Until the early 1960s, this gave the private sector only short reprieve, though repeatedly so and just long enough to permit its gradual institutional integration in a functional and ideologically acceptable fashion. The survival of a sizable private sector, I have further argued, was therefore a result of *unintended consequences,* not of a programmatic overhaul of the SED's social and economic goals. During the 1960s, the institutional and ideological integration reached a qualitatively new level. Institutionally, a fairly successful framework for the regulation and integration of the private sector was in place. Ideologically, this framework seemed to have been firmly established. Its socialist character was continuously reaffirmed, and it became identified with a stage in the development of socialism that would not be superceded until the advent of the final, and increasingly nebulous and distant, communist stage. In fact, the GDR's "mixed economy" or "functional socialism" had become so successful that in the late 1960s it became a vehicle for the SED under Ulbricht to push the claim for the GDR's greater political independence from the Soviet Union and an economic leadership role in Eastern Europe.

Return to Orthodoxy:
Toward the Last Nationalization Drive, 1972

The history of private-sector policy reviewed up to this point has shown that not until the early 1960s had ideological ambitions been sufficiently revised to make the survival of the private economy conceivable as more than the outcome of fortuitous circumstances and temporary compromises. Ideological ambitions, in other words, were so effectively restrained and frustrated by a variety of contingent non-ideological—economic and political—factors that an institutional framework for the private sector could emerge. Notwithstanding official GDR history to the contrary, this institutional and ideological integration of the private sector into the socialist economy was above all an unintended consequence of political actions. Under the New Economic System in the 1960s, the political and economic integration of the private sector had become institutionally established and even ideologically codified. The existence of private firms had become more secure than ever before in the history of the GDR. It is for these reasons that the last nationalization drive in 1972 came as a surprise.

In the late 1960s, the private sector was criticized for a number of problems. None of these, however, were considered serious enough to put in question the basic framework that had been established for its integration into the socialist economy, let alone to inspire calls for its nationalization. The most severe public criticisms from about 1967 were directed at handicraft cooperatives (PGHs), which were increasing their production by hiring additional labour, predominantly from the state sector. At the same time, they showed little enthusiasm for accepting private artisans as members.[85] Under conditions of growing labour scarcity,[86] PGHs were thus violating the interests of the state economy as well as failing to live up to their political task of incorporating private handicraft firms. Both cooperative and private handicraft firms, moreover, were criticized for devoting an inadequate share of their activities to repairs and services for the population.[87]

In contrast to handicraft cooperatives, private and semi-private firms in industry, which had received special subsidies to compensate them for the negative effects of the industrial price reform of 1967,[88] were assured of continued financial assistance for 1969 and 1970.[89] Private and semi-private firms, as well as cooperative and private handicraft firms in the construction sector, were admonished to participate more strongly in "socialist cooperation" in order to avoid falling short of plan targets. They were reminded that it was "socialist cooperation . . . [which] is the guarantee for a secure perspective in the elaboration of the developed social system of socialism, and it is beneficial for all to make their decision soon and consciously to proceed ahead."[90] Despite much more serious charges against the private sector that surfaced in 1971/72, and in the subsequent literature justifying the necessity of a nationalization drive, the private sector seemed safe. An analysis of the integration of semi-state enterprises published as late as 1972 was very positive and contained no clues as to the imminent "socialist offensive" in the form of a renewed policy of nationalization.[91] The fate of the private sector was determined by larger problems with the New Economic System under which it had thrived.

In the late 1960s, there was growing dissatisfaction within the SED with Ulbricht's general approach to economic policy. The gap between East and West Germany had further widened, and by 1970 it had become clear that some basic goals of the 1966-70 plan would not be reached. Labour productivity in 1969 and 1970 rose by only about half the projected increase. There were growing problems in the supply of consumer goods, as well as unfulfilled export obligations to the Soviet Union.[92] The strong emphasis on advanced R & D industries under the New Economic System had led to structural problems in the energy sector, consumer goods industries, and the infrastructure. The Central Committee in December 1970 rejected Ulbricht's "technocratic" economic policies.[93] With respect to the private sector, it decided to make revisions in the regulatory system, as well as to strengthen the party organizations and trade union representation in private and semi-private firms.[94] In addition, new financial measures became effective in January 1971. Among others, tax increases were instituted for the whole private sector, and compensatory subsidies for industrial firms were eliminated.[95] Special commissions at district, county, and municipal levels composed of representatives from state organs, trade unions, the National Front, the Chambers, and banks were set up to expedite the implementation of the new policies. Growth rates in the private sector in 1971 were between 3.5 and 5.3 percent, indicating that the measures were successful.[96]

Aslund conjectures that the session of the Central Committee had gone much further, and had decided already in favour of nationalization. The most convincing piece of evidence he cites in support of his interpretation is the setting up of special commissions at all levels of government.[97] It is difficult to see why such extensive efforts would be required to implement a set of financial measures for the private sector. The simultaneous activation of Party and union representatives in the private sector also suggests that a policy reversal going beyond a tax reform was in the making. Aslund argues that the nationalization initiative was being prepared carefully and quietly in order to avoid disruptions in the production of these firms. An alternative explanation, however, is conceivable.

Two problems which in the subsequent discussion and justification of the nationalization drive were characterized as fundamental (see below) were, first, high incomes in the private sector and, second, the need for substantial infusion of capital in non-state industry and the fusion of private firms in order to make optimal use of their productive capacity. The latter problem, in effect, would have implied a "recapitalization" of private firms and would have tended to boost the incomes of private owners even more. Of course, neither problem was new, and both could have been dealt with on the basis of existing policy instruments—taxes and state participation. The simple explanation for establishing the commissions might be that they were charged with exploring ways of dealing with these problems.[98] Two other possible reasons for their creation should at least be considered. First, given the SED's negative experiences in the past with restrictive measures for the private sector, the commissions might have been enjoined to monitor the effects of the new tax policy and to provide immediate and objective feedback. Second, if the SED sought to prepare the ground for nationalization inconspicuously, how could the private owners themselves be expected not to become suspicious about the work of these commissions in their own firms?

The months following the December 1970 meeting of the SED Central Committee, which had rejected the New Economic System of the 1960s and strongly undermined Ulbricht's position, were characterized by disunity in the Politburo and considerable ambivalence concerning the private sector.[99] As East German economic historian Jörg Roesler has suggested, while the December 1970 meeting was anti-reformist, the February 1971 meeting of the Central Committee of the SED was pro-reformist and pro-Ulbricht again. This was the period during which the struggle over economic reform was waged. It was a purely political struggle within the Party leadership. Political decision makers did not seek the advice of economists, let alone permit a wider debate on the economic issues.[100] Ulbricht's demise was hastened by the growing conflict between his confrontational policy vis-à-vis the Federal Republic and the cooperative atmosphere emerging in East-West relations. Willy Brandt's *Ostpolitik* was bearing fruit in the non-aggression treaties concluded with the Soviet Union and Poland in 1970, undermining the GDR's traditional image of West Germany as an imperialistic and aggressive power. Ulbricht was unwilling to subordinate his conception of the GDR's interests to the new approach favoured by his allies, and it was on this front that his strong claims for the GDR's independence finally were rebuffed by the Soviet Union.[101] In May 1971, Ulbricht was succeeded by Erich Honecker as the SED's First Secretary.

The VIIth Party Congress of the SED in June 1971 made it clear that the SED leadership wanted a fundamental break with the policies of the 1960s, though there was no indication that the private sector would soon be subjected to a "socialist offensive."[102] The emphasis was on the central place of human welfare and the interests of the average citizens under socialism, obviously in contrast to the strong emphasis on technological progress and a response to the growing income differentiation of the 1960s. Under the influence of the worker unrest in Poland in 1970, the SED under Honecker turned to the concerns of lower income groups. Not surprisingly, given the circumstances of Ulbricht's fall and Honecker's rise, the Soviet model was again recognized as absolutely binding for GDR policymakers. After the Congress, the idea of the primacy of politics over technocratic tendencies became dominant in the SED leadership. This was reflected in the demotion of "technocrats" and the promotion of "apparatchiks". The new leadership's resolve to chart a new course was expressed by the disregard of the Ulbricht era and the attempt to emphasize any changes after his departure as significant elements of a comprehensive new policy.[103]

The decision to embark on a sweeping nationalization campaign was taken by the Central Committee in December 1971. The chairmen of the Bloc parties met with Honecker in January 1972, and the specific procedures were agreed upon in a resolution passed by the Council of Ministers in February 1972. Later that month, at the 11th Congress of the LDPD, private part-owners of semi-state enterprises publicly declared that they were offering their shares to the state.[104] Part-owners who were members in one of the Bloc parties had already in the fall of 1971 been called to consultations with regional state organs on the implications of the impending measure. In particular, they were assured that they would be able to maintain a management position in the new state enterprise. "The SED pre-empted opposition and benefited from their earnest assistance in identifying and solving problems beforehand, proving its pragmatic approach even in dogmatic actions."[105]

The "socialist offensive" was carried out swiftly. Within two weeks in late February/early March 1972, the owners of all private and semi-state enterprises selected for nationalization were called before local state organs and informed of the decision.[106] The quick conclusion of the campaign constituted a violation of the agreement between the SED and the Bloc parties, according to which the part-owners' decision to sell their shares to the state was to be voluntary, and the process of nationalization gradual. Liberal-Democratic Justice Minister Kurt Wünsche was forced to resign after protesting the SED's actions.[107]

The nationalization campaign created 11,300 new state enterprises with some 585,000 employees, bringing the share of the state in the industrial sector up from 88.8 percent in 1971 to 99.9 percent in 1972.[108] The labour force in the non-state sector had been almost halved, accounting for 7.6 percent of the total labor force in September 1972.[109] 85 percent of former (part-)owners retained positions as directors or managers in the new enterprises. Capital infusion, special attention and assistance from state organs, and the institutional continuity that was maintained even after the change in ownership insured the successful economic functioning of many of the nationalized enterprises for some time.[110]

The reasons for the nationalization drive that were given in 1972 and after to a large extent represent *post-hoc* ideological justifications, and are therefore only of limited value in ascertaining the actual motivations leading to the decision. At the very least, however, they indicate how and where basic assumptions of the 1960s concerning the private sector had been undermined. In October 1971, three months after the SED's VIIth Congress, Kurt Hager, the Party's chief ideologue, called for the return to a more orthodox understanding of class. Speaking before a congress of GDR social scientists, Hager stated: "It is evidently necessary to start unequivocally with Lenin's class definition, that is from the position of the class or stratum in socialist production and the corresponding level of socialization and organization."[111] The argument was subsequently presented more implicitly, though nevertheless unambiguously. Ulbricht's excessive claims for his "model GDR" had to be dismissed and the Soviet Union's leading role needed to be reaffirmed. Hager argued that Ulbricht's concept of a "developed social *system* of socialism"[112] referred essentially to the same thing as "developed socialist society" (the concept used by the Soviet Union and the other Eastern European countries at that time), namely, to "mature or developed socialism".

> But the following point must be noted: The developed socialist society was first established in the Soviet Union. In the other socialist countries the comprehensive construction of developed socialist society was started during the 1960s.[113]

Hager became more explicit in 1972. He charged that the conception of a "socialist community of man" (*sozialistische Menschengemeinschaft*)— which had symbolized the ideological integration of private entrepreneurs in the 1960s—had glossed over still existing class differences, vastly overrated the actual drawing together of the classes, and ignored the existence of "various capitalist remnants." The concept of the "developed social system of socialism" was declared false, thus the GDR was not in advance of the other socialist countries. "We are therefore in full agreement with the collective wisdom of the CPSU and the other fraternal parties in the socialist countries. In this way the universal validity of Marxist-Leninist theory is once again underscored." Ulbricht's central thesis of socialism as a relatively independent social formation was dismissed as "untenable".[114]

Thus, the entire ideological framework justifying the New Economic System and giving legitimacy to the private sector in the 1960s was being rejected. In part, this was due to Ulbricht's extensive use of the GDR's economic achievements and its special approach to socialism for what turned out to be overly ambitious and ill-fated political goals. In part, it was due to the economic problems generated by the GDR's "functional socialism". Some of the official reasons for nationalization were ideological. These include the existence of a "consciousness gap" between workers in the private sector and those in the state sector. Similarly, it was rediscovered that the existence of a private sector preserved "non-socialist modes of thought and behaviour".[115] Others were related more closely to economic facts, but derived their urgency from a perception of the situation reinvigorated by ideology. Private sector profits and private incomes appeared as excessive and growing.[116] Productivity growth in the private sector was believed to be increasingly lagging behind that of state enterprises.[117] Two problems, however, were serious enough that they would have required action regardless of the prevailing ideological situation. The first was the fact that the private sector attracted workers away from the state sector under conditions of labour scarcity. The second was that in order to safeguard the continued satisfactory performance of the private sector, extensive new investment as well as mergers of some private firms would become inevitable. This would have meant the economic strengthening of, and a renewed political commitment to, the private sector, and in the orthodox view this constituted "recapitalization."[118]

Nevertheless, this option was apparently given serious consideration.[119] There are strong reasons to assume that had the larger institutional (New Economic Policy) and ideological ("socialist community of man") framework successfully integrating the private sector in the 1960s not itself been rejected, these problems could have been resolved without nationalizing private firms. The reorientation towards orthodoxy also entailed a renewed belief in the economic superiority of socialist enterprises, so the assumption may have been that the nationalization would not have any economic costs. Finally, Honecker may have seized the opportunity to add some substance to his claim to initiate a new era[120] through an act of great symbolic significance—staged for the benefit of both his own Party and the hegemonic power. Whether and to what extent these and other factors[121] contributed to the decision in favour of nationalizing large parts of the private and semi-private sector in the GDR is not of crucial importance for the purposes of this study. It is clear that in contrast to earlier "socialist offensives," the last one in 1972 was part of a fundamental reorientation in political, economic, and social strategy, and thus for the first time a by-product, rather than the centrepiece of the SED's political strategy. This interpretation is further supported by the fact that not only was the alliance policy invoked in the justification of nationalization, but it was also expressed in the orderly and ideologically much less embittered approach vis-à-vis private entrepreneurs employed in the process.

Uncertainty and Neglect:
Private-Sector Policy, 1972–1975

The situation for the remaining private firms, predominantly in handicraft and retail trade, in the wake of the 1972 nationalizaton drive was very difficult. They had survived as remnants of an era that had now come to an end. But it was not clear what their position in the "developed socialist society" would be. Ideological fervour at the local level stirred up by the nationalizations was negatively affecting private artisans. It expressed in extreme form that SED policymakers had no adequate conception of a new private-sector policy. The basic objective was to channel the capacity of the handicraft sector increasingly into repair and service activities, while at the same time promoting the transformation of private handicraft firms into cooperatives.

New regulations passed in July 1972 specified how this was to be achieved. Local state organs at county and municipal levels were responsible for the restructuring of the handicraft sector. They were required, in the case of cooperatives, and permitted, in the case of private handicraft firms, to incorporate these enterprises into state planning and administration, regulating the number of employees for private firms and detailing the content and scope of newly-licensed operations. Tax breaks should be made available to promote repairs and services. The wording of the new regulation left no doubt that a restrictive licensing practice was intended: "Licenses [for new private firms] . . . *may* be issued if this is necessary for the supply of the population."[122] Local administrators hardly needed to be restrained. The widespread attitude was that if communism is near, why give financial and other support to private firms?[123]

The private-sector policy from 1972 to 1975 proved to be a failure in all respects. While the ideological goal of promoting the move towards cooperatives was maintained at a rhetorical level, many private artisans, if pushed too hard, would have simply gone out of business. So it was stressed that new cooperatives should only be set up if this was economically justified.[124] The restructuring of the handicraft sector aimed at increasing the share of capacity devoted to repairs and services showed only insignificant results. The share of repairs and services in total handicraft output grew by barely 1 percent between 1972 and 1975.[125] This was due to the fact that production continued to be more lucrative than providing repairs and services, despite the financial incentives. Moreover, a considerable part of handicraft capacity was tied contractually to state enterprises, which often could not find any alternative suppliers.

The neglect by policymakers and the tense ideological atmosphere contributed to a significant decline in the size of the handicraft sector. From 1972 to 1975, there was a net loss of some 17,000 private firms (16 percent) with a workforce of over 50,000. During the same period, only 14 new cooperatives were established, and the workforce of the cooperative sector grew by merely 6,000.[126] The restrictive licensing practice and the uncertain prospects for private firms were the major causes. Few new entrants were recruited, and established artisans often discouraged their children from taking over their firms.[127] Much the same was true for private and commission trade. Between 1972 and 1975, the number of self-employed (including assisting family members) declined from about 53,000 to 43,000 (or by almost 20 percent).[128]

The objective of private-sector policy in the early Honecker era seemed to be simply to let the still existing private firms gradually and naturally expire. The general assumption was that state enterprises would be able to provide the production and services of private firms much more efficiently.[129] Not for the first time in the history of the GDR, however, ideological preconceptions with respect to the private sector proved to be an inadequate guide for policy-making. Increasingly, the need for private firms was implicitly acknowledged in 1975,[130] and a fundamental policy reversal came in 1976.[131] While in the early 1970s the SED had sharply reduced the size of the private sector and severely compromised the credibility of its alliance policy, it was once again in the fortunate position to be able to reactivate the still existing institutional and ideological framework for its new private-sector policy since 1976.

Notes

1. Thus Hermann Weber suggests that there are two distinct periods in the history of the GDR in which ideology, reality, and motivation were given different priority. "Until 1961 ideological norms and programmatic objectives predominantly shaped policy: restructuring of political structures and of society according to the principles of 'Marxism-Leninism' in the concrete application of the Soviet model. This process had been by and large completed in 1961. Since then, the changed social and political reality—particularly the contradiction between modern industrial society and outdated methods of political rule and administration—more strongly affect politics. The objective constraints (*Sachzwänge*) determine changes in politics and even in ideology itself." Weber, *Geschichte der DDR*, p. 10.

2. In addition to the references made in Chapter 2, see for a comparative perspective, J. Roesler, "Die Rolle der Leitung und Planung bei der Zurückdrängung des privatkapitalistischen Sektors in der Industrie der Sowjetunion und einiger europäischer Volksdemokratien (zwanziger und vierziger Jahre)" (The role of planning and administration in restraining the private capitalist sector in the industry of the Soviet Union and various European People's Democracies (1920s and 1940s), *Jahrbuch für Geschichte der sozialistischen Länder Europas*, Vol. 22, No. 1 (1978), 87–95. On Poland, see Aslund, *Private Enterprise*.

3. Aslund, *Private Enterprise,* pp. 154–55.

4. See, for example, W. Mussler, "Die privatkapitalistische Industrie und die ökonomische Politik der Arbeiter-und-Bauernmacht" (Private capitalist industry and the economic policy of the workers' and farmers' power), *Einheit,* Vol. 11, 5 (1956), 530–537 and H. Sandig, "Zur Problematik der staatlichen Beteiligung an privatkapitalistischen Betrieben" (On the problem of state participation in private capitalist firms), *Einheit,* 12, 3 (1957), 308–317 regarding private industry; W. Heinrichs, "Zur Einbeziehung des privaten Einzelhandels in den sozialistischen Aufbau der DDR" (On the incorporation of private retail trade in the socialist construction of the GDR), *Wirtschaftswissenschaft,* Vol. 5, 6 (1957), 835–847 regarding private retail trade.

5. Roesler, "Strategies", 41. The information on semi-state enterprises is based on *ibid.*, 41–44; Aslund, *Private Enterprise,* pp. 153–157; W. Mussler, *Der kapitalistische Sektor der Industrie als Problem der Übergangsperiode zum Sozialismus in der Deutschen Demokratischen Republik* (The capitalist sector in industry as a problem of the transition period to socialism in the GDR) (Berlin: Verlag Die Wirtschaft, 1959), pp. 103–108; S. Wietstruk, *Entwicklung des Arbeiter-und Bauernstaates der DDR 1949-1961* (Development of the workers' and farmers' state of the GDR 1949–1961) (Berlin: Staatsverlag, 1987), p. 122–128.

6. Roesler, "Strategies", 40–41.

7. By 1957, the CDU, for example, had published a special booklet entitled "We are working with state participation" (*Wir arbeiten mit staatlicher Beteiligung*) (East Berlin: VOB Union Verlag, 1957) that explained and highly recommended this new form of mixed ownership.

8. Roesler, "Strategies", 42.

9. Aslund, *Private Enterprise,* p. 156.

10. *Ibid.,* p. 157.

11. *Ibid.,* p. 156.

12. Roesler, "Strategies", 43.

13. *Ibid.,* 42.

14. Heinrichs, "Zur Einbeziehung des privaten Einzelhandels," 835–837.

15. *Ibid.,* 837.

16. *Ibid.,* 838–39.

17. Aslund, *Private Enterprise,* pp. 158–59.

18. Wietstruk, *Entwicklung des Arbeiter-und Bauernstaates,* p. 130.

19. *Ibid.,* pp. 130–31.

20. *Ibid.,* p. 131.

21. *Ibid.*

22. Weber, *Geschichte der DDR,* p. 317.

23. Staritz, *Geschichte der DDR,* pp. 127–28.

24. E. Richert*, *Macht ohne Mandat. Der Staatsapparat in der sowjetischen Besatzungszone Deutschlands* (Power without mandate. The state apparatus in the Germany's Soviet Zone of Occupation), 2nd ed. rev. (Opladen: Westdeutscher Verlag, 1963), pp. 130–131.

25. *Ibid.,* p. 135.

26. Staritz, *Geschichte der DDR,* p. 102.

27. The main exponents were Prof. Fritz Behrens and Arne Benary who with reference to the Yugoslav model of self-managment called for decentralization and democratization of the economy. See F. Behrens, "Zum Problem der Ausnutzung ökonomischer Gesetze in der Übergangsperiode" (On the problem of utilizing economic laws in the transition period), *Wirtschaftswissenschaft,* 5 Sonderheft 3 (1957), 105–140; A. Benary, "Zu Grundproblemen der politischen Ökonomie des Sozialismus in der Übergangsperiode" (On basic problems of political economy in the transition period), *Wirtschaftswissenschaft,* 5, Sonderheft 3 (1957), 62–94. It should be noted, however, that the future of the private sector was not explicitly addressed. It is quite obvious that even these reformists did not question the need for the socialization of the means of production.

28. Weber, *Geschichte der DDR*, pp. 283–85.

29. *Ibid.*, pp. 286–291.

30. This paragraph is based on *ibid.*, pp. 292–94; Staritz, *Geschichte der DDR*, pp. 112–118.

31. *Ibid.*, p. 123.

32. Weber, *Geschichte der DDR*, p. 295.

33. *Ibid.*, pp. 297–98.

34. Staritz, *Geschichte der DDR*, p. 120.

35. Wietstruk, *Entwicklung des Arbeiter-und Bauernstaates*, p. 127.

36. Aslund, *Private Enterprise*, p. 254.

37. K. Steinitz, "Probleme der sozialistischen Umgestaltung des Handwerks in der DDR" (Problems of socialist restructuring of handicraft in the GDR), *Wirtschaftswissenschaft*, Vol.7, 8 (Nov.–Dec. 1959), 1128.

38. Aslund, *Private Enterprise*, p. 161.

39. The favorable lump-sum tax was only available for handicraft firms with a maximum of 3 journeymen, while for larger private handicraft enterprises a higher tax rate applied. Wietstruk, *Entwicklung des Arbeiter-und Bauernstaates*, p. 132.

40. More direct forms of coercion, however, were also used between 1958 and 1960. They included condemning in the press the refusal of private artisans to join a PGH. As Aslund (*Private Enterprise*, p. 164) reports, "[i]n Rostock, a competition between the political parties was launched to win as many artisans as possible for cooperatives. A district council in Leipzig had decided upon a full socialist transformation in 1960."

41. Steinitz, "Probleme der sozialistischen Umgestaltung," 1128.

42. Aslund, *Private Enterprise*, p. 165.

43. See e.g. Staritz, *Geschichte der DDR*, p. 135; Weber, *Geschichte der DDR*, pp. 315–317.

44. *Ibid.*, p. 317.

45. Staritz, *Geschichte der DDR*, p. 135.

46. Quoted in H. Klatke, "Die weitere Einbeziehung des privaten Einzelhandels in den sozialistischen Aufbau der DDR" (The further incorporation of private retail trade into socialist construction in the GDR) (East Berlin: Humboldt Universität, Diss., 1963), pp. 72–73.

47. Staritz, *Geschichte der DDR*, p. 136.

48. *Ibid.*, p. 137.

49. Weber, *Geschichte der DDR*, pp. 299–300.

50. J. Roesler, "Von der Generalperspektive zum Neuen Ökonomischen System. Wirtschaftspolitische Weichenstellungen in der DDR Ende der 50er/Anfang der 60er Jahre" (From the General Perspective to the New Economic System. Fundamental economic policy decisions in the GDR in the late 1950s/early 1960s), *Mannheimer Berichte*, Vol. 33 (August 1988), 9.

51. *Ibid.*, 10.

52. *Ibid.*

53. *Geschichte der SED. Abriss* (History of the SED. Brief Survey) (Berlin: Dietz Verlag, 1978), p. 439.

54. *Protokoll des VI. Parteitages der SED* (Berlin 1963), part 4, pp. 322–323; quoted in Aslund, *Private Enterprise*, pp. 168–69.

55. Roesler, "Generalperspektive," 12.

56. At the end of 1960, the share of PGHs in total handicraft output was 31 percent. *Ibid.,* 16.

57. See also Table 3.1 above.

58. W. Ulbricht, "Einige Grundfragen der Entwicklung der DDR" (Some Basic Questions concerning the Development of the GDR), in *Neues Deutschland,* 24 March 1962, p. 4; quoted in K. Gläss and E. Krey. "Fragen der staatlichen Leitung auf dem Gebiet der halbstaatlichen Betriebe und der Produktionsgenossenschaften des Handwerks," *Staat und Recht,* 1 (1964), 109 (emphasis added).

59. I have drawn on the following useful surveys of the NÖS, see Bundesminister für Innerdeutsche Beziehungen*, ed. *DDR-Handbuch.* 3rd rev. ed. (Cologne: Verlag Wissenschaft und Politik, 1985), Vol. 2, pp. 1488–89; Deutsches Institut für Wirtschaftsforschung*, ed. *Handbuch DDR-Wirtschaft.* 4th rev. (Hamburg: Rowohlt, 1984), pp. 81–83.

60. Paul Fröhlich, "Technischer Fortschritt in der gesamten Industrie" (Technological Progress in all of industry), *Neues Deutschland,* 15 October 1962, p. 4; quoted in Gläss/Krey, "Fragen der staatlichen Leitung," 110.

61. E. Lohse and S. Voigtsberger. "Zur Einbeziehung der halbstaatlichen und privaten Industriebetriebe sowie des allgemeinproduzierenden Handwerks in die perspektivische Entwicklung" (On the incorporation of semi-state and private industry as well as general manufacturing handicrafts into perspectivist development), *Wissenschaftliche Zeitschrift der Hochschule für Ökonomie,* 8, 3 (1963), 259.

62. *Ibid.,* 261.

63. *Gemeinsam zum Sozialismus. Zur Geschichte der Bündnispolitik der SED* (Together Towards Socialism. On the History of the SED's Alliance Policy) (East Berlin: Dietz Verlag, 1969), p. 365.

64. Lohse/Voigtsberger, "Zur Einbeziehung der halbstaatlichen und privaten Industriebetriebe," 273–74; H.-J. Nagel, "Die Einbeziehung der Betriebe mit staatlicher Beteiligung in die sozialistische Planwirtschaft beim Aufbau der entwickelten sozialistischen Gesellschaft in der DDR" (The incorporation of firms with state participation into the socialist planned economy during the construction of the developed socialist society), *Jahrbuch für Wirtschaftsgeschichte,* II (1972), 234–240.

65. *Gemeinsam zum Sozialismus,* p. 368.

66. H. Buske, W. Gahrig, J. Haschker et al. *Bündnispolitik im Sozialismus* (Alliance policy under socialism) (East Berlin: Dietz Verlag, 1981), p. 126.

67. Aslund, *Private Enterprise,* p. 171.

68. *Ibid.,* p. 171.

69. Roesler, "Strategies", 44–45.

70. Aslund, *Private Enterprise,* p. 254.

71. Between 1962 and 1971, the number of private handicraft firms had declined from about 159,000 to 112,000 (employees from ca. 394,000 to 341,000) while handicraft cooperatives (PGH) had increased from 4,114 to 4,480 (membership and employees up from ca. 190,200 to ca. 260,100). While in 1962 private handicraft still accounted for 64.7 percent of total handicraft output, in 1971

PGHs produced the larger share with 51.3 percent. Bundesministerium für Gesamtdeutsche Fragen*, ed. *Fünfter Tätigkeitsbericht 1965/69 des Forschungsbeirates für Fragen der Wiedervereinigung Deutschlands* (Fifth activity report 1965/69 of the research council on questions of the reunification of Germany) (Bonn und Berlin: Bundesdruckerei, 1969), pp. 295, 297; K. C. Thalheim, and M. Haendcke-Hoppe*, "Das Handwerk in der DDR und Ost-Berlin" (Handicraft in the GDR and East Berlin), *Beilage zum Jahresbericht der Handwerkskammer Berlin* (1972), 10. A revision of tax regulations for private handicraft in 1966, which abolished the favorable lump-sum tax for firms with 1–3 employees, was a further cause for the closing of private handicraft firms (7,744 in 1966 alone) and worked as an incentive for some owners to join a PGH. *Fünfter Tätigkeitsbericht,* p. 295.

72. Source: G. Büttner, "Die historische Entwicklung des sozialistischen Staatshaushaltes in der DDR und seine Rolle beim sozialistischen Aufbau" (The historical development of the socialist state budget in the GDR and its role in socialist construction), Dissertation A (Humbold-Universität, Berlin 1982), p. 210.

73. See further on this Aslund, *Private Enterprise,* pp. 172– 173.

74. Staritz, *Geschichte der DDR,* pp. 164–65.

75. *Politische Ökonomie des Sozialismus und ihre Anwendung in der DDR* (Political Economy of Socialism and its Application in the GDR) (East Berlin: Dietz Verlag, 1969).

76. *Ibid.,* p. 175.

77. *Ibid.,* p. 183.

78. *Ibid.,* p. 180.

79. *Ibid.,* pp. 180–181.

80. *Ibid.,* p. 181.

81. *Gemeinsam zum Sozialismus. Zur Geschichte der Bündnispolitik der SED* (Together Towards Socialism. On the History of the SED's Alliance Policy) (Berlin: Dietz Verlag, 1969).

82. *Ibid.,* p. 335.

83. *Politische Ökonomie,* pp. 170–71.

84. Quoted in Staritz, *Geschichte der DDR,* p. 165.

85. See, for example, *National-Zeitung,* 25 October 1967, where it was stressed that no more than 10 percent of the PGH's workforce was to be wage labour, and that only private artisans and their employees were eligible for PGH membership. The same problems were still criticized in 1970. See *National-Zeitung,* 11 March 1970.

86. Weber, *Geschichte der DDR,* p. 398.

87. K.C. Thalheim and M. Haendcke-Hoppe*, "Das Handwerk in der DDR und Ost-Berlin" (Handicraft in the GDR and East Berlin), *Beilage zum Jahresbericht der Handwerkskammer Berlin* (1967–1971).

88. See also Aslund, *Private Enterprise,* pp. 172–73.

89. *Neue Zeit,* 28 December 1968.

90. *National-Zeitung,* 11 October 1970.

91. Nagel, "Die Einbeziehung der Betriebe mit staatlicher Beteiligung".

92. Weber, *Geschichte der DDR,* pp. 402–403.

93. Staritz, *Geschichte der DDR*, pp. 194–95.

94. A. Bauernfeind, "Die Umwandlung der Betriebe mit staatlicher Beteiligung und Privatbetriebe in Volkseigene Betriebe" (The transformation of firms with state participation and private firms into nationally owned firms), *Zeitschrift für Geschichtswissenschaft*, Vol. 23, 1 (1975), 9.

95. *Ibid.*, 10–11; S. Finzelberg, "Die Stärkung der sozialistischen Produktionsverhältnisse und der führenden Rolle der Arbeiterklasse durch die Neubildung volkseigener Betriebe im ersten Halbjahr 1972" (The strengthening of socialist relations of production and of the leading role of the working class through the new formation of nationally owned firms in the first half of 1972), *Jahrbuch für Wirtschaftsgeschichte*, I (1975), 21–22.

96. Bauernfeind, "Die Umwandlung der Betriebe mit staatlicher Beteiligung," 11–12.

97. Aslund, *Private Enterprise*, pp. 182–84.

98. That other solutions for the private sector were being seriously considered is indicated by Bauernfeind,"Die Umwandlung der Betriebe mit staatlicher Beteiligung," 8.

99. Interview with Jörg Roesler, Academy of Science, East Berlin, 19 December 1989.

100. *Ibid.*

101. On the complex conditions in East-West relations and its linkages with the German situation at that time which brought Ulbricht into strong conflict with Moscow and thus precipitated his domestic demise, see Staritz, *Geschichte der DDR*, pp. 192–93.

102. Aslund (*Private Enterprise*, pp. 185–86) interprets this in accordance with his thesis that preparations were to be carried out as quietly as possible in order to avoid disruptions. This is plausible, though it may equally be taken as an indication that the nationalization decision had not yet been finalized.

103. This paragraph is largely based on Weber, *Geschichte der DDR*, pp. 408–409.

104. Bauernfeind, "Die Umwandlung der Betriebe mit staatlicher Beteiligung," 14.

105. Aslund, *Private Enterprise*, p. 187.

106. "Nationalisation proceeded in three steps, beginning with the persuasion of owners to sell their shares to the state, after which owners and employees were given directions, and finally, an inventory was made, directors appointed, and a nationally-owned enterprise legally constituted. By appointing directors last, the state kept open both the hopes and fears of owners who wanted to remain in charge." *Ibid.*, pp. 188–189.

107. Information from Joachim Linstedt, economic expert at the party headquarters of the Liberal Democrats, East Berlin, 22 December 1989. Kurt Wünsche was again Justice Minister in the transitional government under Hans Modrow and has retained his portfolio in the new coalition government formed after the March elections.

108. Bauernfeind, "Die Umwandlung der Betriebe mit staatlicher Beteiligung," 15.

109. Aslund, *Private Enterprise,* p. 189. For further details, see M. Haendcke-Hoppe*, "Die Vergesellschaftungsaktion im Frühjahr 1972" (The socialization drive in the spring of 1972), *Deutschland-Archiv,* Vol. 6, 1 (1973), 37–41.

110. Aslund reports that within five years no more than 30 percent of former owners still held management positions in their previous firms. "Yet the advantages of these enterprises have faded. They stopped excelling in innovation quickly. The private and semi-private dressmaking industry, which had competed well on Western markets for fashion, lost out at once. Thus, activities which required great initiative declined rapidly, but the quality of existing production did not deteriorate significantly in the medium term, as the good work morale lasted longer." (Aslund, *Private Enterprise,* p. 190) This does not seem to be true for the nationalized handicraft cooperatives where, according to two knowledgable interview partners, morale rapidly declined almost immediately after nationalization. Thalheim and Haendcke-Hoppe, on the other hand, have suggested that there was little resistance among members of handicraft cooperatives , since nationalization freed them from the heavy tax load they were carrying, as well as from the need to reorient their activities towards providing repairs and services. See K.C. Thalheim and M. Haendcke-Hoppe*, "Das Handwerk in der DDR und Ost-Berlin" (Handicraft in the GDR and East Berlin), *Beilage zum Jahresbericht der Handwerkskammer Berlin* (1972), 5.

111. K. Hager, "Die entwickelte sozialistische Gesellschaft" (Developed Socialist Society) (presentation given at the congress of social scientists on 14 October 1971 in Berlin), Berlin 1971, p. 25; quoted in P.C. Ludz, "Politische Ziele der SED und gesellschaftlicher Wandel in der DDR," in B. Gleitze, P.C. Ludz et al., *Die DDR nach 25 Jahren* (West Berlin: Duncker und Humblot, 1975), p. 77.

112. EgSS; see Section 4 above of this chapter.

113. *Ibid.,* 25.

114. Kurt Hager, *Zur Theorie und Praxis des Sozialismus. Reden und Aufsätze* (On the theory and practice of socialism. Speeches and Essays) (East Berlin 1972), 173ff.; quoted in Weber, *Geschichte der DDR,* pp. 415–16.

115. Bauernfeind, "Die Umwandlung der Betriebe mit staatlicher Beteiligung," 8; Finzelberg, "Die Stärkung der sozialistischen Produktionsverhältnisse," 17.

116. (Bauernfeind, "Die Umwandlung der Betriebe mit staatlicher Beteiligung," 7–8; Finzelberg, "Die Stärkung der sozialistischen Produktionsverhältnisse," 20–21.

117. Bauernfeind ("Die Umwandlung der Betriebe mit staatlicher Beteiligung," 5) refers to a 20–30 percent productivity gap. GDR economic historian J. Roesler has suggested to this author that available data for the 1960s do not allow any conclusions on this question. Aslund has calculated that labour productivity growth was more rapid in semi-state enterprises than in the state sector, and in semi-state and private construction firms even greater in absolute terms. Moreover, "net capital productivity (the ratio of net product to productive fixed assets) for the whole non-socialised sector was 3.3 times higher than that of the socialised sector." And he concludes: "We can therefore discard complaints about low labour productivity as sheer nonsense." (Aslund, *Private Enterprise,* p. 193) While this may in fact be true, what matters more at any rate is what was considered to be true in the GDR at the time.

118. Bauernfeind, "Die Umwandlung der Betriebe mit staatlicher Beteiligung," 8.

119. *Ibid.*

120. See on this Weber, *Geschichte der DDR,* pp. 406–407.

121. For some possible additional factors and a somewhat different interpretation, see Aslund, *Private Enterprise,* pp. 190–96.

122. See K.C. Thalheim and M. Haendcke-Hoppe*, "Das Handwerk in der DDR und Ost-Berlin" (Handicraft in the GDR and East Berlin), *Beilage zum Jahresbericht der Handwerkskammer Berlin* (1972), 7–8; emphasis added.

123. Information from Prof. J. Roesler (interview 1988).

124. K.C. Thalheim , and M. Haendcke-Hoppe*, "Das Handwerk in der DDR und Ost-Berlin," *Beilage zum Jahresbericht der Handwerkskammer Berlin* (1973).

125. M. Haendcke-Hoppe*, "Handwerkspolitik der SED 1976—ökonomische und ideologische Aspekte der Förderungsmaßnahmen" (The SED's handicraft policy 1976—economic and ideological aspects of the promotion measures), *FS-Analysen,* 9 (1976), p. 8.

126. *Ibid.,* 6–7.

127. Roesler (interview 1988).

128. M. Haendcke-Hoppe*, "Privatwirtschaft in der DDR. Geschichte— Struktur—Bedeutung" (The private economy in the GDR, history—structure—significance), *FS-Analysen,* 1 (1982), p. 54.

129. Roesler (interview 1988).

130. K.C. Thalheim and M. Haendcke-Hoppe*, "Das Handwerk in der DDR und Ost-Berlin," *Beilage zum Jahresbericht der Handwerkskammer Berlin* (1975).

131. This will be discussed in detail in subsequent chapters, esp. Chapter 5.

4

Private Enterprise and Private Entrepreneurs Under GDR Socialism: Scope, Structure, and Social Composition of the Private Economy in the 1980s

The present chapter will provide an analysis of the scope, size, and structure of the East German private economy in the 1980s. It will discuss the incentives for, and obstacles to, becoming a private entrepreneur in the socialist GDR and conclude with an account of the social origins and characteristics of this social stratum. In order to situate the official or legal, full-time private economic actors who are the subject of this study more clearly in their social context, the chapter will begin with an outline of what will be referred to as the margins of the private sector—illegal as well as part-time private economic activities (see Figure 4.1). This snapshot of the GDR private sector in the 1980s will set the stage for the discussion in subsequent chapters of its different forms of *institutional integration* into the larger socialist society—its legal-administrative integration (Chapter 5), its forms of economic integration (Chapter 6), and its political and social integration (Chapter 7). The *institutional continuity thesis* with respect to these various forms of legal, economic, and political integration links the following in-depth analysis of the private sector in the 1980s (Chapters 5–7) with the preceding account of its historical evolution (Chapters 2–3). The rapid political and economic transformation underway in the GDR since November 1989 raises the question whether the analysis provided in this and the following chapters is now merely of historical significance. The general theoretical argument of this study suggests that even in a radical and comprehensive transition process to a new socio-economic order, the institutional elements of the past may have an important and lasting influence on the shaping of the emerging new order. Since the present reform goals assign a central place to the private economy and entrepreneurs, an analysis of the functioning of the private sector under socialism can provide important clues for an understanding

Figure 4.1 Scope of Private Economic Activity in the GDR in 1988

Illegal	Legal Full-Time	Legal Part-Time
informal and illegal trade "black labour"	artisans retailers others (181,700 self-employed)	individual agricultural production rental housing professional services

of the problems and prospects of the transition process.[1] The present chapter assembles the first of a number of elements that together constitute the institutional point of departure of East Germany in its transition to a new socio-economic and political order.

On the Margins I:
"Black" and Other Unregulated Markets

Compared to most other Eastern European socialist countries, the GDR had a fairly sizable legal private sector. H. Brezinski has estimated that—recorded and unrecorded—legal private economic activity accounted for about 5 percent of national income.[2] Most commentators agree that in the GDR there was considerably less illegal private economic activity than in other Communist states.[3] One reason for this was probably the relatively larger size of the GDR's legal private sector until the early 1980s. Other factors are economic (the relatively better supply with goods and services in the GDR)[4] and probably also cultural. On the basis of impressionistic evidence, one might conclude that bribery was kept in check to some extent (e.g. compared to Poland or Hungary) by the survival of cultural norms opposed to such practices. At any rate, shortages in some areas and product types were no less severe in East Germany than in neighboring socialist states so that relatively better economic conditions alone are an insufficient explanation. Small gifts and amounts of money were commonplace for many forms of exchange (between 5 and 100 Marks). Larger sums, on the other hand, were considered indecent by most people in the GDR.[5]

The two most widespread forms of illegal activity were "black labour" (or moonlighting) and violating official price and license regulations. The former was more or less openly tolerated and to some extent legally sanctioned, while the latter was strictly prosecuted and punished. Black labour was in great demand, particularly for home repair, construction, and services. These, of course, were the very occupations promoted by the SED's private-sector policy. But since demand for prompt service could not be satisfied by existing private firms, there was a flourishing market for 'after-work brigades'. These could be state workers, but also employees and even owners of private firms, who could easily charge 3 to 4 times the official wage.[6]

In addition to promoting the private repairs and services sector, in 1972 the SED legalized unofficial and unregistered work for up to 3,000 Marks annually as tax-free income. Exceeding this limit resulted in minor fines only. More recently, a regulation concerning private part-time services in computer software was passed, permitting up to 600 hours of consulting work per year.[7] It was generally recognized that "black labour" was indispensable and therefore had be tolerated. This was reflected in existing regulations and perhaps even more in the 'liberal' way these rules were enforced.

The authorities were much less lenient in cases of black market trading and violations of price and license regulations. The single largest and most important market which may illustrate the fine line between tolerated and prosecuted illegal private activity was the used car market. New cars in the GDR cost between 15,000 and 40,000 Marks (the average gross annual income for an employee in state industry in 1988 was just over 15,000). However, new cars could not be purchased immediately. There was enormous excess demand, and prospective buyers had to enter their names on official waiting lists to become eligible for purchasing a car. Depending on the model they chose, their turn to buy a car finally came after between 11 to 14 years of waiting. These conditions on the market for new cars explain why prices on the used car market were extremely high. In order to restrict excessive pricing of used cars, the state established official list prices. But it was practically impossible to find anyone who was willing to sell a car at the list price. It was generally understood that the private seller would demand additional, informal payment in cash. Practically all used car deals were thus based on illegal pricing. This, however, was accepted as long as buyers and sellers were in the market "for the goods and not for the profit." It is clear at the same time that under existing market conditions, incentives to act as an illegal used car dealer were very high. (No licenses were issued for used car dealerships.) Stiff penalties were imposed on those convicted for illegal car trading.[8]

The private sale of any goods in public places was generally regulated and subject to licensing. Some, as for example gardeners selling their produce on street corners without a license, were tolerated. But on the whole, unofficial private trade, particularly if it was related to violations of currency and customs regulations, was strictly prosecuted and punished. Only pensioners and housewives were allowed to sell home-made or home-grown products without a license, with sales permitted to total up to 3,000 Marks per year.[9] The black market for Western goods, especially clothing, was dominated by Polish citizens because they could freely travel to West Berlin and, if caught, usually only received a warning. There were, however, legal alternatives. Home-produced and inherited goods, for example, could be legally sold at one of the numerous flea markets with the payment of only a small booth fee. The increasingly popular fairs or flea markets during the spring, summer, and early fall were, in fact, the largest organized and officially sanctioned black markets in the country. They differed in size and importance, the largest taking place in Havelberg near Berlin in early September of every year. Between

200,000 and 300,000 people flocked to this fair to buy and/or sell goods at completely unregulated prices.

It is quite obvious that the government was attempting to deal with some of the pent-up demand created by the generally unsatisfactory supply situation in the consumer goods sector by creating more public opportunities for people to buy and sell—mostly used—goods.[10] The SED Central Committee more recently encouraged local state organs at county and district levels to organize such markets "under strict state control . . . to further improve the supply level in accordance with the growing demands of the population."[11]

On the Margins II:
Houseowners and Part-time Farmers

Two further segments of the private sector may be discussed here under the heading of "marginal", not because they were marginally legal (or even illegal). Rather, they may be considered marginal because it was seldom that a person could make a living in them, in part because they were usually engaged in on a part-time basis.

Undoubtedly, the most unprofitable form of private ownership in the GDR was *rental housing*. Still, over 50 percent of housing units in the GDR remained privately owned.[12] This is a surprisingly large share, given the enormous efforts of the Honecker regime since 1971 in the area of housing construction and renovation.[13] There are no statistics available on the share of privately-owned housing units which were not owner-occupied, i.e. which were actual rental units.[14] As a result, only some general observations may be made here. All rental housing, whether publicly or privately owned, was subject to rent regulation. Rates were extremely low—between 1.00 and 1.25 M per square meter in Berlin and 0.80 to 0.90 in the rest of the GDR in modern buildings, even less in old (prewar) buildings.[15] This means that an average household spent a mere 2.4 percent of its net income on rent.[16]

It thus comes as no surprise that private owners of rental housing had practically no financial means—and absolutely no incentive—to invest in repairs and general maintenance. Private house ownership, unless one occupied one's own premises, entailed no privileges, but a number of obligations. Private owners could not rent out their units themselves. In fact, they were not even able to move into their own house if it was already occupied, or if the living space was considered too large for the owner. Private rental housing, just like public housing, was administered by a local housing authority. The "municipal housing administration" (*Kommunale Wohnungsverwaltung; KWV*) was on the whole unable to provide the minimum repair and maintenance necessary for preserving the substance of public housing. It is for this reason that private owners of rental units were not expected or forced to maintain any higher standards of building maintenance than the public authorities, and with the same lamentable results. Tenants of both privately- and publicly-owned housing were encouraged to make their own repairs, the materials being paid for by the housing authority. In some cases, tenants were able to purchase a state-owned house from the public housing authority.

Individual agricultural production, while for the most part not based on the private ownership of the means of production (i.e., mainly land), could be a very profitable form of private economic activity. Since the practically full collectivization of agriculture in 1960/61, private owner-ship of the means of production played a very minor role in individual farming. There were only 5,900 private full-time farmers and gardeners left in the GDR in 1988.[17] In addition, there remained a small number of agricultural cooperatives of the transitional types I and II (i.e., not fully collectivized cooperatives) in which members still owned stables and livestock, but they can be assumed to have been of only marginal quan-titative significance. Finally, the churches operate their own farms, ac-counting for 3.2 percent of GDR farm land in the 1980s.[18] The total workforce in private farming and forestry in 1988 totalled 14,500.[19]

Of much greater importance was individual production by members and employees of collective farms. Until the mid-1970s, the SED consid-ered this to be no more than a temporary concession to collective farmers to boost their incomes and to enable them to grow supplies for their own families. It was expected that with the ultimate success of large-scale "industrial" farming, individual production would gradually disappear. However, the disillusionment with the industrial approach in the face of growing problems during the 1970s led the SED to reverse its approach to individual agriculture.[20] This was reflected in the 1977 Statute for Agricultural Cooperatives. The members' right to a private plot of up to 0.25 hectare/person (or 0.5 hectare/family) was now also extended to workers employed by the cooperative. Restrictions on privately kept livestock were dropped, and loans with favourable conditions were of-fered.[21] In the late 1980s, about two-thirds of cooperative farm families engaged in individual production.

The other major group of private producers of agricultural goods were part-time farmers who usually worked in non-agricultural sectors of the economy or were retired. These were the so-called "small gardeners and lifestock breeders and keepers" who had their own association, the VKSK.[22] Over 1.5 million members organized in more than 20,000 basic cells of the association made use of approx. 60,000 hectares of land.[23] The SED encouraged their individual production in various ways. Private pro-ducers, for example, could send soil samples to central laboratories for analysis and advice. Since 1980 there had been a concerted effort by the state to locate very small patches of unused land (*Splitterflächen*) to be distributed to interested individuals for private farming. According to a resolution of the XIth Party Congress in 1986, another 150,000 plots were to be made available by 1990, particularly to working class families and large families, 20,000 of these in Berlin alone.[24]

Very considerable increases in individual production in the 1980s were in large part achieved by a generous price policy. Large increases were granted to private producers in 1978 and 1984.[25] Individual producers were encouraged to sell their products on a contractual basis directly to institutional consumers (e.g. to local supermarkets, holiday facilities, and enterprise kitchens). Moreover, there was a dense network of purchasing depots (*Aufkaufstellen*) specifically charged with buying up the products of individual producers and getting them as quickly as possible to the consumer. Many of these purchasing depots were retail outlets of state, as well as a small number of private, retail firms.[26]

The annual maximum tax-free income from private cultivation and animal breeding was 7,000 Marks. However, there was no strict control of individual incomes derived from part-time agricultural production[27] in order not to discourage the additional production of crops. Generally, it seemed to be most advantageous for the individual producers to take their produce to a local *Aufkaufstelle* where the highest prices were paid. In fact, the state subsidized individual agricultural production to such an extent that retail prices were lower than what the individual producer received from the state purchasing depot. There is little doubt that the government believed the benefits of ensuring a better supply of the population with fresh products to be greater than the costs of promoting individual agricultural production.[28] Private production of agricultural products in the 1980s was officially and unabashedly portrayed as an integral part of GDR agricultural policy.[29] This is understandable, given the private sector's share in total agricultural output—ranging from 10 percent in beef and vegetables, approximately 30 percent in fruit, some 50 percent in eggs to 99.9 percent in rabbits.[30] Nevertheless, compared to most other Eastern European countries, the GDR, along with Czechoslovakia, had the most highly collectivized agricultural sector.[31]

The Free Professions and Other Private Entrepreneurs

Table 4.1 provides an overview of the quantitative significance of different sectors of the private economy and their change during the 1980s. In contrast to the handicraft and retail trade sectors which will be described in the following sections, private enterprise played a very minor role in a number of other economic sectors. Private farming and gardening

Table 4.1 Number of Self-Employed* by Economic Sector in 1980 and 1988

	1980	1988
Agriculture and Horticulture	6,200	5,900
Retail and Wholesale Trade	37,700	39,000
Handicraft	112,500	111,700
Free Professionals	10,700	12,600
Others	12,900	12,500
Total	180,000	181,700

* incl. assisting family members
Source: *Statistisches Jahrbuch 1981, 1989*, p. 111.

have just been mentioned, and as Table 4.1 indicates, the 5,900 self-employed farmers and gardeners and assisting family members accounted for only a very small fraction of individual agriculture, which was predominantly part-time.

The 12,600 free professionals may be divided into two main groups according to their tax bracket. The larger group, the so-called "free-lancing intellectuals" (*freischaffende Intelligenz*), was subject to a maximum 30 percent tax rate. This group consisted of writers, scientists, physicians, dentists, veterinarians, midwives, and inventors.[32] The remaining free professionals were subject to a tax rate of up to 60 percent. This group included graphic artists, engineers, architects, filmmakers, translators, tourist guides, lawyers, and others. The almost 20 percent increase in the number of free professionals in the GDR between 1980 and 1987 was primarily due to a more liberal licensing practice and more favourable tax regulations since 1980.[33]

The "other" 12,500 private entrepreneurs ran businesses that were not regarded as handicraft or trade. They paid the highest tax rates with a progression of up to 90 percent. For instance, in the transportation and communications sector, there were 7,900 self-employed persons with a total of 7,000 employees. These were mainly taxi and truck drivers, driving schools, transportation companies, and inland waterway carriers. With an average of less than one employee, the size of these firms was very small. The state did not seem to be very interested in expanding this part of the private sector. For example, it was very difficult to set up a private trucking business, even if it was only a one-man operation. One problem was fulfilling numerous and very strict regulations as a precondition for being licensed by the local department of transport. But perhaps the most difficult problem was to acquire a used truck or any other transport vehicles.[34]

The situation was quite similar in the area of private taxis. A 1986 regulation[35] permitted private car owners to offer taxi services on a part-time basis on commission from a state taxi enterprise. There were strict rules governing the licensing of taxis by the county council. These pertained to the driving record of the applicant and the technical condition of the car. As well, the approval of the applicant's full-time employer had to be obtained. Great regional disparities in the supply of taxi services persisted.[36] Even in Berlin itself, it was a trying experience to attempt to flag down a cab or to order one by phone at practically any time of the day. The supply gap was filled to some extent, especially late at night, by private unlicensed (thus illegal) drivers offering their services at rates usually below the official level.

There were some 200 private industrial enterprises (with a total of 1,700 employees) that survived the 1972 nationalization. The private business community, in addition, included pharmacies and a considerable number of other specialized and in some cases rather peculiar occupations. A private medical-technical laboratory in East Berlin had 60 employees.[37] The Chamber of Trade and Commerce, a state-supervised organization for private businesses outside the handicraft sector, was responsible for some 100 different occupations, including such odd trades as animal intestine sorter (1 in Berlin) and public washroom operators (254 in Berlin).[38]

Retail and Wholesale Trade

A total of 39,000 self-employed persons with 51,700 employees operated businesses in the domestic trade sector in 1988.[39] Private wholesale firms, which very early in the history of the GDR were squeezed out,[40] accounted for only a very small fraction of the private trade sector. No statistics are published, but in the whole of Berlin, for example, there were only 35 private wholesale enterprises left. While they had a good reputation on account of their flexibility, generally no new licenses were issued except in some cases for children of the owners of existing firms.[41]

The bulk of the private trade sector was made up of retail shops, restaurants, and small hotels. In 1987, 20 percent of retail outlets and 41 percent of restaurants and pubs in the GDR were privately operated. Their shares in total retail trade turnover were, respectively, 8.5 percent and 16 percent.[42] Private enterprises could be found in practically all areas of retail trade, and their numbers were particularly strong among drugstores and hardware stores.[43] Within the private trade sector, two basic ownership forms existed, private firms with and without a commission contract. At one time ideologically important, this differentiation had become by the 1980s largely a matter of economic preference on the part of the owner. A private firm without commission contract owned or rented its own premises, owned the inventory and equipment, and determined its own selection of goods offered.

A private firm with a commission contract may be compared to a franchise operation where the private operator receives a share of the profits from its contracting partner, usually one of the large state retail or wholesale trading enterprises. The working of the commission system may be briefly illustrated with the help of two examples. The first is a small liquor and tobacco commission shop. The shop's inventory was owned by the commission partner, the *Staatliche Handelsorganisation* (state trade organization, HO). It had an inventory of roughly 30,000 Marks and its annual revenue was approximately 500,000 M. As in virtually the whole private sector, the state set prices and profit margins, which here was 10 percent. The HO retained about half of the profits, the rest went to the commission retailer. His annual income before taxes was approximately 25,000 M. There were very strict limitations on temporarily exceeding the 30,000 M inventory limit as a disincentive to hoarding. A 15 percent penalty on overstock was charged and deducted from the owner's commission.

A hardware store may serve as a second example. Its commission partner was the *Staatliche Grosshandelsgesellschaft* (state wholesale company, GHG). Most of the goods the commission trader picked up himself at the regional GHG outlet every two weeks. This commission trader owned his business premises, for which he received rent from his commission partner. He paid 2.5 percent of the annual gross wage sum into a social and cultural fund run by the GHG, which his employees received as a bonus at the end of the year. Employees in the retail trade sector received very low wages—2.15 M/hour plus a monthly bonus of 150 M. 460 M per month was the maximum a sales person could earn in his store. One advantage he had to offer was that people could work part-time. Another apparently more general benefit of working for a private employer was that there was no political interference and no political activity required. Many people found this attractive. It was an obvious advantage for individuals who had applied for emigration. In a state firm, they would have been subject to various forms of special supervision and pressure. This hardware store owner reported that in the 1950s and early 1960s commission retailers received preferential deliveries compared to private retailers. Now that the supply situation had worsened, there was no difference. Another reason for the absence of any difference was that the distinction between private and commission trade was no longer ideologically relevant in the 1980s. The two forms of trade were put on an equal ideological footing by government decrees in 1984 and 1988.[44] A private shop often yielded more revenue for the state than a commission shop, which had to deduct a portion of its profit for its state commission partner.

In the private retail trade sector, about one-third of all firms operated without, and two-thirds with, a commission contract. In the private restaurant and hotel sector, the share of firms with commission contract was even higher.[45] Of a total of just under 27,000 public restaurants, there were about 8,000 private enterprises with, and about 3,000 without, commission contract.[46] And of the 450 private hotels (with 26 percent of total lodging capacity in the GDR), by far the largest number operated under commission contract.[47]

The Handicraft Sector

With 111,700 self-employed, 82,234 firms, and 153,975 employees in 1988,[48] the handicraft sector constituted by far the single largest part of the private economy in the GDR. It was also that part of the private sector which had received the most positive attention from the state since 1976. Finally, it is the part of the private sector for which the most detailed structural data are available.[49] The handicraft trades have a long tradition in Germany, not only as traditions of skills and techniques, but also as traditions of work attitudes and of economic and political organization. While the majority of artisans in the GDR worked in the private sector, there were some 2,719 cooperative handicraft firms (*Produktionsgenossenschaften des Handwerks,* PGH) with a total of 162,169 members.[50] Handicraft cooperatives, which for many years were specially promoted and portrayed as the handicraft organization of the future, had been stagnating and even slightly declining in numbers. The 1972 nationalization of many cooperatives had negative effects on the surviving cooperatives and further reduced the incentive to join them.[51] The state seemed to have no intention of promoting them by encouraging the formation of new cooperatives. In fact, state plans made provision for annually increasing the quantity of supplies and materials designated for private sector handicraft firms. This suggests not only that private firms were considered more lucrative for artisans, but also that they worked more effectively than handicraft cooperatives.

Table 4.2 provides a survey of the structure of the most important handicraft trades. There are three general categories according to which handicraft trades were classified. First, the so-called *producing handicraft trades,* i.e., those primarily engaged in the processing or manufacturing of products. More than 61 percent of the total production was accounted for by the food processing trades, primarily meat processing (2,239 private

Table 4.2 Structure of Major Handicraft Branches in 1986

Handicraft Branches	Share in total sales revenue in billion Marks	handicraft output in percent	percent share of		number of firms		number of employees(2)	
			private	PGH(1)	private	PGH	private	PGH
Meat processing	2.88	14	10	4	2,239	66	17,300	3,600
Bakeries	1.50(3)	7	6	1	6,540(4)	57(4)	33,000	4.000
Machine and vehicle construction	3.82	18	11	7	13,297	341	44,700	20,100
Electrical/electronic	2.56	12	5	7	7,246	320	22,600	23,200
Services	1.19	6	2	4	9,639	400	25,800	41,100
Construction	5.59	27	12	15	13,469	1,064	36,000	53,100
Total	17.80	85	47	38	53,275	2,256	182,500	145,800

(1) PGH = handicraft cooperative; (2) rounded figures; (3) estimate; (4) in 1985
Source: Based on M. Haendcke-Hoppe, "Struktureffekte der SED-Handwerkspolitik seit 1976," *FS-Analysen* (1988), p. 17.

firms and a workforce of about 17,300 employees) and bakeries (6,540 private firms and a workforce of about 33,000). The baking trade (i.e., private and cooperative firms) produced 43 percent of freshly baked goods.[52] In view of German preferences for freshly baked bread and buns, this is certainly one of the most vital handicraft trades.

Second, there are the *repair and service trades* (excluding building repairs which fall under the third category). Automobile repairs, radio and television repairs, and the services trades (e.g. laundry services, dry cleaning) were the three main branches, accounting for 84 percent of output in this category (and 36 percent of total handicraft output). The repair and service trades were very important in the GDR because consumer goods were often of poor quality and not cheaply or easily replaceable. This is why it was politically very important to insure a relatively easy access to such services at low cost.[53]

The third and the single largest handicraft branch is made up of *construction trades* (25 percent of total handicraft output). These include those engaged in the production of building materials, in construction, and in building repairs. In 1988, there were 14,295 private firms with a workforce of 45,240.[54]

All told, the handicraft sector in the GDR consisted of some 140 different trades. In many highly specialized crafts, only a few master artisans were left—e.g., bronze casters, crystal glass workers, jewellers, mould makers, glass painters, bell casters, builders of musical instruments, and lace makers. In recent years, however, the state had been specially promoting apprenticeship training in 47 rare artisanal trades.[55]

Incentive and Disincentive Structures in the Private Sector

What were the incentives to become a private entrepreneur in a socialist society? What were some of the major obstacles and difficulties? With its basic positive policy approach to the private sector after 1976, the SED had created one important precondition for making private business an attractive option in principle. The restrictive licensing practice of the state in the early 1970s and, more important, the psychological climate in the aftermath of the 1972 nationalization drive did not encourage the starting up of a private business. Many owners of existing private firms discouraged their children from taking over. On the other hand, even under the favourable general conditions, it was still difficult in many respects to secure a license for a private enterprise. Local administrative departments at county and municipal levels had the right to determine whether there was demand for the product or services offered by any particular applicant, and this political assessment of economic demand followed its own rather restrictive logic.

A systematic analysis of the policy and regulatory framework and its effects will be the subject of Chapter 5. Some positive and negative incentive factors for established and prospective private entrepreneurs need to be mentioned here, however. A crucial factor attracting individuals to the private sector was the prospect of a relatively high income. In the absence of published income statistics for the private sector,[56] it is of course not possible to provide more than a general and impressionistic picture. H. Vortmann has estimated that until 1970 the average gross income of a self-employed artisan continually increased to a level two-and-a-half times that of employees in industry.[57] Haendcke-Hoppe conjectures that during the period of restrictive handicraft policy in the early 1970s, the average income may have dropped somewhat.[58] Aslund suggests that the minimum income of private entrepreneurs was approximately equal to the average wage in the GDR, while the median entrepreneurial net income was about 2-2.5 times as much, and maximum incomes may have been around twenty times the average wage.[59] Finally, Brezinski believes that the promotion of the private sector was resulting in growing income disparities between private entrepreneurs and the population at large.[60]

The average gross annual income of employees in the state sector, including social benefits, in 1988 was just over 15,000 Marks.[61] According to the estimate of an expert in the GDR, an average private entrepreneur, such as an optician or a butcher, with an assisting family member had an annual net income of about 35,000 Marks.[62] Others, such as private master shoemakers and bicycle mechanics, earned considerably less. Special subsidies for these trades were established in 1986 to improve financial incentives, but they met with only partial success.[63] It is obvious that in trades where a private entrepreneur was unlikely to earn more than an average state sector wage, there was no financial incentive to start one's own business. But additional factors have to be taken into account.

Thus bakers, for example, earned about an average private sector income, and they could easily earn above average if they specialized in pastries or opened up a cafe on the side. However, in many—particularly rural—regions of the GDR there was a severe shortage of private bakeries.[64] Local councils often offered special benefits, such as making available a modern home, a weekend cottage, etc. to attract master bakers to their community. The fact that in spite of these favourable conditions there continued to be a lack of applicants suggests that there were strong limits on the effectiveness of purely financial incentives in attracting people to the private sector. It was widely recognized that operating a private business demands a significantly greater amount of effort and time than was required of any employee in the state sector. Even the prospect of doubling one's income was not always sufficient reason to make a career in the private sector a desirable option.

A good indicator for the lack of incentive for many private entrepreneurs in the restaurant and retail sectors to put in extra work was reflected in their opening hours. Often, they tried to keep their opening hours to a minimum, which sometimes could take on extreme forms, such as in the case of an ice cream parlour where the owner applied for permission to close down for the whole month of July.[65] There are a number of reasons why private entrepreneurs were unwilling to keep their premises open for long hours. First, they may not in fact have increased their earnings substantially by doing so, either because they would have had to hire additional labour or because their additional revenue put them in a higher tax bracket. Second, they may have been content with their income and unwilling to work longer hours because the value of money in East Germany (as in many other socialist countries) was rather limited. That is, many luxury goods, trips to foreign countries, etc. were simply not availabe for money, or for money alone. Given their already privileged material position, the value of spare time may have been much higher than additional income. On the other hand, many private entrepreneurs as well as representatives of the state, the Bloc parties, and the Chambers suggested that one of the strongest disincentives to expansion and increased performance in private sector firms was the structure of the tax system.[66] Thus, the favorable lump-sum tax available to small handicraft firms with up to one employee represented a strong disincentive for business expansion. More generally, the tax progression became so prohibitive from a certain level of income[67] that the logic of negative incentives described above applied with even greater force. In addition, there were other disincentives to firm expansion which compounded the effects of the tax regulations. Expanding a firm usually meant that an owner had to spend proportionally more time securing supplies, which often resulted in more aggravation and frustration than the extra income seemed to justify.

Prices for the products and services supplied by private entrepreneurs in the GDR were generally set by special departments at various state levels. In many cases, prices were fixed at very low levels for political reasons, i.e., to make these goods and services easily affordable for all. Bread and shoe repair services are a case in point. One result of this general policy was that the state, in order to attract private entrepreneurs for such trades, had to provide a variety of subsidies. Another implication was that affordability led to high demand which, since prices rarely changed, simply resulted in long waiting periods or in unsatisfied demand.[68] This explains why some private entrepreneurs, such as hairdres-

sers, actually complained about excessive demand for their services.[69] The
rigid and low price level also explains in part why state organs were, on
the whole, fighting a losing battle in their attempt to satisfy the demand
for services that could be provided by private firms. Purchasing power
under such conditions of "artificial" scarcity is virtually unlimited.

Another problem for private sector firms was finding employees. There
was a general and worsening labour shortage in the GDR in the late 1980s,
due mainly to the negative growth of the population as well as the constant
emigration (legal and illegal) of citizens to the West. In addition, the
private sector was handicapped vis-à-vis the state sector by not being
allowed to pay equal wages for the same work. Private owners were forced
to resort to other forms of additional remuneration in order to attract and
keep their employees. They were allowed to pay higher wages than
provided for by the official rate, but only if they were willing to take a
corresponding cut in their own profits. Such additional wage payments
were not tax-deductible. Frequently, they offered employees additional
time off or paid them tax-deductible overtime which they had not actually
worked. Other benefits depended on the trade in question.[70] Generally, it
was very difficult for private firms to lay off workers for any reason but
misconduct. However, due to the voluntary character of many of the
benefits employees of private firms received, a private employer could
simply withhold those benefits as an incentive for the employee to quit.[71]
The Council of Ministers' resolution of March 1988 provided for small
wage increases for full-time employees working in the private retail and
restaurant sectors and equal pay for part-time employees.

These were some of the major problems and disincentives in the GDR
private sector in the 1980s. Nevertheless, it would be wrong to conclude
that there were few incentives to become a private entrepreneur. Unless
the trade in question happened to be characterized by particularly un-
pleasant working conditions (e.g., bakers) or afforded barely an average
income (e.g., shoe or bicycle repair), material incentives to start a business
were in fact quite strong. However, the non-material rewards of private
entrepreneurship in the GDR should not be underestimated. Most private
entrepreneurs greatly valued their relative independence. In a system
where the state played a dominant role in practically all aspects of working
life, the private sector offered one of the few niches in society where
personal initiative and full-time work could be combined. As a result, the
demand for licenses in most private-sector trades far exceeded the state-
assessed demand for the goods and services of private firms. More
important, it exceeded the available infrastructure (especially space) and
supply of materials and equipment the state could allocate.[72]

Who Are the Private Entrepreneurs?

There are no socio-structural studies or data available on private entrepreneurs in the GDR. All that can be provided is a very general characterization of this social stratum, the full-time self-employed, particularly those owning their own businesses in the handicraft or retail sectors, based on observations, experiences, and conversations in the GDR.[73]

Private entrepreneurs—in the GDR usually referred to as *Handwerker und Gewerbetreibende*—were generally regarded as a distinct social stratum, and they seem to have had their own group (if not class) consciousness. This consciousness of forming a distinct group in society was a function of various objective and subjective factors. Objectively, private entrepreneurs were among the wealthiest in East Germany. By virtue of being self-employed, they had a certain degree of independence not enjoyed by most citizens. In short, they objectively held a privileged position in society. Subjectively, in addition to a sense of proprietorship, they generally felt a strong sense of responsibility for their work; they were committed to standards of quality, honesty, and reliability. In short, they believed that ownership entails obligations. These attitudes on the part of private entrepreneurs were to some extent reinforced by regulations and official standards of performance, and they could be explained in part by the fact that there was a financial incentive for them. Nevertheless, in view of the quasi-monopoly position of many private sector firms, which would have made a much less conscientious approach at least feasible, I believe the existence of these attitudes can only be understood in terms of surviving traditions from pre-socialist times.

Until the early 1970s, the majority of private entrepreneurs had learned their trade and even started their business before the war and in the immediate post-war period. This is where the link of tradition is most evident and direct. Often in the history of the GDR, new licenses were issued only to very few new applicants, and private entrepreneurs were repeatedly subjected to unfavourable political treatment. As a result, they remained a fairly stable social group, sharing a common sense of identity—an identity threatened by the existing order. Moreover, it had been the strategy of the SED from the start to incorporate these strata into socialism and win them over gradually. This situation of partial acceptance and partial threat allowed entrepreneurial traditions and identities to survive, while at the same time heightening their members' awareness of belonging to a distinct, "petty-bourgeois" group. Thus, rather than weakening and ultimately eliminating traditions of social life, and with it standards of professional practice, the SED approach encouraged the private entrepeneurs' commitment to their values. Put differently, being under siege ideologically and politically, though still with some hope for survival, private entrepreneurs could ill-afford to be viewed as exploiters and profiteers, for example by taking advantage of their quasi-monopoly position or by neglecting professional standards in order to increase their profits.

The ranks of this first generation of private entrepreneurs were thinning rapidly in the 1970s. The 1976 policy reversal with its measures for stimulating the private sector was a belated response to an emerging crisis in the reproduction of private firms. The political-ideological atmosphere and the technological optimism of the early Honecker period hardly made the fate of private firms a reason for concern for the regime. Although there is no clear evidence for this, the SED leadership may even have welcomed the natural depletion of this middle class as a painless form of socializing the remaining private sector. It is, however, more likely that the problem was simply not understood until the economic effects became more visible. More specifically, the population voiced discontent with the shortages in repair and service capacity, and this clashed all too obviously with the Honecker regime's professed political priority of improving the living conditions of the broad masses.

Failure in the late 1960s to ensure the rejuvenation of the private sector and the unfavourable atmosphere of the early 1970s severely interrupted the continuity in the recruitment of new entrepreneurs, particularly in successors for existing firms. The gap in the number of new entrants compared to retiring entrepreneurs was closed only recently. Who is this new generation of private entrepreneurs? To what extent did they follow in the tradition of the older generation, what were their motives for running a private business, and what were their attitudes?

After 1976, SED policy explicitly encouraged children of private entrepreneurs to take over the parental business. A good portion of the "new" entrepreneurs thus came from entrepreneurial families—there was a considerable degree of inter-generational continuity. In such cases, we may assume social traditions and work attitudes to have been passed on at least to some extent. In addition to attitudes and expertise that were passed on from parents to children, a crucial factor is that the means of production could be taken over. During the periods when the private sector was subject to discriminatory legislation and administration, securing a license was the major barrier. During the more favourable period since 1976, the main obstacles for a new entrepreneur have been space and equipment.

An important benefit of inter-generational continuity in the private sector resulted from the fact that not only skills, premises and equipment could be passed down, but also that crucial connections were maintained. This obviously was of advantage for the individual private entrepreneur who did not have to build such ties anew. It was also of general economic advantage because it kept functioning economic relations alive.[74] It was also for this reason that in numerous cases the children of private owners taking over their parents' business had a university education and a career in the state sector prior to deciding in favour of running the family business. For example, the recent case of a son who had been an engineer in a large ship-building company in Rostock taking over his father's small leather goods store suggests that it was still (or again) attractive to be a private entrepreneur in the GDR. Moreover, the willingness to release scarce and highly trained labour from the state to the private sector indicates the seriousness on the part of the government to ensure the continuity and survival of existing small family businesses.[75]

Individuals entering this social stratum "from the outside", i.e., those who had no family background of private entrepreneurship, conversely cannot be assumed to have brought the same values and attitudes to their work. The licensing requirements ensured that they fulfilled high professional standards—i.e., that they held a master artisan certificate in the case of private handicraft firms, or that they had completed formal training in the retail or restaurant sector. In addition to professional qualifications, however, solving the "logistical" problems of setting up a new business— particularly those related to securing business premises as well as equipment and machinery—required a significant amount of effort and personal initiative. This group of "new" entrepreneurs thus could be expected to be, on the whole, made up of exceptionally flexible and achievement-oriented individuals.

The "new" entrepreneurs, whether the sons or daughters of "old" entrepreneurs or new entrants, had all grown up and been socialized under the GDR regime. The education system had treated private entrepreneurs probably more unfavourably than had SED policy. For lack of better examples and in the absence of a more accurate understanding of SED alliance policy with private entrepreneurs, some school teachers singled out the children of private entrepreneurs as representatives of the exploitative capitalist class. While the relatively high standards of professional performance could be expected to be continued by the "new" entrepreneurs, the same is probably not true with respect to basic attitudes. The "new" middle class never experienced life under a different social order where they would have counted themselves among the "better people". And the "new" entrepreneurs, at least since 1976, had never experienced the kind of political attack which reinforced the commitment to traditional values among the older generation. As a result, the "new" entrepreneurs tended to be more self-confident about their social position and status than the old generation, and they constituted a distinct social group not so much by virtue of their social values and culture as by virtue of their income and level of consumption.

Notes

1. These implications will be more systematically discussed in Chapter 8.

2. H. Brezinski, "The Second Economy in the GDR—Pragmatism is Gaining Ground," *Studies in Comparative Communism,* 20, 1 (1987), 85.

3. See, for example, W. Gaertner, A. Wenig, eds., *The Economics of the Shadow Economy* (West Berlin: Springer, 1985).

4. Brezinski, "The Second Economy".

5. This was the general consensus of all interview partners.

6. Quite frequently, only remuneration in West German marks was considered adequate (Brezinski, "The Second Economy," 91). Thus a brick layer on the black market could cost 22 Marks per hour, and if the job was be done immediately, it could cost 12 West German Marks. (The black market exchange rate between East German and West German Marks was between 4:1 and 6:1 in the 1980s.)

7. *GBI.I,* No. 28, pp. 273–275.

8. For instance, three people who in a period of 8 years had made profits of several hundred thousand Marks each received prison sentences ranging from two-and-a-half to 4 years. "Gerechte Freiheitsstrafen für spekulativen Handel mit PKW" (Just prison terms for speculative car trade), in: *Freiheit,* Nr. 241, 12 October 1988.

9. A man who bought up articles from Western visitors—fashion jewellery—and resold them at a profit (less than 10,000 Marks in the course of several months) was sentenced to 21 months in prison and a penalty of 5,000 Marks. A housewife in a similar line of business was sentenced to a year and a half on probation, and her profit was confiscated (she had made 4,725 Marks in 3 months). Reported in *Berliner Morgenpost*,* 13 April 1986.

10. Cf. also in this respect an increase in recent years in the licensing of so-called "Purchase and Retail Shops" where people could sell and buy used goods. This growth in the number of second hand stores was largely accounted for by private shops. *Volksstimme* (SED), Magdeburg, No. 224, 23 September 1987.

11. E. Wildner, K. Müller, "Dynamische Entwicklung des Marktgeschehens im Ostseebezirk" (Dynamic development of local markets in Baltic district), *Handel,* 3 (1988), 11.

12. Bundesminister für Innerdeutsche Beziehungen*, ed. *DDR-Handbuch,* 3rd rev. ed. (Cologne: Verlag Wissenschaft und Politik, 1985), Vol. 1, p. 157.

13. Since 1971, over 1.9 million new apartments have been completed and over 1 million apartments have been renovated. Cf. W. Stinglwagner*, "Noch überwiegt der Jubel" (Still mainly jubilation), *Deutschland-Archiv,* 21, 11 (1988), 1143.

14. The only figures available are for new housing construction. Between 7 and 10 percent of new housing construction annually since 1976 was individual (private) construction. *Statistisches Jahrbuch 1989,* p. 168.

15. *DDR-Handbuch,* p. 157.

16. *Statistisches Jahrbuch 1989,* p. 293.

17. *Statistisches Jahrbuch 1989,* p. 111.

18. Bundesminister für Innerdeutsche Beziehungen*, ed., *Informationen,* No. 19 (1989), p. 6.

19. *Statistisches Jahrbuch 1989,* p. 112.

20. For more on this, see K. Eckart*, "Die Bedeutung der privaten Anbauflächen für die Versorgung der Bevölkerung der DDR" (The significance of privately cultivated land for the population of the GDR), *Deutschland Archiv,* 16, 3 (1983), 415f.

21. K. Hohmann*, "Entwicklung und Bedeutung der privaten Agrarproduktion in der DDR" (Significance and development of private agricultural production in the GDR), *FS-Analysen,* 3 (1984), 12, 19.

22. Verband der Kleingärtner, Siedler und Kleintierzüchter (Association of Small Gardeners, Homesteaders, and Small Animal Breeders, VKSK).

23. Up from 0.96 million members in 1970. *Ostsee-Zeitung* (SED), No. 82, 7 April 1988.

24. "Freude, Erholung, Ertrag" (Joy, recreation, yield), in: *Neues Deutschland,* No. 246, 18/19 October 1986.

25. Cf. Klaus Siegmund, "Zur individuellen Produktion landwirtschaftlicher Erzeugnisse" (Concerning individual production of agricultural products), *Einheit,* 43, 6 (1988), 568.

26. In 1983 there were 15,300 such purchasing depots for private producers. Eckart, "Die Bedeutung der privaten Anbauflächen," 418.

27. Information from private producer.

28. In addition to the price subsidies, there were other costs of stimulating private production, e.g. the private use of collective property (such as feed for livestock) or feeding subsidized bread to privately raised animals. See Hohmann, "Entwicklung und Bedeutung der privaten Agrarproduktion," 19. The issue of ideological costs did not even pose itself in view of the great popularity and recreational value of individual production.

29. See, for example, *Kooperation* (Zeitschrift für sozialistische Landwirtschaft und Nahrungsgüterwirtschaft), Vol. 21, No. 6 (June 1987), 280–282.

30. Approximate average shares for 1980–87; own calculations, based on *Statistisches Jahrbuch 1988,* pp. 205–208.

31. Hohmann, "Entwicklung und Bedeutung der privaten Agrarproduktion," 45.

32. M. Haendcke-Hoppe*, "Möglichkeiten und Grenzen privatwirtschaftlicher Betätigung in der DDR" (Opportunities and limitations for private economic activity in the GDR), in Göttinger Arbeitskreis, ed., *Wirtschaftsverfassung und Wirtschaftspolitik in der DDR* (West Berlin: Duncker & Humblot, 1984), p. 151. The same author points out (*ibid.*) that there are no figures available breaking down this group of self-employed by occupation. However, in 1979, there were 953 physicians and 1,148 dentists with a private practice.

33. *Ibid.,* p. 151.

34. Personal information from owner of a new small trucking company.

35. "Anordnung über die nebenberufliche Tätigkeit von Bürgern als Taxifahrer" (Regulation concerning the part-time work of citizens as taxi drivers), *GBl.* 4.9.86.

36. "Hallo, Taxi bitte . . ." *Märkische Volksstimme* (SED), No. 64, 16 March 1988.

37. Personal information from M. Haendcke-Hoppe from the West Berlin Forschungsstelle für gesamtdeutsche wirtschaftliche und soziale Fragen. She is the leading West German authority on the GDR private sector.

38. Information from Werner Sommer, Vice-Chair, East Berlin Chamber of Trade and Commerce, interview, 23 November 1988.

39. See *Statistisches Jahrbuch 1989*, pp. 111–112. There are practically no structurally and regionally-differentiated data on the private trade sector available. This section pulls together some of the randomly and sparsely published data in the GDR, combined with calculations and estimates made by Western experts.

40. See Chapter 2.

41. Sommer (interview).

42. "Private Händler und Gastwirte mit guten Leistungen an der Versorgung beteiligt. Zahlen und Fakten" (Private retailers and restaurant operators participate with good performance in supply), *Presse-Informationen*, No. 62, 31 May 1988, p. 6.

43. See M. Haendcke-Hoppe*, "Neueste Entwicklungen im privaten und genossenschaftlichen Handwerk der DDR sowie in der sonstigen Privatwirtschaft" (Most recent developments in private and cooperative handicraft of the GDR as well as in the remaining private economy), *FS-Analysen*, 2 (1984), 20.

44. See also Chapter 5.

45. See Haendcke-Hoppe, "Möglichkeiten und Grenzen," pp. 152–153 and Haendcke-Hoppe, "Neueste Entwicklungen," 21.

46. Estimated shares for 1985, following A. Scherzinger* (Deutsches Institut für Wirtschaftsforschung), "Das Gaststättengewerbe in der DDR" (The restaurant sector in the GDR), *DIW Wochenbericht*, 55, 22 (2 June 1988), 296. In 1982 private retailers without contract accounted for 5.6 percent and those with contract for 5.8 percent of total retail turnover, private pubs/restaurants without contract had a 2.8 percent share and those with contract a 13.7 percent share in the total turnover of their sector. Calculated by Haendcke-Hoppe, "Neueste Entwicklungen," 21.

47. Haendcke-Hoppe, "Möglichkeiten und Grenzen," p. 153. In addition, there were thousands of private lodgings renting rooms on contract with the trade union (FDGB) which organized much of the vacation sector in the GDR. Responsible for the administration of these private hotels were county and municipal organs. In the district of Erfurt, for example, there were 7,120 such private lodgings in 1987. *Das Volk* (SED), No. 199, 23 August 1988.

48. *Statistisches Jahrbuch 1989*, p. 178; employees not including apprentices.

49. See, for example, *Statistisches Jahrbuch 1989* in which special sections are devoted to the handicraft sector, which is not the case for the rest of the private sector.

50. *Statistisches Jahrbuch 1989*, p. 176. For the purposes of this study, cooperatives are not counted as part of the private sector.

51. Information from Eberhard Engel, CDU Hauptvorstand, East Berlin, 29 November 1988.

52. M. Haendcke-Hoppe*, "Struktureffekte der SED-Handwerkspolitik seit 1976" (Structural effects of SED handicraft policy since 1976), *FS-Analysen* (1988), 16.

53. The shortage in output of new cars and the modest extent to which cars were imported explains the fact that large sums of money were spent on regenerating old cars in private automobile repair shops. That this was an extremely wasteful practice in terms of labour was generally acknowledged. Much of the repair capacity was thus spent on rebuilding cars basically from scrap. Frequently, state or collective firms with money to spend—such as an agricultural cooperative (LPG)—tied up the repair capacities of private shops. (Personal information from owner of a private car repair shop.)

54. *Statistisches Jahrbuch 1989*, p. 161.

55. *Neue Zeit*, 26 March 1985.

56. There are no published income statistics for the private sector although, as one economics professor at Humboldt University assured me, the Finance Ministry has a detailed data set. In general, these income statistics were not even available to GDR researchers. The fact that they were treated as classified information gives some indication that the incomes of private entrepreneurs were considered politically sensitive material.

57. H. Vortmann*, "Geldeinkommen in der DDR von 1955 bis zu Beginn der achtziger Jahre" (Monetary incomes in the GDR from 1955 to the early 1980s), *DIW-Beiträge zur Strukturforschung*, No. 85 (West Berlin: Duncker & Humblot, 1985), p. 122ff.

58. M. Haendcke-Hoppe*, "Das private Handwerk in der DDR" (Private handicraft in the GDR), *Deutschland Archiv*, Vol. 20, No. 8 (1987), 849.

59. Aslund, *Private Enterprise*, p. 208. Interesting in this context for comparative purposes is Aslund's suggestion that in Poland the average entrepreneurial income until the early 1980s was about five to eight times the average while maximum incomes may have been as high as 200 times the national average wage. *Ibid.*

60. Brezinski, "The Second Economy," 100.

61. *Statistisches Jahrbuch 1989*, pp. 110, 129.

62. Engel (interview).

63. *Idem.*

64. See, for example, "Leserecho zum Thema 'Brot'" (Readers' voices on the subject of bread), in *Das Volk* (SED), No. 243, 16 October 1987.

65. Information from a former local administrator of private restaurants and pubs in East Berlin who had emigrated to the West.

66. Information from Eberhard Schwarz, Chamber of Handicraft, interview, East Berlin, 23 November 1988.

67. For details on the tax system and its progression, see Chapter 5.

68. Information from Vera Fleischer, editor of *Das Neue Handwerk*, interview, East Berlin, 22 November 1988. Another example was pedicure services, where demand had strongly increased due to low prices.

69. According to Fleischer (interview).

70. For example, a car repair shop may have let employees use equipment and workspace in their spare time to work for their private customers—a benefit that was not available to those working in cooperative or state repair shops.

71. Information in this paragraph is based on interviews with private entrepreneurs.

72. According to the Chamber of Trade and Commerce, East Berlin (Sommer, interview) and the Chamber of Handicraft, East Berlin (Schwarz, interview), respectively, the demand for licenses was greatest in the restaurant and industrial or mass-produced goods retail sectors and in the automobile repair sector.

73. The lack of data also does not permit an analysis of the position of women in the private sector. A small number of women operated private firms in the retail trade, restaurant, and hotel sectors as well as in selected handicraft trades in the service sector, such as hairdressers. In the rest of the private economy, they can be assumed to have had only a negligeable share. Frequently, women had the status of "assisting family members" in private enterprises operated by their husbands. They could not even be hired as regular employees and only a small tax deduction was granted to the firm's owner by the state (see further on this Chapter 5).

74. This was suggested to the author by East German economic historian Professor Jörg Roesler, Academy of Sciences, interview, East Berlin, 30 November 1988.

75. The Ministry for Trade and Supply's comments on licensing regulations state that: "As a rule, there is no societal interest in issuing licenses to citizens with university or college education." (Ministerium für Handel und Versorgung, ed. *Zur Gewerbetätigkeit privater Einzelhändler und Gastwirte. Erläuterung gesetzlicher Bestimmungen* (Berlin: Verlag Die Wirtschaft, 1986), p. 13.

5

The Policy Framework:
Government Regulation and Planning

The stability, legality, and security in the East German private economy since the adoption of a positive private-sector policy in 1976 significantly distinguished it from developments in the private sectors of other Communist countries in the 1980s and poses one of the explanatory problems for the present study. This relative success of SED policy is all the more astounding since, as will be shown in this chapter, the policy measures for the private sector since 1976 were modest and certainly much less liberal and radical than those adopted, for example, in Poland and the Soviet Union in the 1980s.[1] In fact, in the late 1970s and the 1980s, the SED followed an incrementalist approach vis-à-vis the private sector. As the *institutional continuity thesis* proposed here suggests, incrementalism was a policy choice for the SED—and one that even met with relative success— because a legal-administrative framework and corresponding bureaucratic practices regulating the private economy and integrating it into the socialist economy were in place. This chapter will describe the regulatory framework within which the GDR private sector operated in the 1980s and explore who made private-sector policy, which agencies implemented it, and what were the central issues and problems.

The fact that a policy framework for the private sector existed explains why there were no political and ideological obstacles to be overcome after 1976, when the SED leadership decided to reaffirm its alliance policy with the remaining private entrepreneurs. It is also for this reason that the policy-making central level of Party and government occupied a marginal position in the policy framework compared to the local level, which was responsible for policy implementation and the regulation of private firms. This is the level where licenses were issued, equipment and material were allocated, and where private firms were supervised and controlled. In the present period of restructuring, many restrictive regulations for the private sector are quickly being eliminated and the regulatory framework as a whole is radically being overhauled. The practice of licensing private firms is being replaced by the more simple process of registration based on the right to establish a private business, and the administrative system of allocations is to be replaced by a market allocation system.[2] For two reasons, the analysis presented in this chapter will be of relevance for understanding this transition process. First, for an intermediate period, elements of the old regulatory system will coexist with newly introduced elements. Second, and more important, at the local level, there will be considerable continuity in the administrative personnel and, to a greater or lesser extent, in bureaucratic practices and attitudes. In both respects, an understanding of the point of departure for the private economy in the new era can be expected to be of more than merely historical significance.

The Role of the Power Centre

The politics of private enterprise in the GDR were to a large extent played out at the local level. Particularly during periods in which the general policy direction was not controversial, the Politburo and the Central Committee Secretariat did not seem to be prominently involved in private-sector policy-making. As they touched upon sensitive political-ideological issues, however, basic resolutions adopted by the Council of Ministers with respect to the private sector had in fact been determined already by the Central Committee, on the initiative, or at least with the approval, of the Politburo.[3] Since 1976, the basic policy direction had been clarified through four major policy resolutions issued by the Council of Ministers for the private sector.[4]

While it is impossible to establish whether there had been any opposition in the central Party apparatus to the adoption of a more positive private-sector policy, there are at any rate no indications that support such a conjecture.[5] The high political cost of not preserving a private handicraft and trade sector had become all too obvious by the mid-1970s when, contrary to Honecker's promise to improve significantly the living conditions of the working people, the situation in a number of services traditionally supplied by private entrepreneurs was rapidly deteriorating. There seemed to be no real alternative to preserving the private sector by way of promoting it. Given the institutional and ideological legacy of past private-sector policy, it was not difficult to construct a political and ideological justification for a more positive and active private-sector policy. Any ideologically-motivated resistance that had existed, and to some extent still survived, was at the local level. The reasons for this will be explored in more detail below, but one major cause may be mentioned here. The implementation of the SED's private-sector policy at the local levels confronted the functionaries and administrators with a variety of problems and dilemmas, while at the same time demanding from them initiative and special effort for its successful implementation. It is to some extent understandable that an ideological reorientation connected with new and additional responsibilities did not everywhere generate the necessary enthusiasm.

In light of this, the central leadership's engagement in private-sector policy-making occurred, above all, at the level of symbolic reinforcement and bureaucratic mobilization. The Party frequently stressed the integral role of its alliance policy in its overall social policy approach, as well as the important contribution of its private-sector policy to satisfying the needs of the population. Thus, for example, an SED report on the Party's social policy underscored the central importance of the development of services for the population. It listed various private sector incentive programs, such as tax breaks, training programs, and special bonuses, in the context of measures for the achievement of broad social policy goals.[6] Similarly, General-Secretary Honecker had gone on record promising a safe future for the country's 80,000 private handicraft firms with its 250,000 employees as well as the 25,000 private shopkeepers and restaurant owners.[7] He had also visited a private shop—the first Party leader in the GDR's history to do so.[8]

In his annual speech before the First Secretaries of the Party's county executives—an important annual event where local Party leaders were provided with a basic political orientation—the SED leader regularly reaffirmed the party's commitment to promoting the private sector.[9] In conferences with county and municipal government leaders, Politburo members stressed the responsibility of local organs for improving the supply situation in the consumer goods sector. They demanded greater attention from local organs as well as increased "socialist cooperation" between enterprises of different ownership forms. Phrases such as "there are still significant reserves", "further perfection of planning, direction, and accounting on the part of local organs carry special political weight," or "the existing instruments must be used more effectively"[10] were indirect criticisms by the central level of the performance of local authorities. Local organs were under considerable pressure from the centre to show tangible successes in the promotion of the private firms, particularly in the handicraft sector.[11]

The General Policy Framework

With the number of private firms dwindling in the early 1970s in an atmosphere of uncertainty, a fundamental reversal in the deteriorating conditions for the private sector required both a new symbolic commitment to private enterprise from the state, as well as specific measures and programmes for stimulating economic development in the private sector.

The 1976 resolution of the Politburo and the Council of Ministers, entitled "For the promotion of private retail businesses, restaurants, and handicraft firms for services in the interest of further improvements in the supply of the population," was aimed at fulfilling both these functions. In the 1980s, the Council of Ministers issued three more sets of policy measures for the private sector—in 1984, 1986, and 1988—which, together with the 1976 resolution, represent the basic policy framework within which the private sector operated. They included the following specific sets of measures:

- liberalization in licensing
- preference in the allocation of apprentices
- promotion of the children of private entrepreneurs to take over the parental business
- special start-up and expansion loans
- tax exemptions and credits
- special performance subsidies for selected trades
- wage increases for employees in the private sector
- possibility of converting socialist retail outlets to private management

These sets of policy measures will now be analyzed in greater detail, beginning with the SED's financial as well as planning and structural policies in the present section. The subsequent section will be devoted to an examination of how private-sector policy was implemented at the local level. Figure 5.1 provides a general representation of the responsibilities of different Party and state organs in the policy-making and implementation of private-sector policy.

Financial Policy

H.E. Haase has suggested in his discussion of GDR handicraft cooperatives that "in a system with imperative economic planning, the incentive effect of tax policy is to be regarded as extremely low. Rather, direct plan orders prove to be the policy instrument which is adequate to the system."[12] This thesis seems to be borne out by the fact that GDR tax policy for the private sector since 1976 introduced only relatively minor readjustments, whereas the production and services of private firms were increasingly incorporated into state plans (which set direct plan orders).

The handicraft sector was subject to special tax regulations, which for the most part are already contained in the Law on Taxation of Artisans of 16 March 1966.[13] The decree of 15 December 1970 imposing additional "production" taxes on private handicraft firms was to encourage them to shift their activities to repairs, services, and supplies for the population, rather than production or services for industry. A supplementary decree

Figure 5.1 Policy Making and Implementation

Fundamental decisions prepared/cleared by	Politburo Central Committee	
		POLICY MAKING
Laws and decrees	Council of Ministers	=
	Ministries	CENTRAL LEVEL
Pass regulations, direct, assist in, monitor implementation	Finance, Price Admin. District/Food Industry Trade, Construction Traffic	

Coordinate implementation for territory long-term planning, control	District Council + its administrative departments	
		IMPLEMENTATION
Material/output planning price control and applic. manpower, licensing	County Council + its administrative departments	=
		LOCAL LEVELS
Plan control, business hours, business space, licensing	Municipal Council + its administrative departments	

on taxation of the private sector was passed on 5 April 1976[14] in the wake of the Politburo's reversal of private-sector policy. It provided for a favourable lump-sum tax for handicraft firms with no more than one full-time employee which, in addition, had at least a 70 percent share of their total output in repairs and services for the population. Moreover, the decree exempted private retailers and restaurant and hotel operators from trade tax. A Council of Ministers resolution passed in 1984 made it possible to claim special tax exemptions for an assisting spouse.

Private artisans not subject to the lump-sum tax were taxed on their annual profits.[15] Private retailers and restaurant operators, while exempt from the trade tax, had their profits taxed according to the—less favourable—income tax schedule. Here, private retail and restaurant businesses operating with a commission contract paid at significantly more favourable tax rates than those operating without a commission contract.[16] While no attempt had been made since 1976 to achieve the SED's policy aims by general and significant tax reductions—and to this extent Haase's thesis quoted above seems to be correct—there was a growing realization and even consensus on the fact that the existing tax regulations for the private sector had some serious disincentive effects.[17]

It was extremely unlikely that a private business venture in the GDR would fail for financial reasons. Credit was readily available at low interest rates and with long amortization periods once all other regulatory and organizational hurdles had been overcome. The credit-extending institution—either the Cooperative Bank for Handicraft and Trade or the Savings Bank—assessed loan applications from the private sector. A general criterion for acceptance was the usefulness of the planned investment, particularly in terms of rationalization and extension of services for the population. The applicant had to demonstrate to the credit institute that all state licenses, allocations (e.g., for the necessary material or machinery), and approval for the project had been obtained.[18]

Since 1984, financial policy has also included price subsidies for special trades. As many prices of goods and services for the population were heavily subsidized or simply fixed at low levels, the income potential of a number of private occupations was extremely low. As a result, an attempt was made to attract more applicants to fields such as shoe repair, clothing alterations, and bicycle repair by paying special subsidies to the owners of such firms.[19] Finally, in March 1988 the Council of Ministers passed a resolution which among other things provided for a greater equalization (if not yet full equality) of wages paid in the state sector and in the private sector. This is remarkable because the GDR in the 1980s suffered from a general labour scarcity. It thus underscores the SED's commitment to the further promotion of the private sector.

Planning and Structural Policies

While financial incentives to private entrepreneurs were of some importance for increasing the numbers and performance of private firms, their effectiveness was fundamentally circumscribed by systemic conditions. Private firms were situated not in a more or less free and competitive market context, but rather in the restrictive framework of a state-administered economy. Put simply, money was of only minor significance in stimulating performance and in allocating resources. For instance, a master mechanic who wanted to start his own business may have had the financial means for purchasing the necessary equipment, but the local administration in charge of ordering and distributing such equipment may have been unable or unwilling to supply this private entrepreneur. Similarly, since business space was usually scarce, he may not have been able to set up a new operation because local authorities were unable or unwilling to allocate the appropriate business premises. Problems such as these at the local level will be explored more systematically in the next section. What is already evident at this point, however, is that financial measures alone could do very little to stimulate the development and increased productivity of private sector firms in an environment where so much depended on the actions and decisions of local bureaucrats in charge of distributing scarce resources. This is why the political actors at the central level engaged in a variety of measures in addition to financial policy to overcome such systemic and local administrative obstacles.

Since 1972 the private sector had increasingly become subject to various forms of planning. As practically all private firms were administered by local rather than central state organs, planning was, at the central level, at best a marginal policy instrument in the hands of the central government actors responsible for the private sector: the Council of Ministers, the Planning Commission, the Price Office and, above all, the "industrial" Ministries—the Ministry for District Directed Industry and the Food Industry (handicraft sector), the Ministry of Trade and Supply (retail and restaurant sector), and the Ministry for Construction (building trades) (see Table 5.1). These central level state organs set general priorities and also allocated funds for specific objectives, such as housing repairs, to the districts, which in turn allocated funds to their county administrations.[20] For the most part, however, the central government had little direct influence on how local governments distributed resources to the private sector—e.g., whether and how workspace or equipment were provided to the private sector in a particular county, or what share of supplies was to be allocated to private, as opposed to cooperative or state, firms.

Much of the activity of central government agencies, in particular the responsible ministries, seemed to consist in mobilizing and coordinating the work of local state councils and administrations, as well as of other institutions involved in private-sector policy. The central agencies used a combination of political pressure on local organs and the provision of organizational and logistical support when tackling what seemed to be chronic impediments to better economic performance in the private sector. The top policy priorities were thus of an exclusively economic nature, and may be summarized under the heading of increased labour productivity through various forms of rationalization. As U.D. Wange, head of the Ministry responsible for most of the handicraft sector, put it: "Political-ideological work [has achieved its goal] when there are tangible economic results."[21]

There was another issue of great importance to the central authorities. The private sector was tied economically into the state sector at two crucial points: the supply of production equipment and the supply of materials. In both areas, the state sector was unable to maintain a sufficient and reliable supply. This was the most important obstacle to a stronger performance of private firms. Administrative hurdles, financial problems, or lack of incentive and competition were, by comparison, only secondary factors. Even if they had not existed as buffers to market entry, the shortage of production equipment and materials produced by the state sector would have nevertheless severely limited the growth potential in most private sector trades. The political actors at the central level, in particular the Ministries, attempted to intervene at these two crucial points. That they did so with only very limited success, however, is in large part due to the fact that they could not allocate what the state economy failed to produce, and that they could only encourage, instruct, and assist local actors to help themselves as best they could.

The Ministries undertook a wide variety of policy initiatives.[22] In addition, the Ministries appealed on a regular basis to the various local actors to "exploit their reserves" and to "implement central policy even more effectively". For instance, the Ministry for District Directed Industry and the Food Industry issued basic policy guidelines for discussion at the annual membership meetings of the private firms' purchase and delivery cooperatives (ELG). Moreover, the head of this Ministry announced the government's political priorities and goals at special conferences on the private sector convened by the National Front. Such policy statements provide a good indication of the kinds of problems the central government considered most significant. Judging from the same recurring themes one encounters in such basic policy guidelines, the basic problems of increasing performance of the private sector were persistent.

The ineffectiveness of the work of the responsible Ministries, to the extent that they were not simply due to systemic problems which only broader political initiatives could have addressed, was also a result of a political non-decision. The jurisdiction over the private sector at the central level was split between at least three Ministries with responsibility for different economic branches. In addition, there were the Finance Ministry and the Price Administration which partly regulated the private sector. What was conspicuously absent, however, was not only a central government agency to develop and coordinate initiatives for the private sector, but also a Chamber of Handicraft or a Chamber of Trade and Commerce at the central level which might have represented more effectively the interests and problems of private firms at the central level. The organizations which came closest to a central-level interest representative for the private sector were the Bloc parties. How seriously and successfully they played this role will be discussed in Chapter 7.

Private-Sector Policy at the Local Level

Legislation affecting the administration of the private sector at the local level was passed in 1985 and 1986. It gave greater authority and responsibility to local state organs and redefined the responsibilities of the purchase and delivery cooperatives, the wholesale enterprises for private handicraft firms. The 1985 Law on Local Popular Assemblies firmly placed the responsibility for all major aspects of policy implementation related to the private sector in the hands of local governments at district, county, and municipal levels. The important tasks of planning, licensing, and supervision were carried out by various departments, primarily at the county and municipal levels of local government. The functioning and effectiveness of local government in these areas, and some basic problems and conflicts, will be discussed in the following.

Planning and Prices

Local state organs were responsible for three types of planning with respect to the private sector. First, they incorporated the required material and equipment for private firms into their annual material plans. Second, they planned the output of private firms in certain branches. Third, they worked out medium-and long-term development conceptions for the private sector. (1) Material planning was the most important form of state planning for the private sector. The reason is that the bulk of material and equipment needed by private firms was produced by state enterprises and, as a rule, could not be sold directly to private firms. In other words, since there was practically no official market for most of the basic supplies required by the private sector, private firms, like state enterprises, depended for their supply on being incorporated into the state plan. Here, very much the same logic applied as in the state sector. That is, due to the chronic shortages and regularly emerging bottlenecks, private firms tried to stockpile as many supplies as they could, and in order to get as much as they needed, they had to demand more than they planned to use. The local planning administrations, in turn, had to decide how to distribute what was allocated to them among the various state, cooperative, and private enterprises in their territory. The question of whether private firms were systematically discriminated against in the distribution of supplies will be discussed below.

(2) The second type of planning, i.e., planning the output of private firms, has been gradually introduced since the 1970s. Through output planning, state authorities hoped to control the tendency of private firms to seek customers in state industry rather than serving the population directly. How specific and detailed such output plans were depended to a large extent on the particular private-sector trade. Not all private trades were included. Thus, private retail shops, for example, were not subject to output planning unless they worked under a commission contract.[23] Others, such as auto repair shops, received a monetary output target which was increased every year. The most detailed form of output planning was applied to the construction trades, such as plumbers and electricians. Up to 100 percent of their capacity was planned for specific projects. The main motivation behind these different types of output planning was the structural reorientation of the private sector after the 1972 national-

ization. Private firms were to serve the population directly, which required that they would reduce significantly their work for state industry.

However, even planning the relative share of services to be rendered to state industry, and to the population, was fraught with difficulties. The reason was that the policy of private-sector reorientation assumed that state enterprises which formerly utilized the production and services provided by private firms could simply develop their own internal capacities. For example, in order to free car repair capacity for the population, private repair shops had to reduce the services for state firms. The latter were required to build up their own internal repair capacity. A car repair firm in a rural area, for instance, received a plan order stipulating that it provide 95 percent of its services to private citizens. A local agricultural cooperative, which in the past had relied to a large degree on the services of this private firm for its car repair needs, had been unable to arrange for adequate alternatives. The owner of the private repair shop was approached by the cooperative. Legally, he would not have been able to provide the services. Since he had a long-standing business relationship with the cooperative, and wanted to help, he approached the County Council. If the Council Chairman and the department head for traffic had given official permission to the private owner to provide a greater share of services to state firms, they would have been in violation of the directives issued by the district and central government levels. They resolved the dilemma of conflicting local needs and central directives informally by giving tacit approval to the private owner to increase the share of services to state firms. The actual share of services to state firms provided by this private owner amounted to roughly 50 percent.[24]

The issuing of plan orders by local state organs to private firms thus was in part a purely symbolic or ceremonial affair. All parties involved knew that it was impossible to fulfill detailed production or service plans. Moreover, there were no penalties on falling short of a plan target. On the other hand, both local administrators and private entrepreneurs depended on a minimum of good will and cooperation from the other side to achieve their specific goals. Firm owners receiving detailed plan orders were invited to the county administration once a year for a "plan discussion." Such a meeting usually lasted no longer than two hours.[25] Another method of keeping closer contact with the private sector was reported by the County Council of Karl-Marx-Stadt. Representatives of the local government regularly consulted with and visited private firms in their territory, and more recently have adopted the practice of personally delivering plan orders to each private auto repair shop in the county.[26]

(3) The third type of private sector planning carried out by the local state organs was the drawing up of longer-term development conceptions for their territory. Since below the district level only one-year rather than

five-year (financial and material) plans were made, such development conceptions were to assist county and municipal authorities in establishing their territorial needs for the production and services of private firms and in designing corresponding long-term strategies. These were not as binding as the national economic plans, but, as a former local administrator explained the logic of these development conceptions, "one has to demand the impossible in order to achieve the possible."[27]

A pilot project for private sector development planning was initiated by the county SED leadership in the Baltic city of Stralsund soon after the policy reversal of 1976. The municipal government passed a resolution on "further improving the supply of the population with services and repairs" and initiated a collective effort for its implementation involving the major actors concerned with private-sector policy. The framework for consultations was provided by the Working Group on Handicraft and Commerce at the Stralsund county committee level of the National Front, a "corporatist" forum which had traditionally fulfilled this coordinating function. Here, representatives of the municipal departments with jurisdiction over private firms (Finance, Local Supply Economy, Traffic and Communications, Construction, and Trade and Supply) met together for consultation with private entrepreneurs, and representatives of the Chambers and the Bloc parties.

The Stralsund initiative was discussed twice in the SED's theoretical organ *Einheit*,[28] which suggests that it was intended as a model for how to implement the SED's new private-sector policy of 1976. At national level, the Working Group on Handicraft and Commerce of the National Front had played a similar political role in the past, particularly in times when the relationship between the private sector and the state had been strained, or when a new policy had been adopted. While the working group at central and local levels of the National Front was still formally in existence in the 1980s, there is no indication that it played the leading role in policy implementation as presented in the Stralsund model.[29] Rather, it seemed to be a forum for local bureaucrats and functionaries to discuss their problems with very little input from representatives of the private sector.

It is always somewhat puzzling to read that the decision to increase the number of private firms in a particular city or region depended on the "objective need" of the population for their services. In the absence of market surveys and systematic popular input, there was a danger that local authorities, as the ultimate arbiters of "objective need", would also be influenced by the potential difficulties involved for them in attracting and establishing new private firms, not to mention the influence of "subjective factors." One objective criterion for determining popular need was the so-called performance comparisons (*Leistungsvergleiche*). Different counties and municipalities were compared with respect to criteria such as variety of services available, the level of supply—as a whole and in specific services (e.g. shoe repair, chemical cleaners, tailor-made clothing, late and weekend services)—as well as number of licenses issued. In this way, the territories that were lagging behind in providing a reliable supply for the population could be identified. As a result, they might receive concrete orders from the responsible organ of the District Council to redress the imbalance.[30] The importance attached to these territorial development conceptions was underscored by the Council of Ministers' 1988 Resolution on the private sector, which required all districts and counties to present detailed analyses on the state of repairs and services until 1990.[31]

Licensing

Licensing had always been a powerful tool in the hands of local state organs for implementing a restrictive private-sector policy, or even for the "cold socialization" of private firms. In the early 1970s it was often impossible even for the children of private entrepreneurs to take over the parental business. But after 1976, the children of private owners were particularly encouraged by the state to continue the family business. The 1988 Council of Ministers' resolution once more called on local governments to grant new licenses in an expeditious fashion. Even under very favourable political and ideological conditions, however, securing a license for private commercial activity in the GDR was more than a mere formality.

An application had to be submitted to the municipal government, stating among other things what business premises and equipment were available to the applicant.[32] Moreover, the application had to contain a certificate of professional qualification (usually a master's certificate, in some cases a skilled worker's certificate), as well as police clearance.[33] The application was examined by the responsible departments of the municipal government and passed on to the county council. The final decision was made here after consulting with the Chamber of Handicraft or the Chamber of Trade and Commerce and the responsible supply or product groups.[34] For some trades, the District Council reserved the right to issue licenses.[35] In general, however, the trend was towards devolution of the licensing authority to the lowest (municipal) level of local government.

The most fundamental criterion upon which the decision on a license application was based was the "objective need" for the services of the particular private trade. While the need for particular services varied from territory to territory, there were some types of business which were in high demand almost anywhere in the GDR. These included bakers, tailors, shoemakers, bricklayers, roofers, stove builders, plumbers, car wash, fruit and vegetable trade, and fast food outlets.[36] The urgency of the local need for a particular business may even have led local authorities to relax or modify otherwise strictly-enforced licensing prerequisites. Similarly, local authorities frequently were very forthcoming in providing scarce business space and even procured equipment if they felt under political pressure in a particular area of local supply. Generally, however, obtaining a license for a private business was considerably more difficult. Where, for example, a handicraft cooperative (PGH) of, say, electricians already existed in the town, local authorities were unlikely to grant a license to a private electrician. Instead, the applicant would be advised to apply for membership in the local cooperative.[37] Usually, it was the applicant's task to demonstrate the availability of suitable business space, of which there was a great shortage in the GDR. Similarly, the applicant had to provide the necessary equipment to run his or her business. For many types of machinery, there were long waiting periods after posting an application with the local department responsible for their procurement. Prospective entrepreneurs had to find their way around these systemic obstacles, such as by finding and purchasing used equipment or by developing the right contacts with state suppliers.

The "objective" need for a particular service in a given territory would also be limited by the available supplies necessary to run a private business. In this respect, new entrants to the local trade would be not only an additional source of problems for the local departments in charge of material planning, but they would also represent potential competition for scarce resources for their private-sector colleagues. In principle, the established private firms had some influence on the licensing process in their territory through their occupational groups (*Berufsgruppen*) and the Chambers, which had some input in the decision.[38]

The following example from the restaurant sector is an illuminating instance of what it meant for local organs to make their decisions on a license application in light of "objective needs." The criteria included a restaurant's "social fit" into the neighborhood. That is, if it was a predominantly workers' section of town, an applicant for a restaurant with a higher price level was not likely to be granted a license. This was not so much because there would not be enough customers, but rather because the lower-income population in that area would have resented such a higher-price restaurant and sent submissions (*Eingaben*) to the local authorities complaining about the fact that no lower-price place had been established.[39]

Supervision and Control

In addition to the tasks of planning and issuing licenses for private firms, local authorities had a whole range of supervisory and control functions in the private sector, ranging from price classification to the allocation of labour and the organization of "socialist competition."

Prices for many products and services were determined at the central level. However, for a whole range of products and services, only approximate pricing guidelines existed on the basis of which particular products were priced. The Price Administration (*Amt für Preise*) at the local level was responsible for monitoring and supervising price calculations and price levels for private firms. The price structure and the range of goods and services to be offered were usually specified in the initial licensing process. Any changes in these initial conditions had to be cleared with local government organs.[40] The control and supervision of pricing gave local authorities a considerable amount of power to influence the operation and profitability of certain private businesses. In contrast to earlier years, however, prices tended to be set such that the firm could make a reasonable profit in order to stimulate future investment.[41] The local goverment was also responsible for enforcing strict health and safety regulations. In fact, many of these standards were practically impossible to fulfill for a private firm. This exposed an owner to the danger of arbitrary harassment and even closure if a local official was intent on narrowly enforcing such rules. On the other hand, if health and safety standards required the renovation of business premises (especially in the food sector), it was encumbent upon the local government to provide for a temporary alternative business location.[42] Another responsibility of local organs was in the area of training and the allocation of apprentices to the private sector. The number of apprentices was determined by the county council each year for each trade, or group of trades, and they were assigned to the state, cooperative, and private sectors. Within the private sector firms of each trade, the occupational group decided on its own internal allocation of apprentices. It is interesting to note that in the 1980s, in a period of declining numbers of high school graduates, the share of apprentices for the private sector actually increased.[43] This was the result of a specific central policy. Clearly, there was a need to train a sufficient number of artisans in order to preserve and gradually expand the ranks of private handicraft businesses. These had been depleted as a result of the restrictive private-sector policy in the first half of the 1970s.[44] Indeed, the general labour shortage in the GDR may in part account for the fact that the private sector was not allowed to expand more vigorously.

Finally, local organs initiated and supervised various forms of "socialist competition". These included performance comparisons (*Leistungsver-*

gleiche) whose purpose was to make productivity differences between firms visible. The responsibility for performance comparisons was with the respective department (e.g. traffic, construction, local service economy) at the county and district levels. They were usually conducted within the same, rather than between different, ownership forms.[45] Participation in such comparisons was voluntary and symbolically expressed a private entrepreneur's loyalty to the state. However, they otherwise generated little enthusiasm in the private sector, not least because participation implied additional work. Furthermore, there was no guarantee that self-evaluation led to honest reporting on performance.[46]

Ideological Factors and the Logic of the Local Administrative Process

In view of the crucial importance of the local authorities for both central policy makers and individual entrepreneurs, the question arises as to what generally motivated and constrained the decisions and actions of these local-level actors. More specifically, to what extent did ideological attitudes play a prominent role. First, the question of the continuing influence of an anti-private sector ideology among local bureaucrats will be considered. Next, some additional factors which shaped the administration of the private sector at the local level will be discussed.

Historically, whenever the SED moved from a restrictive to a more liberal private-sector policy, the political leadership regularly had to admonish local officials to beware of "sectarianism", i.e., an excessively harsh approach to the private sector. In order to distance themselves from the negative effects of restrictive measures vis-à-vis the private sector, the SED leaders laid part of the blame at the doorstep of local organs, which presumably had misinterpreted the policy and overstepped their boundaries. Whether as perpetrator of or scapegoat for past policy mistakes, local authorities at any rate played a key role in how private-sector policy was implemented. Their political understanding and ideological preconceptions with respect to the role of the private sector under socialism had always strongly shaped the conditions under which private entrepreneurs operated.

While the SED's alliance policy with all "non-monopolistic" classes of society had gone some way towards eliminating the stigma of "class enemy" from East German private entrepreneurs, the Party's nationalization drives and its failure to reconcile the existence and future of small capitalists within socialism and communism with its official ideology,[47] left sufficient room for ambivalence. Had the SED's pragmatic and positive approach to the private sector since 1976 given a clear and effective signal to local officials that any ideological reservations towards promoting private firms contradicted the spirit and the intention of the central policy?

Generally, there seemed to be very little ideologically-motivated prejudice against private entrepreneurs on the part of lower-level bureaucrats.[48] The official whose attitude towards the owners of private firms can be summarized as "we will use them as long as we need them" was the exception rather than the rule. There continued to be some distrust of, and aversion towards, private entrepreneurs on the part of some local officials, but the main motivation was not so much political or ideological as it was simple envy of their privileged position. After all, the average income of private owners was usually at least twice as high as that of a lower-level bureaucrat, and in many cases the income differential was considerably greater. As a rule, the relationship between the local administration and the private sector depended on individual circumstances and personal factors. It should be remembered that, quite apart from the official policy which required local bureaucrats to support and promote private firms, many private entrepreneurs had services to offer that the local officials themselves would need sooner or later. It might be quite inconvenient to have all the plumbers in the town against you.

A good indicator of the general ideological climate with respect to the private sector has always been how vigorously handicraft cooperatives and retail commission contracts were being promoted. For many years these institutions were portrayed as a higher stage of development. Thus, private artisans and private retailers found themselves under pressure from local organs to take this important step towards socialism, thus proving their more highly-developed political consciousness. In recent years, however, handicraft cooperatives (PGH) very rarely have been referred to as a higher and superior form of organization, nor have private artisans been urged or even encouraged to join a handicraft cooperative. Their numbers as well as their memberships have been stagnating for years.[49] On the contrary, there was a strong trend in favour of licensing applicants for private firms. Only where in a given territory cooperative in the sector was strong were private applicants encourged to join. Reprivatization of PGHs, however, as a rule did not occur.[50]

Similarly, commission contracts with a socialist enterprise in the private retail sector used to be considered an important and inevitable step in the transition process. In the 1980s, even the terminology reflects the de-ideologization of these different organizational forms in the private sector. They were now indiscriminately called "private retailers". It was up to the applicant whether s/he wanted to work with or without contract, and even an established private retailer could cancel his/her contract. An even more significant recent development in the retail sector was the reprivatization of a number of state retail shops.

This is not to say that all was well for the private sector, or perhaps even that it received preferential treatment from local administrators over state enterprises. The contrary was generally true.[51] The basic point, however, is that ideological reservations did not seem to play a major role in the decisionmaking of local authorities. A much more serious obstacle to the implementation of the SED's policy of favouring the private sector were simple bureaucratic inertia. The successful implementation of the policy of promotion required considerable initiative and effort on the part of local governments, ranging from the allocation of space to the procurement of production equipment. New regulations, moreover, designed to give an impetus to private sector development did not always encounter the dynamic and competent bureaucrat that could effectively put them into practice.[52]

It would be one-sided, however, to highlight only the bureaucratic attitudes which slowed down or obstructed the effective implementation of private-sector policy. Local governments also had a number of incentives to actively work for the consolidation and growth of private firms in their territory. In addition to the political pressure which party and state organs at the centre could bring to bear, the Law on the Local Popular Assemblies of 1985 had given local organs greater financial autonomy over the enterprises in their administrative jurisdictions.[53] As a result, they had a greater financial incentive to increase the tax base in their territory.

Local governments financed well over half of their budgets through local revenue[54] (from the private sector, as well as from cooperative and state enterprises under their jurisdiction). Thus, most private sector firms submitted their tax payments directly to their county and municipal governments. The GDR's 1989 budget anticipated a private sector revenue of 4.458 billion Marks, while expenditures for financial measures for the promotion of the private sector were to amount to only 235 million M.[55]

There were other tangible benefits for a local bureaucrat or council to expand the private sector. It may just have been the simplest and most effortless way to improve the level of services for the local population. For example, there was a special incentive for a county or municipal government to grant a license to a private restaurant rather than a state restaurant. For getting a state restaurant operational, the municipal council had to provide, and thus plan, for the materials, labour, and special equipment. This was often difficult and may have exceeded the plan allocations available to these local authorities. Private restaurant owners, on the other hand, were usually prepared to arrange for their own materials and labour and invest considerable work and initiative. They were thus no extra burden on the budget, while at the same time the firms' output raised the level of supply to the population in the territory. Although state officials at the local level tended to prefer state restaurants, they were for the above reason quite prepared to make compromises.[56]

Finally, applicants for a private firm were not alone in facing a sometimes less than cooperative local department. At least in principle, both the Chambers and the Bloc parties assisted and pushed for the interests of the private sector. This and other aspects of their work will be discussed in the following chapters.

Notes

1. Developments in the private economies in Poland and the Soviet Union are discussed in greater detail in the introductory chapter of the present study.

2. These issues are discussed in greater detail in Chapter 8.

3. Interview with Prof. Hartmut Zimmermann, Free University of Berlin, one of the leading West German experts on GDR politics, 28 June 1988.

4. The policy resolutions will be further discussed below.

5. Staritz, *Geschichte der DDR,* pp. 216–217 suggests that among the Party leadership under Honecker there had always been a consensus on the major political issues—at least until the mid-1980s.

6. "Zur Sozialpolitik der SED," *Neues Deutschland,* 29 January 1987.

7. "Leistungsfähiges Handwerk und Gewerbe in der DDR," *Aussenpolitische Korrespondenz,* 8 August 1986, 246–47.

8. M. Haendcke-Hoppe*, "Das DDR-Handwerk am Beginn einer neuen Fünfjahrplanperiode 1986–1990" (GDR handicraft at the beginning of a new five-year-plan period 1986–1990), *FS-Analysen,* 3 (1986), p. 5.

9. "It is our firm standpoint to promote the cooperative and private artisanal sector in a determined fashion. The artisanal sector is a significant economic factor." *Der Morgen,* 3 April 1987.

10. See, for example, Conference of the CC of the SED and the Council of Minsters with the chairpersons of the county councils and mayors (24 October 1986 in Berlin), Egon Krenz (member of the Politburo and CC secretary), "Erfolgreiche kommunalpolitische Entwicklung—von großem Gewicht für Frieden und Volkswohl" (Successful municipal development—of great importance for peace and national welfare), *Einheit,* Vol.41, No.12 (1986), 1079–1092.

11. Engel (interview).

12. H. E. Haase*, "Aktuelle Fragen der Steuerpolitik in der DDR," (Contemporary issues of tax policy in the GDR), *Deutschland Archiv,* 10, 6 (1977), 631.

13. *GBl.* I, No. 8/1966, p. 71.

14. *GBl.* Nr. 13/1976, p. 193.

15. The progression reached 50 percent at an annual profit of 60,000 M; additional profits above 60,000 and below 100,000 fell under a tax rate of 75 percent; anything above 250,000 M a year was subject to the maximum profit tax rate of 90 percent. "Rechtsnormen für das Handwerk. Gesetze, Verordnungen, Kommentare" (Legal norms for handicraft. Laws, decrees, commentaries), *Das neue Handwerk,* special issue, 2nd ed. (1978), 163.

16. Ministerium für Handel und Versorgung, ed. *Zur Gewerbetätigkeit privater Einzelhändler und Gastwirte. Erläuterung gesetzlicher Bestimmungen* (On the commercial activity of private retailers and restaurant operators) (Berlin: Verlag Die Wirtschaft, 1986), pp. 143, 194–208.

17. Interviews with private artisans; Schwarz (interview); Sommer (interview).

18. Loans of up to 25,000 M per investment project were usually provided at an interest rate of 5 percent, though lower rates were available, particularly to new businesses and "problem trades" (e.g. bakeries). Moreover, in order to offer special incentives, even interest-free loans with extended amortization periods and special tax deductions could be made available. H. Gerlach, "Die Förderung des Handwerks durch Kredit und Zins" (The promotion of handicraft through credit and interest), in *Rechtsnormen für das Handwerk. Gesetze, Kommentare, Verordnungen,* ed. *Das Neue Handwerk* (Berlin: Verlag Die Wirtschaft, 1978), pp. 182–184.

19. In the case of shoe repair services, for instance, the state granted a 60 percent subsidy to private firms. Müller (interview).

20. H.H. Kinze, H. Knop and E. Seifert, eds. *Sozialistische Volkswirtschaft* (Socialist Macroeconomics) (Berlin: Verlag Die Wirtschaft, 1983), pp. 92–98; Deutsches Institut für Wirtschaftsforschung, ed. *Handbuch DDR-Wirtschaft* (Handbook GDR Economics) (4th rev. ed. Hamburg: Rowohlt, 1984), p. 85ff.; Interview with Prof. Klaus Steinitz, economics section of the GDR Academy of Sciences, West Berlin, 21 November 1988.

21. *Das Neue Handwerk,* 4 (1988), 3.

22. Organize the production and procurement of equipment by the state sector to the private sector; prioritize which private trades were to receive special promotion; oversee the establishment of "consultation points" throughout the country for the introduction of new technologies and know-how; encourage and facilitate various forms of information exchange; establish commissions (e.g. for the application of computer technology in private handicraft firms); designate local Chambers to coordinate trades at the central level; encourage the private sector to produce increasingly its own rationalization equipment; call for the freeing of private sector capacity producing for the state sector to be fully committed to the needs of private firms; propose the recycling of equipment to the private sector used or discarded by the state sector; call for "performance contests" to be organized between private sector firms at the local level to reduce productivity differentials; urge local organs to develop conceptions for the development of the private sector in their territory; lay down basic guidelines and curricula for apprenticeship training and further training in private sector occupations.

23. "Kommissionshandelsverordnung", (Decree on Commission Trade), esp. Paragraph 3, Ministerium für Handel und Versorgung, pp. 32–33.

24. Information from owner of private car repair shop.

25. Information from private entrepreneur.

26. *Neue Zeit,* 11 February 1988.

27. Engel (interview).

28. See H. Lehmann, "Der Beitrag des Handwerks zur Erfüllung der Hauptaufgabe" (The contribution of handicraft to fulfilling the Main Task), *Einheit,*

Vol. 32, 7 (1977), 877–880; H. Schütze, "Handwerk und Gewerbe—Zwischenbilanz einer Initiative" (Handicraft and Commerce—interim report of an initiative), *Einheit*, Vol. 34, 6 (1979), 651–654.

29. This assessment is based on the observation that in the more recently published literature, the Working Group, if it is mentioned at all, is not portrayed as a particularly important organ. This impression was further confirmed by responses from various interview partners. My request for an interview with a representative of the National Front headquarters in East Berlin was unfortunately denied.

30. *Neue Zeit*, 11 February 1988.

31. Bundesminister für innerdeutsche Beziehungen*, ed. *Informationen*, No.8/1988, p. 3.

32. See "Antrag auf Erteilung einer Gewerbegenehmigung" (Application for the Issuing of a Commercial License), Ministerium für Handel und Versorgung, pp. 23–25.

33. As a rule, a private entrepreneur was required to hold a master's certificate which concludes a period of 5–6 years of formal vocational training (composed of apprenticeship and master training). In the handicraft sector, the master's programme extends over a two-year training period held at training institutions (*Betriebsakademien*) of the Departments of Local Service Economy (*örtliche Versorgungswirtschaft*) at the county level (for rare trades at special district centres).

34. See Chapter 6.

35. Paragraph 16, "Gewerbeverordnung", in *ibid.*, p. 15.

36. Cf. *Liberal-Demokratische Zeitung* (LDPD), No. 233, 3 Oct. 1987. The 1988 Council of Ministers' resolution on the promotion of private retail trade stipulates that priority be given to the following businesses: sales points for fruit and vegetables which also buy up produce from individual producers; icecream parlours, fast-food and fish restaurants, pubs, bakeries with small cafes, pubs with slaughterhouses, shops for metal products, tools; drug stores, small shoe shops with service; arts and fashion shops which also buy up goods privately produced on a part-time basis; and running restaurants/pubs, food stands, etc. on a part-time basis. Bundesministerium für innerdeutsche Beziehungen, ed. *Informationen*, No.8/1988, p.3.

37. Fleischer (interview).

38. See further on this, Chapter 6.

39. Information from a former deputy of the East Berlin city government, Department of Supply (*Amt für Versorgung*), interview, West Berlin, 1 July 1988.

40. For example, restaurants were divided into several levels of quality and service, simple restaurants having a low price level while more sophisticated ones had a correspondingly higher price level. Private owners could not simply change the price structure of their menu, nor could they independently decide to move to a different level of service and price. Even minor changes had to be authorized by the responsible local organs. Decisions on changes in the price level and price structure of a restaurant, for example, were taken by a committee composed of respresentatives from the Department of Finance, a bank (if investment funds

were required), the Chamber of Trade and Commerce, and the local council. The commission members visited the project for a detailed evaluation. The committee also examined and authorized the menu with respect to the price structure.

41. Information from former local administrator (interview).

42. Schwarz (interview).

43. Haendcke-Hoppe, "Struktureffekte," pp. 10–11.

44. See Chapter 3.

45. Fleischer (interview).

46. This was the consensus among all private entrepreneurs I asked about these performance comparisons.

47. The most far-reaching step in this direction proposed to reconceptualize the small-scale private property of artisans and shopowners as (functionally) "socialist" property. See Falconere, "Zur Rolle der Handwerker und Gewerbetreibenden".

48. The following assessment is based on the responses received from private entrepreneurs, the Chambers, Bloc parties, and academic experts (cited earlier).

49. Schwarz (interview). In fact, state plans made provision for annually increasing the quantity of supplies and materials assigned to the ELG (the purchase and delivery cooperatives for private handicraft firms).

50. Fleischer (interview).

51. On the contrary, the private sector was systematically discriminated against in terms of the allocation of equipment and supplies. But ideological reasons do not seem to have been primary. First, many state enterprises were considerably larger and economically more important than private firms. Second, it was easier to deal with a small number of large units than with a large number of small firms in the allocation of materials. This was also why state wholesalers often preferred dealing with state retailers, which received larger deliveries. This also underscores the importance of the purchase cooperatives (ELG) in the private handicraft sector, which handled supplies for a large number of small firms.

52. Interview Manfred Bogisch, Liberal Democratic Party, Zentralvorstand, East Berlin, 1 December 1988.

53. See Gesetz über die örtlichen Volksvertretungen (Law on Local Popular Assemblies) (3rd ed. Berlin: Staatsverlag der DDR, 1986), Article 64.

54. According to Egon Krenz in Neues Deutschland (25/26 October 1986), this share was 62 percent of total local budgets.

55. According to the Budget, local governments were to increase their own revenues by making additional deductions from enterprises under their jurisdiction, as well as obtaining greater tax revenues from handicraft cooperatives and private firms. The revenue structure of local state budgets shows that there have been some positive developments, mainly as a result of the improved performance of state enterprises as well as private firms. H.-O. Schützenmeister, "Haushalts- und Finanzwirtschaft und sozialistische Kommunalpolitik," Staat und Recht, Vol. 37, 2 (1988), 152–163.

56. Engel (interview). A new law effective since 1 July 1989 ("Gesetz über die Zuständigkeit und das Verfahren der Gerichte zur Nachprüfung von Verwaltungsentscheidungen"; Law on the Jurisdiction and Process of Courts in Examining

Adminstrative Decisions) allowed applicants for a commercial license who had been rejected by the local council to appeal this decision before a court—previously such decisions could only be questioned by filing a formal "request" (*Eingabe*) with the next higher state organ. See *Einheit,* No. 3 (1989) and Bundesministerium für innerdeutsche Beziehungen, ed., *Informationen,* No. 11 (1989), 7–9.

6

Patterns of Cooperation and Subordination: The Economic Integration of the Private Sector

Private firms under socialism have led a precarious existence, even under the most favourable political and ideological conditions. State enterprise managers, local administrators, and Party functionaries as well as significant segments of the population, will frequently oppose openly or undermine quietly the implementation of a policy favourable to the private sector if private economic actors are seen as violating "socialist norms". Various activities of private enterprises create resistance and opposition to the implementation of a "liberal" private-sector policy.[1] The most important of these are:

1. competition with state enterprises for markets, supplies, space, and/or for labour;
2. voluntary or involuntary recourse to illegal supply channels due to a shortage of official state supply;
3. accumulation of large profits/incomes; charging high prices;
4. catering to markets that do not have political priority.

This chapter will provide an overview of the economic institutions and organizations that linked the GDR private sector to the rest of the economy. It is evident that in a centrally-planned economy consisting predominantly of large state enterprises, private firms, in order to be able to operate legally, at a minimum must be connected to the material and technical supply systems. In addition to fulfilling this economic function, the private sector's integration into and subordination to the state economy is a task of eminent political importance.

Economic integration is here defined as the existence of an institutional framework which allows and/or compels private firms in a socialist economy to operate without generating the problems noted above beyond what are generally considered acceptable limits in that society. It should be emphasized that this definition does not assume the rationality of such a framework in strictly economic terms. Obviously, restrictive regulations and institutions will have adverse effects on the economic performance of private firms by stifling their initiative and depriving them of some, or even most, of their dynamism and flexibility. The decisive point is that where this degree of economic integration of the private sector is not achieved, the resulting political problems can endanger the private-sector policy and may lead to its ultimate failure. To put it simply, reformist policy makers at the central level are confronted with a trade-off between the potential economic gains of a relatively freely-operating private sector, and the potential political costs of opposition created by the social and economic effects engendered by their policy. The values of this trade-off are shaped by the concrete ideological, political, and economic situation at the time of the policy's adoption. Thus, the utter bankruptcy of "socialist norms" and the desperate economic conditions in present-day Poland seem to have raised the general level of tolerance with respect to the four types of problems described above. In the Soviet Union, by contrast, the greater legitimacy of "socialist norms" has led to strong opposition against the reformists' private-sector policy.[2]

A crucial variable in this trade-off is the existing institutional framework at the time of the policy's adoption. When in 1976 the SED leadership decided to embark on a new course with respect to the country's private sector, it was able to do so in the context of an existing institutional structure for the economic integration and subordination of the private economy. Through this institutional framework, the new policy could be implemented without generating any of the basic problems discussed above. Specifically,

1. competition for supplies, space, and labour was minimized by subordinating the needs of private firms to those of state enterprises (e.g., by applying a lower wage scale to private firms);
2. supply channels, though far from abundant, were legalized and regularized through a special network of supply firms for the private sector;
3. tax regulations kept a ceiling on profits and incomes, and discouraged large turnovers; prices were strictly controlled;
4. licensing practices ensured that private firms were at least minimally admitted to those occupations that were most desired, and the qualifications and performance of private entrepreneurs were strictly controlled.

The most important institutions and organizations through which the East German private sector cooperated with, and was subordinated to, the state economy were: (1) purchase and delivery cooperatives (*Einkaufs- und Liefergenossenschaften*; ELG), whose central function was the supply of private firms with material and technical resources; (2) Chambers of Handicraft and Chambers of Trade and Commerce, the major functions of which included logistical and training support and economic interest representation; (3) product and supply groups (*Erzeugnis-und Versorgungsgruppen*; EVG), whose main function was the vertical sectoral integration of private firms (see Figure 6.1). The discussion in this chapter will also touch upon such "institutions" as performance comparisons, occupational training, technological assistance, and social security for private entrepreneurs.

The relative success of the SED's policy since 1976 of promoting the private sector, including the fact that this policy was, for the most part, uncontroversial ideologically, was largely a result of its successful integration into, and subordination to, the state economy. By assisting in supplying private firms with resources, and by promoting the special state objectives with respect to the output assigned to the private sector, the institutions to be discussed in the present chapter made it possible for private firms to operate relatively efficiently and, on the whole, in a legal fashion.

Purchase and Delivery Cooperatives (ELG)

ELGs are cooperatives whose members are private handicraft firms. Their main function was to procure material supplies for their members. As such, they formed the main link between local state planners and private firms. In the 1980s, there were some 1,100 ELGs in the GDR. They served one or several related trades in a limited territory. Like individual private handicraft firms and cooperatives (PGH), ELGs had compulsory membership in the Chamber of Handicraft which supervised and controlled their work.

Handicraft cooperatives of the purchase-and-delivery type were the first cooperatives to emerge in the Soviet zone of occupation in 1946. Very early in the history of the GDR, the ELG assumed the basic functions which it continued to play until the late 1980s: a wholesale organization for private handicraft firms which interacted on their behalf with state enterprises and planners for supplies. The ELG's role as a marketing agency for its members was of minor significance.[3]

The ELGs worked under the direction of the county councils in close cooperation with the district Chambers of Handicraft.[4] Generally, their scope of operation was confined to a county territory. Any expansion of

Figure 6.1 Economic Integration of the GDR Private Sector

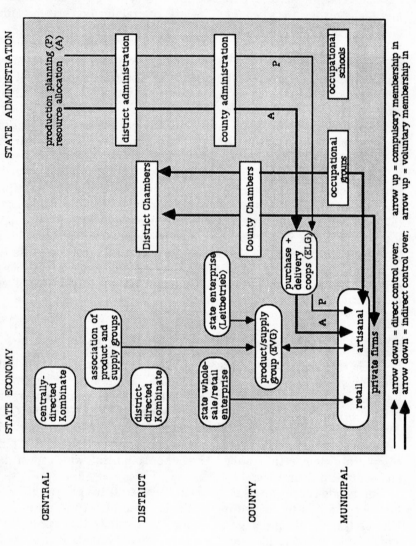

business operations into other counties or districts required the approval of the district council. ELGs were organized as "basic materials" cooperatives (e.g., metal) or as "special cooperatives" (e.g., opticians). About 90 percent of an ELG's annual turnover was accounted for by sales of materials, raw materials, spare parts, and auxiliary materials to member firms.[5] For the more effective supply of member firms with materials, and for influencing the determination of the output profile, the county councils provided the ELGs with a summary of plan targets and plan requirements for their firms as part of the annual plans. Moreover, ELGs were expected to make contracts directly with material suppliers on a regular basis.

Membership in an ELG was open to private artisans and business operators who were members of the district Chamber of Handicraft, whose firm was located in the territory served by the ELG, and who did not hold a membership in another ELG. Each member had to purchase a specified number of shares upon joining the cooperative. Through the ELG, the private handicraft sector was thus integrated into the local planning system by territory and by product line. Integration meant being incorporated into the "logic of shortage." That is, private firms were dependent upon supplies being secured by their ELG through the planning system, as well as subject to planners' targets for their sector. In addition, ELGs, as cooperatives of *private* entrepreneurs, were often last in line in the distribution of scarce resources.[6] On the other hand, there was no better alternative for private firms in the *existing* system. With a maximum firm size generally not exceeding 10 employees, most private handicraft firms could not possibly hope to secure their supplies if they themselves had to deal directly with state suppliers and local planning authorities. Moreover, many ELGs seemed to be run more like private businesses than state enterprises. They had a reputation for operating very flexibly in an environment of shortage.[7] It was common knowledge that they procured for their members not only supplies which were officially allocated to them, but also hunted down materials and equipment through informal channels.[8]

Another important consideration is that in the more favourable political environment after 1976, local planning authorities had a strong incentive to ensure that private handicraft firms were able to provide their products and services to the population.[9] Integration and subordination of the private sector at the same time implied greater direct responsibility of the state for its functioning.[10] The value of ELGs for the private handicraft sector can be illustrated with reference to private artisans who could not rely on an ELG for their supplies. Artistic and rare handicraft trades, which in recent years had been particularly encouraged by the state,[11] because of their special needs were usually not able to secure their supplies through local ELGs. In such cases, the individual artisans had to establish their own connections with the relevant state enterprises, as well as negotiating with the local planners to be incorporated into the supply system. Thus, despite a positive political climate for the operation, the start-up costs of establishing the necessary links, as well as the continuing costs of maintaining them, added up to a large investment of time. Constant attention was thus required just to have the requisite supplies available. This is not to say that private firms that were able to receive supplies through an ELG had no supply problems. Quite the contrary. The central problem for private artisans was that of supply. The ELG appeared as the final link in a chain of shortage-administering agencies, a link that provided fairly regular and legal supply services exclusively for the private sector. These, of course, could be—and very frequently were— supplemented by the private firm's own efforts to secure materials or equipment through alternative channels.[12]

Private retail[13] businesses did not have any supply agencies comparable to ELGs. Working with a commission contract,[14] which until the late 1970s was officially portrayed as an ideologically-progressive step towards socialism, implied that the private retailers received the bulk of their supplies directly through the contracting state retail or wholesale enterprise. Private retailers without a commission contract, by contrast, were in principle free to find their own suppliers. In practice, this greater potential flexibility rarely translated into better access to supplies, for in most sectors there were almost no alternative channels of supply outside the state wholesale enterprises. As a result, commission retailers, as a direct part of the state trading network, in some cases may have had better, or at least easier, access to supplies.[15]

The Chambers

Like the ELG, the Chambers of Trade and Commerce (until 1983 called Chambers of Industry and Trade) and the Chambers of Handicraft are organizations whose activities are devoted exclusively to the private and cooperative sectors.[16] Like the ELG, they represent elements of institutional continuity in the GDR. They have traditionally played an important role in the economic integration and subordination of the private sector.

The *Chambers of Industry and Trade* were established in 1945/46 in the five *Länder* of the Soviet zone of occupation.[17] As part of a comprehensive administrative reform in 1958 which gave greater economic responsibilities to local governments, the central institutions of the Chamber were dissolved. The district Chambers were subordinated to the district councils, with the county Chambers answerable to the district Chambers as well as to county councils.[18] Thus by 1958, the Chamber of Trade and Industry's basic administrative structure and functions as well as its forms of subordination to the state had been established. The significance of the Chambers of Industry and Trade was further reduced after 1972 when the nationalization of most remaining private and semistate industries reduced their jurisdiction to a small private retail sector.

In 1946, the reorganization of the *Chambers of Handicraft* began with the transformation of the independent local guilds (*Innungen*) into subordinate departments and occupational groups (*Berufsgruppen*) within the Chambers.[19] As part of an administrative reform in 1952, the five *Land* Chambers were reorganized into 14 district Chambers (plus one Chamber for East Berlin). Since 1953, the Chambers have worked under the control of district councils.[20] The basic structure and function of the Chambers of Handicraft had been established by the late 1950s. In contrast to the Chambers of Industry and Trade, they were not as strongly affected by the 1972 nationalization. They lost relatively fewer members in their jurisdictions. Moreover, the greater importance attached to the handicraft sector since the inception of the promotion policy of 1976, the larger number of member firms,[21] as well as the greater organizational presence of the Chambers of Handicraft at the county level (see below) explain why the Chambers of Handicraft played a more prominent and apparently more effective role than their counterparts in the trade sector.[22] The main functions of the Chambers may be described as monitoring and planning, coordination, technological development support, training, and interest representation. Each function will be briefly discussed with reference to examples.[23]

The Chambers were, on the whole, not directly involved in input and output planning. One exception were Chambers that fulfilled the role of the purchase and delivery cooperatives (ELG) for specific handicraft trades. The main *monitoring and planning function* of the Chambers concerned the territorial supply of consumers with services. In particular, the county branches of the Chambers attempted to keep track of the availability of specific services in their territory, the age structure in "problem trades," the number of apprentices required, etc. They designed long-term (usually five-year) development programmes, which were incorporated into the county's five-year "conceptions."[24] Among others, these determined which community needed new private or cooperative firms, prepared for the establishment of suitable business premises and the training and further training of employees.[25] To promote action on acute problems, the Chambers organized conferences dealing, for example, with the sharp decline in private shoe repair services in a given territory.[26] Where the demand for services offered by private handicraft firms was on the decline for structural reasons, the Chambers frequently set up, or assisted in, access to retraining programs or alternative business opportunities for the affected individuals.[27]

The Chambers were also responsible for monitoring the adequacy of performance on the part of their member firms. Much of this quality control was carried out by self-control organs set up through the occupational groups of the individual trades. In Berlin, for example, there were 199 occupational groups, 95 percent of which had their own self-control groups.[28] In addition, all formal citizen complaints (*Eingaben*) filed with public authorities regarding the performance of handicraft firms were routinely passed on to the Chamber. R. Berghammer, Chairman of the Berlin Chamber of Handicraft, reported that in 1984 his Chamber received 299 such *Eingaben*. The following statement he made in the context of professional standards is interesting because it highlights widely-shared public expectations of the private sector. "If the reason for the citizen's complaint is impolite behaviour or low quality work on the part of the handicraft firm, then this is incompatible with the pride and traditions of handicraft. The secure perspective of handicraft in the GDR entails an obligation to work according to high standards, to preserve traditions such as quality, honesty, and courtesy in dealing with clients. The great majority of Berlin artisans work in accordance with this."[29] The *Eingaben* concerned failure to meet deadlines (27 percent); demands for higher quality work (26 percent); and impolite treatment (16 percent). However, only in one case was the transgression serious enough for the Chamber to propose to local authorities that the private entrepreneur's license be revoked.[30]

The Chambers' *coordination function* concerns what in official GDR parlance was referred to as *sozialistische Gemeinschaftsarbeit* (socialist cooperation). The goals of efficiency and economic development were to be promoted by joint initiatives of collective actors—associations, unions, enterprises.[31] A district Chamber was frequently also charged by a Ministry to act as the coordinating Chamber for a particular trade in the GDR as a whole, setting priorities and organizing cooperation and the division of labour between private and cooperative firms.[32] The Chambers, furthermore, were responsible for *technological assistance* to the private sector and for this purpose established special "departments for rationalization." Technological assistance entailed providing information on existing technologies, often through the occupational groups. A widely used way of disseminating information on new technologies was the establishment of so-called consultation points. A handicraft firm in a territory which was working with advanced technology was selected to be available to other private artisans for the testing of new equipment and for advice on its effective use. (Often such new technological solutions were not ready-made products that could simply be purchased, but merely instructions for how to do it yourself.) The Chambers also organized the serial production of certain new technologies for which there was great demand among its members.[33]

A vital element in the SED's private-sector policy since 1976 has been *occupational training*. Attempts were made to stimulate interest among young people, particularly among the children of private entrepreneurs, in a career in private handicraft. The major reason why this continued to be so important is that by the mid-1970s, the age structure of private artisans had become extremely top-heavy. In order to preserve the size of the handicraft sector, a large number of apprentices had to be recruited every year. A major role of the Chambers of Handicraft was to monitor the age structure in specific trades in their territory, articulate the needs of the private sector for apprentices in the future, and provide local manpower planners with the corresponding information. In addition, since not all handicraft occupations enjoyed the same popularity among the young as did hairdressers, auto mechanics, or electricians, the Chamber of Handicraft had to engage in special efforts to stimulate interest in, and recruit apprentices for, less-favoured trades, such as bakers, tailors, or bricklayers. For this purpose, the Chambers established special occupational counselling centres, organized information sessions for students as early as Grades 6 and 7, created opportunities for students to visit handicraft firms, as well as encouraged master artisans to appear in schools to introduce their trades.[34] Moreover, the Chambers were responsible for establishing, financing, maintaining, and updating special training facilities and programs, in particular programs for further training.[35]

Finally, the Chambers engaged in a range of activities that may be broadly described as their *interest representation function*. First, *qua* organizations, they provided a focus and platform for private artisans to interact and define their common interests. Here, the occupational groups as trade-specific and local forums were most important from the point of view of private artisans.[36] The Chambers of Handicraft organized annual artisanal conferences where delegates from the various occupational groups participated. Finally, the Chambers published regular bulletins with information ranging from legal regulations and technical information to professional news and statements and appeals by Ministries. They even offered a travel service.

Second, the Chambers provided legal advice and representation to their members through special departments at the district Chamber level. Specific areas in which the Chambers represented the interests of private entrepreneurs are the licensing process and the renegotiation of terms under which a private firm operated. Licenses were issued by county and municipal administrations, but the Chambers were to be consulted particularly concerning an applicant's professional qualifications. In the past, local governments frequently did not consult with the Chamber. More recently, however, the Chambers have been asserting their prerogative more forcefully.[37] The SED's explicit policy of encouraging a more active licensing practice, and its consistent appeals to local state organs to do everything in their power to help establish new private businesses, strengthened the position of the Chambers as representatives of private entrepreneurs vis-à-vis local authorities. The Chamber was usually also a strong ally of business operators who wished to renegotiate the terms under which they worked, e.g., regarding the number of workers they could employ, or the price level for their products and services.[38]

The Chambers had little formal autonomy, were answerable to county and district councils, and were explicitly charged with assisting in the implementation of government policy. Formally at least, they should be seen as representing the interests of government rather than the interests of the private sector. However, the situation was considerably more complicated. In addition to potentially conflicting interests between central and local levels of goverment, the Chambers obviously had an organizational self-interest. A more differentiated analysis of this situation will be offered below. A simple point may be briefly noted here. As organizations exclusively devoted to private and cooperative firms, their own importance, size, and activities were likely to be curtailed if the size and appreciation of the private sector declined. Moreover, like virtually all organizations, the Chambers constantly attempted to extend their influence. One of the organizational goals that was being discussed within the Chambers in the 1980s was the establishment of a *central* GDR Chamber of Handicraft. There would have been certain functional benefits (in addition to the greater prestige and influence such a central organization would provide), as the *de facto* use of individual district Chambers as GDR-wide coordinating agencies for specific trades indicates. The Chambers were also interested in developing exports of certain private- and cooperative-sector products. However, on the part of central Ministries responsible for private firms, there was considerable resistance to a central-level Chamber which inadvertently would have interfered in their jurisdictions.[39]

Generally, the Chambers of Trade and Commerce fulfilled the same functions for the private retail sector as did the Chambers of Handicraft for private and cooperative artisanal firms. But the public profile, the areas and level of activity, and the political influence of the Chambers of Handicraft were considerably higher than that of their counterparts in Trade and Commerce. There were some obvious reasons for this. As already mentioned above, the number of private and cooperative handicraft firms was more than three times the number of private retailers.[40] The 1972 nationalization had depleted the membership of the Chambers of Trade and Commerce and deflated their importance. Since Chambers were financed on the levy principle, they also had less operating funds than the Chambers of Handicraft, as well as smaller staffs. Related to this was the organizational presence of each: about 80 percent of all counties had a branch of the Chamber of Handicraft, whereas only some 40 percent had county Chambers of Trade and Commerce. Finally, the emphasis in the early phase of the 1976 policy was clearly on the handicraft sector.[41]

Product and Supply Groups

The product and supply groups (*Erzeugnis-und Versorgungsgruppen*; EVG) are associations of enterprises in the same or similar lines of production. They were to ensure the balanced technological and economic development in their sectors. They had a predominantly coordinating function. Private firms participated on a voluntary basis.[42] In 1985, only one in eight private firms and one in three handicraft cooperatives participated in EVGs.[43] For the private sector, EVGs were of particular importance until the last nationalization in 1972, which eliminated a sizable private sector in industrial production. In the 1980s, they continued to play their traditional role for the economic integration of the private and cooperative handicraft sector into the state economy.

The establishment of the product and supply groups in 1963–1964 went hand-in-hand with the launching of the New Economic System.[44] The EVGs relevant for the private and cooperative sector were generally coordinated by district-directed *Kombinate*.[45] Any one such *Kombinat* could be simultaneously responsible for a number of EVGs. Individual EVGs were usually organized at county levels and there coordinated by a state enterprise acting as the *Leitbetrieb* (guiding enterprise). The state enterprise, in turn, belonged to a district-directed *Kombinat*. Thus, the Consumer Service *Kombinat* Karl-Marx-Stadt (Werdau) oversaw the work of 6 supply groups organizing 1,300 handicraft cooperatives, purchase and delivery cooperatives, and private handicraft firms.[46] The Consumer Service *Kombinat* Berlin supervised 7 supply groups, the VEB Radio and Television in Dresden was responsible for 9 supply groups.[47] Individual product or supply groups in the same sector could form an association of EVGs (*Erzeugnisgruppenverband*).[48]

Individual supply groups of the auto maintenance sector, like most other EVGs, operated at the county level. The supply group of the auto maintenance sector in Oranienburg may serve as an example. The Chairman of this supply group at the county level was the branch manager of a state automobile enterprise, the supply group's *Leitbetrieb*. The work of the supply group was at least once a year the subject of discussions in the county assembly. As a state enterprise, the *Leitbetrieb* pulled weight in such cases as procuring important equipment (e.g., diagnosis and measuring technology). However, it also ordered for its member firms more basic equipment and ensured its distribution and delivery. All tools, machines, and equipment for all member firms passed through the hands of the *Leitbetrieb* secretary reponsible for rationalization who also provided assistance to private firms in acquiring the necessary skills. The supply group coordinated training programmes and participated in decisions on the issuing of new licenses. The state enterprise provided training for apprentices from cooperative and private firms in the area of auto electrical maintenance. The supply group organized the exchange of know-how, as well as provided guidance concerning price regulations and related legal issues.[49]

Product and supply groups, furthermore, determined the intrasectoral division of labour.[50] Similarly, the issue of service hours was frequently regulated through EVGs.[51] More generally, the EVGs had to decide on whether a specific service fell under the purview of a state enterprise or that of a private firm.[52] Given the fact that only a minority of handicraft firms participated in product and supply groups, it is clear that their relevance in this respect was confined to specific trades where private firms offered the same services as state enterprises.

Other Forms of Economic Integration and Subordination

There were other ways in which the private sector was incorporated into the larger state economy, specifically with respect to occupational training, technological assistance, and social security. Some of these have already been touched upon in this chapter, since one or more of the formal organizations of private sector integration discussed above were involved.[53] As these functions were essential for the private sector's economic integration and subordination, they will now be addressed more directly and systematically.

Occupational training was important for the private sector because an indispensable precondition for obtaining a license was the possession of professional qualifications—in the handicraft sector that of a master artisan, in the retail and restaurant sector that of a certified manager. While the handicraft sector provided much of the training for most of the private and cooperative artisans in the GDR, the private retail sector played an insignificant role in training apprentices. In both handicraft and retail sectors, however, state training centres provided the theoretical schooling of future private entrepreneurs. Examinations were conducted by special commissions approved by the county Department of Vocational Training.[54]

In both handicraft and retail sectors, the theoretical training component for apprentices was provided by municipal or county occupational schools (*Berufsschulen*), by local enterprise academies (*Betriebsakademien*), and by district or central-level occupational schools (particularly in highly specialized trades). In order to ensure a high level of occupational training for apprentices in small cooperatives and private handicraft firms, it was the responsibility of district and county councils, in cooperation with the Chambers and the product and supply groups, to organize the temporary exchange of apprentices between firms and other forms of cooperation.[55] The costs of apprenticeship training were, for the theoretical component, borne by the state, while private and cooperative firms had to finance the practical component.[56] Admission to master training programs for the private handicraft sector was granted by county councils, based on their "development conceptions" and in consultation with the district Chamber.[57]

The *introduction and application of new technology* is obviously an essential process for the economic performance of any firm. The various ways in which attempts were made in the GDR to facilitate this process in the private sector constituted another significant aspect of its economic integration. The formal organizations already described, in particular the Chambers and the product and supply groups, played a central role in this area of economic incorporation as well. The same was true for central ministries and local administrations, which had to ensure that in the private sector, too, performance was constantly being improved through rationalization. The variety of actors involved in the process of rationalization may be illustrated with reference to an example from the baking trade.

The Ministry for District Directed Industry and the Food Industry entrusted the *Zentrum für Rationalisierung und Kleinmechanisierung* (Centre for Rationalization and Small-Scale Mechanization; ZRK) to play a coordinating function for the introduction of new technology in the private and cooperative baking sector. The manufacturing of machinery and equipment for the baking trade was organized by the product subgroup Rationalization Equipment, Manufacturing which since 1982 has been under the direction of the state enterprise Maschinenbau Fürstenberg/Havel. Special rationalization equipment for the baking trade was also produced by approximately 60 private and cooperative firms of the machine-building trades. For first-time users, new technologies were demonstrated at so-called *consultation points,* i.e., in leading cooperative and private firms which had been selected for this purpose. For the baking trade, there were 27 such consultation points in the GDR.[58] It may be assumed that this level of activity was not typical for the private sector as a whole. The baking trade enjoyed high priority in the GDR. Moreover, it should not be concluded that efforts in the area of rationalization were generally successful. The major stumbling block to rationalization in the private sector, as private bakers did not hesitate to point out,[59] and as was officially acknowledged,[60] was the level of supply of such new technologies.[61]

Finally, the private and cooperative sector in the GDR had full access to the country's *social security system*—in fact, like employees, they had compulsory membership in various social insurance programs such as health, disability, old-age, and maternity.[62]

Formal Economic Integration and Its Significance for the Private Sector

The general argument underlying the analysis presented in this chapter was that the viability of a legal private sector in a socialist economy depends almost by definition on its integration into the official allocation system. Competition with state enterprises, recourse to illegal supply channels, entrance into only the most profitable markets and resulting high incomes will, quite apart from their overall economic effects, raise a host of political problems. In order to operate legally and with some degree of stability, a private sector under socialism must be integrated into the larger state economy of which it forms a part. To some extent, private firms in the GDR derived benefits from this institutional framework. While it placed additional constraints on private entrepreneurs, they were nevertheless frequently able to manipulate it for their own purposes.

The two institutions which were most beneficial for private firms were the purchase and delivery cooperatives (ELG) and the Chambers. While the socialist state tried to use both for achieving the economic goals it set for the private sector, they were the closest allies of private firms in the institutional framework described in this chapter. There are two basic reasons for this. First, both fulfilled important economic functions for private firms. Second, due to their organizational structure and function, they had a manifest interest in strengthening the private sector by fulfilling their functions effectively.

Purchase and delivery cooperatives had a long history as wholesale suppliers for their private member firms. They had acquired considerable skill in dealing with state organs allocating the material and technical resources needed by their member firms. More important, they had established direct relationships with enterprises in the state sector which, through their flexibility, they could exploit to supplement the generally inadequate official allocations they received. As a result, the small member firms benefited by having the ELGs, with their "economies of scale", deal on their behalf with the state administration and with state enterprises. If, in other words, private firms with usually no more than 10 and often only 3 employees had had to deal with the system of shortages on their own, they would have had to invest considerably more time and effort, make do with fewer supplies, and/or resort increasingly to illegal supply channels. ELGs, moreover, had an incentive to increase turnover because they could reinvest their profits.

The Chambers fulfilled equally important, though more general economic functions for the private sector. As organizations *for* the non-state sector, they influenced the various forms of structural planning—development programmes at the local levels, training, retraining, licensing and establishment of new private firms—carried out by local governments which did not always assign the resolute implementation of private-sector policy high priority.[63] As organizations *of* the non-state sector, the Chambers provided a framework for the professional and social interaction of their members—e.g., through the trade-specific and local occupational groups or by organizing handicraft conferences. They offered individual members legal advice and assistance, supplied information on available technical equipment, and at least attempted to improve the highly unsatisfactory situation with respect to the production and allocation of rationalization technology specifically for the private sector. Increasingly, they were willing to assert their mandate as organizations of and for the private sector vis-à-vis local state organs. Despite their limited autonomy, they had an organizational interest in strengthening the private sector, if only to enhance their own influence and importance. As the more marginal and insignificant existence of the Chambers of Trade and Commerce compared to that of the Chambers of Handicraft shows, however, they could play their positive role for the private sector only to the extent that they were consistently and explicitly supported by a strong commitment to positive private-sector policy from the centre.

The role of the product and supply groups (EVG) for the private sector is more uncertain. As noted, only a small fraction of private and cooperative firms belonged to product and supply groups. The latter were dominated by the always much larger state enterprises, which also acted as the formal guiding enterprises of these groups. Their central function was coordinating the intrasectoral division of labour, such as in the automobile, the baking, or the photography sector. The participation of private firms in product and supply groups was often necessary because the leading state enterprises were in charge of distributing technical equipment. In general, the interests of the small private firms were subordinated to those of the state firms. Sometimes, this meant that private firms were assigned less lucrative or more labour-intensive tasks, that innovation by private firms was discouraged if it showed the state enterprises in an unfavourable light, or that bureaucratic barriers were erected or defended for purely political reasons. On the whole, however, the influence of the product and supply groups on the work of private firms was sufficiently limited, ineffectual, or simply symbolic[64] that its negative effects at any rate did not threaten the existence of participating private firms. The economic integration of the private sector with respect to training, further training, and retraining, as well as its incorporation into the public social security system, was in general beneficial for private firms and entrepreneurs.

The fundamental restructuring of the East German economy that is now occurring as part of the German unification process will make the institutional framework for the integration of the GDR private sector largely obsolete with respect to the political-economic functions described in this chapter. Ideologically and structurally, the East German private economy will no longer require integration into, and subordination to, a larger socialist economy. Rather, as a rapidly growing, and perhaps as the eventually dominant, sector of the economy, the private economy will be integrated into the West German and world capitalist market. However, the existing framework of institutions will not simply disappear. Some institutions, such as the Chambers, have been at the forefront of the political struggle for private sector economic reform from the beginning of the political revolution in the fall of 1989, and they are transforming themselves into genuine interest representatives of private entrepreneurs.[65]

While the institutional framework described in this chapter placed a variety of restrictions on private firms by subordinating them to the state economy, it also protected private entrepreneurs under socialism from the negative, and potentially fatal, consequences of having to operate in the context of a larger state economy[66] by integrating them. The transition to a new economic order will liberate the East German private sector from many of the restrictions of the past, thus creating new opportunities for its expansion and growth. At the same time, the transition process can be expected to create previously unknown problems for East German private entrepreneurs, in particular competition with much more efficient and market-experienced West German firms. It is conceivable that the Chambers, especially, may continue to play a protective role for the existing private firms vis-à-vis radical political reformers and powerful economic competitors.

Finally, the analysis presented in this chapter may contain some valuable lessons for East-bloc countries that will move away from the socialist economic system less rapidly and less radically than East Germany, in particular the Soviet Union. The four basic problems that create resistance and opposition to private-sector policy under socialism identified at the beginning of this chapter—competition with state enterprises, recourse to illegal supply channels, high profits, and entry into only the most profitable markets—may in part be alleviated by forms of institutional integration as they have evolved in the GDR. For example, while competition of private firms with state enterprises may be desirable, it may be easier to reduce the political opposition from the state sector, and thus to protect weak private firms, by institutionalizing compromise solutions, e.g., on a division of labour, or forms of private/state-enterprise cooperation, along the lines of the East German product and supply groups. The problem of illegal supply may be reduced by strongly promoting the establishment of wholesale firms serving specifically the private sector, similar to the East German purchase and delivery cooperatives. Most important, a system of Chambers could serve the double function of representing the interests of private firms vis-à-vis local administrations and the central government, as well as the regulation and control of their members' firms (e.g., for maintaining professional standards and for the protection of the consumer).

Notes

1. For examples from the history of the GDR, see Chapter 2. For evidence from other Communist countries, see Chapter 1.

2. See for further details Chapter 1.

3. Müller, "Bedeutung und Formen der Integration des Handwerks," p. 45 reports that the share of output sales by ELG never exceeded 18 percent of their total turnover. G. Röder, "Zu einigen Aufgaben der Einkaufs-und Liefergenossenschaften des Handwerks," (On Some Tasks of Handicraft Purchase and Delivery Cooperatives) in *Rechtsnormen für das Handwerk. Gesetze, Kommentare, Verordnungen,* ed. Das Neue Handwerk (Berlin: Verlag Die Wirtschaft, 1978, p. 190) states that about 90 percent of the ELG's annual turnover of 4 billion marks was accounted for by sales to their member firms.

4. "Beschluß über das Musterstatut der Einkaufs-und Liefergenossenschaften des Handwerks vom 6. Februar 1986" (Resolution on the Model Statute of Handicraft Purchase and Delivery Cooperatives of 6 February 1986), *GBl.*I No. 7, p. 65. See also M. Haendcke-Hoppe, "Das private Handwerk in der DDR" (Private Handicraft in the GDR), *Deutschland Archiv,* Vol. 20, 8 (1987), 850.

5. Röder, "Aufgaben der Einkaufs-und Liefergenossenschaften," p. 190.

6. It is of course difficult to ascertain to what extent ELGs were subject to systematic discrimination in the distribution of supplies. On the one hand, it is hardly surprising that state enterprises received preferential treatment—both for political (ideological) and economic (size) reasons. On the other hand, in an economy of shortage what may appear as systematic discrimination may just be a "normal" effect of the system. All interview partners agreed that there was unequal treatment of ELGs in the allocation of supplies.

7. Schwarz (interview).

8. See, for example, the Address of the Chairman of the ELG for the construction trades Meissen on the occasion of its 40th anniversary, n.d., p. 4. Without tapping into such informal channels, he said, we would be once again where we started with our ELG after the war, "scraping empty barrels."

9. See Chapter 5 on the logic of local level administration of the private sector.

10. For example, an electricians' ELG near Potsdam had to declare bankruptcy because it was not allowed to stay profitable. The state price authorities had reduced its sales margins, and authorities failed to assure a sufficient supply of materials. Given the great need for electricians' services, it was clear that the onus would ultimately be on county and district governments, as well as the Chamber of Handicraft, to find a solution to the problem of supplying the members of the bankrupt ELG with supplies—whether by refinancing the existing ELG or by amalgamating it with an electricians' ELG in a neighboring county. Reported by Schwarz (interview).

11. See, for example, *Das Neue Handwerk,* No. 5 (1987), p. 3.

12. I am referring here to activities in the "shadow economy", i.e., semi-legal or illegal economic exchanges—e.g., the private exchange of services for equipment or rare materials, etc. This "informal" aspect of the economic integration of the private sector will be discussed at the end of this chapter. In some trades for which special ELGs did not exist and would not have been feasible, the Chamber of Handicraft frequently fulfilled the function of an ELG by arranging for the material supply of private firms. In East Berlin, for example, the Chamber of Handicraft played this role for some 70 private handicraft firms which do not have their own ELG. Schwarz (interview).

13. Retail here also includes restaurants and hotels.

14. See Chapter 4.

15. All interview partners questioned about this agreed that in the 1980s, the difference in terms of receiving supplies between commission retailers and private retailers was insignificant. Thus, a former local bureaucrat responsible for food and beverage supplies to state and private restaurants reported that private restaurants received lowest priority from both planners and suppliers—not so much for ideological reasons as for the fact that it was more convenient to deal with larger state enterprises than with small private restaurants. East Berlin administrator (interview).

16. That is, in addition to private firms, the Chambers of Handicraft are also responsible for PGH and for ELG.

17. H. Schlenk*, *Der Binnenhandel der DDR* (Domestic trade in the GDR) (Cologne: Verlag Wissenschaft und Politik, 1970), pp. 31–32.

18. The "Verordnung über die Bildung von Wirtschaftsräten bei den Räten der Bezirke und über die Aufgabe und Struktur der Staatlichen Plankommission bei den Räten der Kreise" (Decree on the Formation of Economic Councils at the District Councils and on the Work and Structure of the State Planning Commission at the County Councils) of 13 February 1958 determined this general administrative reorganization.

19. SMAD order 161 of 27 May 1946.

20. *GBl.* 1953, p. 942.

21. Since the Chambers were financed through levies imposed on their member firms, the Chambers of Handicraft also had greater financial resources than the Chambers of Trade and Commerce.

22. I am here reporting the views of interview partners (Schwarz, Sommer, Engel, as well as private entrepreneurs).

23. The following description of the Chambers' major functions primarily refers to the Chambers of Handicraft.

24. There were no five-year plans at the county level, only one-year plans, so for a longer term perspective county administrations drew up so-called development conceptions (*Entwicklungskonzeptionen*). See H.H. Kinze, H. Knop and E. Seifert, eds. *Sozialistische Volkswirtschaft* (Socialist Macroeconomics). East Berlin: Verlag Die Wirtschaft, 1983, pp. 575–578.

25. See, for example, M. Müller (Chairman of the Chamber of Handicraft, Suhl), in *Das Neue Handwerk*, No. 3 (1986), p. 5.

26. See, for example, "Wird der Schuhmacher ein seltener Beruf?" (Will the Shoemaker become a Rare Profession?) in *Märkische Volksstimme*, No. 230, 28 September 1988.

27. For example, stove builders were increasingly shifted into the floor-tiling trade, which involved little retraining; private dry cleaning businesses were reoriented towards other laundry services; radio and television technicians were retrained for new fields in electronics. Schwarz (interview).

28. Interview with Rudi Berghammer, Chairman of the Chamber of Handicraft of East Berlin, in *Das Neue Handwerk*, No. 5 (1985), p. 4.

29. *Ibid.*

30. *Ibid.*

31. For example, the particularly unfavourable supply situation for the consumer in many rural regions of the GDR led the Cottbus District Chamber to establish links with the Farmers Mutual Aid Society (VdgB). By setting up fully operational bakeries, a joint effort was made to attract qualified bakers who otherwise might have had to invest considerable time and money of their own to establish a new business. See *Das Neue Handwerk*, No. 5 (1988), p. 4 and *Das Neue Handwerk*, No. 7 (1987), p. 1.

32. For example, the Ministry of District Directed Industry and the Food Industry designated the district Chamber of Karl-Marx-Stadt as coordinating Chamber for private and cooperative photography firms. *Das Neue Handwerk*, No. 10 (1987), p. 4. This also raises the question of the need for a central level Chamber in the GDR, an issue which will be briefly discussed below.

33. *Das Neue Handwerk*, No. 2 (1988), p. 4.

34. *Das Neue Handwerk*, No. 10 (1987), p. 6 and No. 11 (1984), p. 6.

35. K. Grabarse, "Die Aus-und Weiterbildung im Handwerk" (Training and Further Training in the Handicraft Sector), in *Rechtsnormen für das Handwerk. Gesetze, Kommentare, Verordnungen*, ed. Das Neue Handwerk (East Berlin: Verlag Die Wirtschaft, 1978), pp. 123, 128.

36. The final allocation of apprentices to individual private firms was also discussed and decided here. Schwarz (interview).

37. Schwarz (interview). See also "Computer ziehen auch im Handwerk ein" (Computers also making their entry in the handicraft sector; interview with Alfred

Köhler, Chairman of the Berlin Chamber of Handicraft), *Berliner Zeitung,* 5 April 1988.

38. Schwarz (interview).

39. This paragraph and this footnote are based on information from Schwarz (interview). A clear example of where the interests of such a central-level Chamber might have clashed with state organs is the following. If such a central Chamber of Handicraft had had the authority to organize the export of products from the private and cooperative handicraft sectors, they would have attempted to "liberate" certain cooperative or private firms with the requisite production potential from the basic repairs and services which the SED's private sector policy required them to focus on. For instance, a handicraft cooperative with a long and successful tradition in shoe manufacturing was forced to commit itself almost exclusively to shoe repairs, a service that was in short supply in the GDR. A central-level Chamber would have lobbied the Ministry of District Directed Industry and the Food Industry to exempt this cooperative from its local repair duties in order to increase the country's export earnings.

40. See Chapter 4.

41. The discussion in this paragraph is based on interviews (Sommer, Schwarz, and Engel).

42. U.J. Heuer, *Wirtschaftsrecht* (Commercial law) (East Berlin: Staatsverlag der DDR, 1985), p. 158f.

43. According to M. Haendcke-Hoppe*, "Struktureffekte der SED-Handwerkspolitik seit 1976" (Structural effects of SED handicraft policy since 1976), *FS-Analysen* (1988), p. 24.

44. See Chapter 3.

45. A *Kombinat* is an association of state enterprises. As a result of the *Kombinatsreform* of 1979/80, the East German economy was organized into 173 centrally-directed and 141 district-directed *Kombinate. Statistisches Jahrbuch 1988,* p. 103.

46. *Das Neue Handwerk,* No. 5 (1986), p. 7.

47. *Das Neue Handwerk,* No. 8 (1985), 4.

48. For example, there was an association of EVGs in the auto maintenance sector which, among other things, regularly published a substantial information booklet containing general information, technical information, and news on EVG activities. This association of EVGs closely cooperated with the Postdam District Chamber of Handicraft, the designated coordinating Chamber for the private and cooperative auto service firms. This high degree of centralization and coordination, however, was typical only for specific very large and important economic sectors where cooperation with central-level industries (e.g., the auto manufacturers and state importers) was crucial (e.g., for the organization of a comprehensive service network for the various car makes available in the GDR).

49. *Das Neue Handwerk,* No. 7 (1986), p. 4.

50. For instance, in photography services the supply group determined the specialization of state enterprises and handicraft firms, respectively. While the state sector took over mass development, the handicraft sector provided custom services such as portraits. *Das Neue Handwerk,* No. 5 (1987), p. 3.

51. The state enterprise, Radio and Television in Dresden, discussed the issue of extended service hours with the three large Radio and TV cooperatives in Dresden, together with council members from the Department of Local Supply Economy in the city districts. At a subsequent supply group meeting the endorsement of the private firms was obtained. *Das Neue Handwerk,* No. 8 (1985), p. 4.

52. The product group of the baking sector, for example, determined that private bakeries would concentrate on specialized goods while the state enterprise would produce mass goods such as regular bread. Schwarz (interview).

53. Thus, occupational training was the responsibility of the Chambers and the product and supply groups, technological assistance was defined as important formal tasks of purchase and delivery cooperatives, Chambers, and product and supply groups.

54. Based on the Regulations for the Examination of Skilled Workers (*Facharbeiterprüfungsordnung*) of 7 August 1973 (*GBl.*I, No. 40, p. 414); K. Grabarse, "Die Aus-und Weiterbildung im Handwerk" (Training and Further Training in the Handicraft Sector), in *Rechtsnormen für das Handwerk. Gesetze, Kommentare, Verordnungen,* ed. Das Neue Handwerk (Berlin: Verlag Die Wirtschaft, 1978), p. 124.

55. Grabarse, "Die Aus-und Weiterbildung," p. 122f.

56. Anordnung über die Finanzierung der Berufsausbildung vom 17.10.1969 (Regulation on the Financing of Vocational Training of 17 October 1969, *GBl.*II No. 88/1969, p. 541. County councils may grant temporary training subsidies to private and cooperative firms (*GBl.I* No. 10/1974, p. 87); Grabarse, "Die Aus-und Weiterbildung," p. 125.

57. Grabarse, "Die Aus-und Weiterbildung," p. 126.

58. Based on a report by the Deputy Minister for District Directed Industry and Food Industry, published in *Der Morgen,* 9 March 1988. There was a total of over 250 consultation points for all handicraft trades. *Neue Zeit,* 4 August 1987.

59. Interview material.

60. Schwarz (interview).

61. The waiting period for a personal computer in the private handicraft sector, for instance, was 5 years. Information from private entrepreneur.

62. The right to social security was already established in the first GDR Constitution of 1949 (Article 16). Until 1951, when the trade union FDGB was entrusted to resume full control of the social insurance funds, they were self-administered by representatives of the workers (two-thirds) and the self-employed (one-third). In 1956, the social insurance funds for private entrepreneurs, members of cooperatives, and the self-employed were placed under the authority of the *Deutsche Versicherungs-Anstalt,* subsequently *Staatliche Versicherung der DDR.* G. Wachner, "Die Sozialversicherung für Genossenschafts-und private Handwerker" (Social Insurance for Cooperative and Private Artisans), in *Rechtsnormen für das Handwerk. Gesetze, Kommentare, Verordnungen,* ed. Das Neue Handwerk (East Berlin: Verlag Die Wirtschaft, 1978), pp. 129–135.

63. See also Chapter 5 where the problems of policy implementation at the local level are discussed more systematically.

64. E.g. when state enterprises "proveed" in performance comparisons within the product and supply groups that they worked more efficiently and productively

than its members from the private sector by bringing to bear its superior material and technical capacity. Personal information.

65. A detailed account of these developments is provided in Chapter 8.

66. I am referring to the general problems identified at the beginning of this chapter.

7

Patterns of Mobilization and Representation: The Political and Social Integration of the Private Sector

The GDR's own peculiar history of private-sector policy from the late 1940s to the late 1960s had left not only a legacy of economic integration. When in 1976 the SED adopted its policy of promoting private handicraft and trade, it did so in the context of traditions of political mobilization and representation and the social integration of private entrepreneurs in socialism. In the 1970s and 1980s, this legacy shaped the elaboration and implementation of general policy, and contributed significantly to the social acceptance of private firms. The present chapter is devoted to an exploration of these political and social aspects of the private economy. The analysis will address the following questions: How were private entrepeneurs politically organized and represented; how, and how effectively, were their interests formulated and included in the policymaking process? What was the social status of private entrepreneurs in GDR society; how were they perceived by their fellow citizens, and how did they see themselves?

The primary political organizations in and through which private entrepreneurs were represented in the GDR were three of the SED's four allied parties (*befreundete Parteien*). They were generally referred to as Bloc parties because together with the SED and the major mass organizations, they formed the Democratic Bloc of Parties and Mass Organizations.[1] The three Bloc parties which played a role for the private sector were the Christian Democrats (CDU), the Liberal Democrats (LDPD), and the National Democrats (NDPD). (The fourth Bloc party, the Democratic Farmers Party (DBD), played no role for the private sector in the 1980s because its membership base was in the virtually fully collectivized agricultural sector.)[2] Given their strong political dependence on the SED, these political parties are best understood as mass organizations of a special type rather than as traditional political parties in the Western

145

sense.[3] Their special mission was the mobilization and integration of social groups outside the working class. Like other mass organizations in Communist societies, they had a double function. On the one hand, they assisted in the implementation of Party policy ("transmission function"), on the other they represented the interests of special groups in society ("interest representation function"). As these two basic functions often conflicted with each other, and as the leading Communist party, with rare exceptions, did not tolerate autonomous organizations,[4] the interest representation function of mass organizations tended to be seriously compromised. This also applied to the Bloc parties in the GDR. Their interest representation function was subordinated to their transmission function. The scope and nature of the "objective" (i.e., legitimate) interests of the non-working class strata were defined and determined by the SED. It would be easy to conclude that these organizations only imposed further restrictions on private entrepreneurs in the GDR, that they merely represented an extended arm of the Party, and that they had neither the autonomy nor the interest to become active on behalf of the private sector. This view seems to be supported by what has already been discussed in the historical part of the analysis: one traditional task of the Bloc parties had been to prepare nationalization campaigns, even giving the impression that they, together with Bloc party members from the private sector, had in fact initiated such policies.[5]

There are at least two reasons why an analysis of the political integration of the private sector—primarily through the Bloc parties—is nevertheless indispensable for an understanding of private-sector policy and politics in the GDR. First, the economics of the private sector were an eminently political matter. Not only was this sector ideologically sensitive, but it operated in the context of a planned economy with its numerous state organs, controls, and detailed regulations. As has been seen in Chapter 5, the private sector was not confronted by a unified state, but rather by a number of state organs at various levels with different functions and interests. The assumption that the Bloc parties were nothing but an extended arm of the Communist state would not have any clear implications as to their actual role for the private sector. It leaves open important questions. For example, did these parties help resolve some of the conflicts between central policy and local implementation?

There is a second reason why the role of the Bloc parties for GDR private-sector policy bears some closer examination. Even if their autonomy and scope for action were strictly limited, it is important to investigate how they used what little autonomy they had for representing the concerns and interests of private entrepreneurs. Since their *raison d'etre* required that they attempt to attract new members from the strata in which they were allowed to recruit, they had to offer some concrete benefits to those willing to join. Similarly, from the SED's point of view, in order to fulfil their transmission function successfully, the Bloc parties had to be granted a minimum of independence if they were to enjoy any credibility among private entrepreneurs.

Indeed, a closer examination of the role of the Bloc parties for the private sector reveals a considerably more complex and differentiated picture than the dependent status of these Bloc parties would seem to suggest. The Bloc parties in the GDR fulfilled a whole range of important functions for the private sector, from contributing to its ideological acceptability to assisting in solving day-to-day administrative problems. While their room for maneuvre was strictly limited, the Bloc parties did see themselves as representatives of special groups in society whose interests they sought to advance. The argument that the various forms of *economic* integration and subordination of the private sector ran counter to the interests of private entrepreneurs, which was discussed and qualified in the previous chapter, also has a parallel with respect to the private sector's *political* integration. The corresponding argument would thus stress the negative aspects of private owners' political integration and incorporation through the Bloc parties: the Bloc parties were relatively powerless, and in light of the role they had played, for example, in the nationalization of private firms as recently as 1972, it is difficult to see how they might be conceived as genuine representatives of the interests of the private sector.

This argument, however, underestimates the political importance of the Bloc parties. Their importance for the private sector did not derive from their relative autonomy as political parties, or from their determined defense of the special interests of private entrepreneurs. Even the official theoretical-ideological conception of their role in the political system of the GDR leaves little doubt of their subordinate position. Their importance might be gauged in a different way. First, the Bloc parties should be considered as the organizational form of the alliance policy, a policy which defined private entrepreneurs as political partners under socialism. The survival of this "socialist corporatism" was, as I have argued, largely a result of *unintended* consequences and developments. That is, it is conceivable that in spite of the existence of an alliance policy and the allied parties, the private sector might have been eliminated earlier in the history of the GDR. After all, the specific content of the alliance policy was authoritatively defined by the SED and not negotiated with the Bloc parties.

In fact, however, the ideological (alliance policy) and organizational (Bloc parties) shell had remained intact. This leads to the second consideration. While the Bloc parties could be, and were, used to implement a restrictive private-sector policy in the early 1970s, they were also included in the implementation of a positive private-sector policy. In other words, while it is correct to say that the role, significance, and potential of the Bloc parties with respect to the private sector always depended on the basic policy adopted by the SED, it follows that this role would be all the more significant and constructive, the more the SED sought to promote those sectors of society for which the Bloc parties were politically responsible. The potential inherent in the ideological tradition and in the "organizational shell"—and thus the importance of institutional continuity—was most forcefully demonstrated in the fall of 1989 when the Bloc parties immediately seized the new opportunities created by the SED's rapid political decline. They immediately set new priorities for the private sector, and within only a few weeks after the fall of the Honecker regime ensured that new measures were adopted. One of the former Bloc parties, namely the CDU, has emerged as the strongest party in the GDR's first free elections. These developments will be further explored in Chapter 8.

The Official Role of the Bloc Parties:
Principles and Institutions

An analysis of the role played by the Bloc parties for the political integration of the private sector must begin with a brief summary of their official status in theory and ideology; and their formal organs and functions, as well as their membership, structure, and participation in state and government. This will provide a basis for the discussion of the actual role of the Bloc parties in the next section.

In the SED's official ideology, including the theory of the state, there was a continuity in the conception of the Bloc parties since their *Gleichschaltung* in the early 1950s when they had been made close and subordinate allies of the Communist party. This reflected the accepted view of the leading role of the working class, and the associate role of other classes and strata, in the construction and development of socialism. What had changed over time was the relative importance the SED had in fact granted the political work of these allied parties. Private-sector policy since 1976 was one of the reasons why the weight of the Bloc parties had been continually growing after many years of decline and very marginal political existence.

Official state theory and ideology explicitly rejected pluralist conceptions of politics as being based on the false assumption of a basic equality of interests.[6] The primacy of the Communist party over both state and all societal organizations was formulated in the recently published work *The State in the Political System of the GDR* in the following way:

> [T]he collective interest of the working class as articulated by its Party is at the same time the fundamental interest of all labouring classes and strata, it constitutes the standard and guideline for the formation of political will . . . for determining the basic direction of societal development. [. . .] The analysis and the decisions of the Party which are based on it always come about by utilizing the state, through the incorporation of the state organs. The results of their work, in addition to the positions, analyses, and views of other politically organized forces, the allied parties, and the mass organizations, form an important basis for the decisions of the Party.[7]

Clearly, the definition of the interests of private entrepreneurs was exclusively the prerogative of the SED. The role of the Bloc parties, like that of other organizations, was of a consultative nature. They assisted in the formulation of basic development goals and strategies by submitting proposals. Thus, when the Bloc parties portrayed themselves as interest representatives for the private sector, it was generally understood that they could only represent those interests that had been—implicitly or explicitly—recognized by the SED as legitimate interests of private entrepreneurs under socialism.

With the new private-sector policy of 1976 having just been launched four years after the last extensive nationalization drive, there was still widespread and understandable confusion and uncertainty in the surviving private sector concerning its future. The Bloc parties' main task was to clarify among its members and other private entrepreneurs that the SED had decided on a continued and constructive cooperation with the remaining private firms. The NDPD daily, *National-Demokrat,* for example, published a letter from a private retailer who inquired whether the new private-sector policy could be reconciled with the fact that "we are creating the fundamental preconditions for the gradual transition to communism". The response by the editors illustrates both the political-ideological function of the Bloc parties, and the major points of the alliance policy towards private entrepreneurs after 1976. It started out with a general theoretical statement:

> This question clearly has to be answered in the affirmative. The fundamental preconditions . . . emerge only through the full development and utilization of all advantages and driving forces of developed socialist society. [. . .] Among the most important driving forces of our socialist society is the alliance . . . with [among others] members of the private and cooperative sectors. As working people they are natural alliance partners of the working class.

At a more concrete level, and probably also more reassuring for private entrepreneurs, it continued:

[T]he [SED's general] policy . . . aimed at the further improvement of the material and intellectual-cultural living conditions of the working population does not exclude the participation of the artisans, but rather includes it . . . precisely because the work of the private and cooperative sectors stands in a direct relationship with the improvement in the living conditions of all working people.

After stressing the opportunity for, and importance of, democratic participation in politics by members of the private economy, not least through membership in the NDPD, the editors concluded:

All this happens with the aid of socialist state power on the basis of the undivided rule of socialist relations of production. They do not exclude the promotion of the work of artisans and the self-employed and the personal development of the members of this social group. Rather, and by contrast, they form its societal foundation.[8]

The official history and ideology of alliance policy from the perspective of the Honecker regime was published by the Academy of Social Sciences at the SED Central Committee.[9] It justified the continued existence of and cooperation with the allied parties in the following terms:

Based on consciously-continued traditions and the realization that other labouring classes and strata will for a long time stand with the working class, the SED drew the conclusion for the formation of the developed socialist society to come out fully in favour of long-term cooperation with the allied parties. The regular comradely discussions of the General Secretary of the Central Committee of the SED with the Chairmen of the allied parties signify the higher stage of this political cooperation and the open consultation on all important problems of domestic and foreign policy. In the same way, there are trustful discussions between the leading functionaries of the SED and the allied parties in all districts and counties of the GDR.[10]

While in the official perspective comradely relations up to the highest level between the SED and the allied parties were stressed, the concrete contributions of the Bloc parties and their actual influence on policymaking received scant attention. The past achievements of alliance policy with respect to the private sector were described almost exclusively as successes of the SED. The only mention of the work of the Bloc parties since 1972 are brief references to "numerous personal conversations" and "central level consultations," as well as a Bloc party-initiated discussion on the "professional honour of the artisan". Whether the Bloc parties played an active role in the policy process is not made clear. The authors merely speak of the Bloc parties' "active contribution in working out resolutions and measures of the SED and the government concerning the comprehensive development and promotion of private entrepreneurs through numerous studies and proposals."[11] It is an indication of the greater importance the SED attached to the Bloc parties in the 1980s that their achievements and political significance and contributions have recently found more explicit and frequent recognition.[12]

Representatives of the Bloc parties held a small number of government positions at the rank of deputy minister (a total of 8), and the office of the Vice President of the GDR National Assembly (*Volkskammer*) was occupied by long-time CDU Chairman Gerald Götting. Bloc party representatives were chairing 6 out of a total of 15 Assembly Committees (*Volkskammerausschüsse*), none of which however dealt with areas directly related to private-sector policy. Moreover, Bloc party deputies had seats in all of the GDR's popular assemblies. In the National Assembly, for example, each of the four Bloc parties had 52 seats, together accounting for over 40 percent of all seats.

The Bloc parties' shares were determined behind closed doors in the SED-dominated Democratic Bloc of Parties and Mass Organizations, a function fulfilled for local assemblies by the corresponding lower-level committees of the Democratic Bloc. The Bloc parties' share of seats was not affected by "election results." Similarly, government policy was not affected by the number of Bloc party officeholders or representatives, for they could not pursue their own policies and were subject to orders and guidelines from the SED.[13] The large representation of the Bloc parties in the GDR's National Assembly was therefore not an indication of their political influence, but rather an expression of the insignificance of the popular assembly. However, the lower the level of the popular assembly, and the more local and de-politicized the issues, the greater was the independence and influence of Bloc party deputies.[14] The SED's formal "power sharing" was apparently necessary so that the Party could invest its alliance policy with a modicum of credibility and reassure the Bloc parties that they were needed.[15] With some exceptions that will be discussed below, this formal participation of the Bloc parties in East German government had practically no bearing on private-sector policy-making.

Another formal institutional channel for the Bloc parties' participation in GDR politics was the National Front (NF). The NF was an "umbrella organization," or a form of national association of all parties and important organizations in the GDR. There was no individual membership. The NF had a large number of committees of various types in towns, cities, counties, districts, and at the national level in which some 400,000 citizens were said to be participating on a voluntary basis, 90,000 of whom were members of one of the Bloc parties. At the NF's National Council, as well as in district and county committees, there were special "working groups"

Table 7.1 Bloc Party Members in State and Government

	CDU	LDPD	NDPD
Elected representatives, candidates, citizens appointed to commissions of popular assemblies	22,686	12,919	10,407
Members of the State Council, the Council of Ministers, district and county councils, mayors, municipal councillors	3,615	2,262	2,132
Members of the National Front and members of commissions, secretariats and working groups	44,362	35,743	27,578

Source: Weichelt, *Der Staat im politischen System der DDR*, pp. 304-305.

for the private sector. Their main task was to activate the private sector politically so as to achieve higher economic performance. Those individuals who did not belong to one of the Bloc parties were particular targets. The "working groups" collaborated closely with state organs and the Chambers. The Bloc parties also used the NF "working groups" to recruit new members from the ranks of the self-employed. In 1985, the "working groups" for the private sector had 8,073 members.[16]

The quantitative extent of the Bloc parties' formal participation in the political system in 1984/85 is represented in Table 7.1. Table 7.2 shows the development of Bloc party membership from 1945 to 1987. The two "classic" Bloc parties, CDU and LDPD,[17] reached their highest levels in 1948, sharply declined in the 1950s, and only slightly recovered between 1961 and 1965. Positive membership trends in all three Bloc parties representing private entrepreneurs can be observed again only after 1975, when the SED was well on its way towards its new private-sector policy. The very significant membership growth in the decade from 1977 to 1987—in the case of the LDPD as much as 38.7 percent—is shown in Table 7.3.

Due to the lack of additional published membership statistics on the Bloc parties, it is not possible to draw any firm conclusions as to how

Table 7.2 Bloc Party Membership, 1945-1987

	CDU	LDPD	NDPD
1945	68,000	88,000	--
1946	207,000	180,000	--
1948	211,000	198,000	10,000
1950	180,000	199,000	100,000
1953	145,000	125,000	233,000
1954	136,000	100,000	172,000
1955	105,000	100,000	120,000
1961	70,000	67,000	100,000
1966	90,000	80,000	110,000
1975	100,000	70,000	80,000
1977	115,000	75,000	85,000
1982	125,000	82,000	91,000
1985	131,000	92,000	98,000
1986	135,000	100,000	103,000
1987	140,000	104,000	110,000

Source: Lapp, *Die 'befreundeten Parteien' der SED*, p. 146.

much of this membership growth is accounted for by members of the private sector.[18] The available statistics, as represented in Table 7.4, can serve at least as a rough indication of the relative share of members of the private and cooperative sectors in these parties. The private and cooperative artisanal sectors and the private business sectors accounted for 12

Table 7.3 Bloc Party Membership Growth, 1977-1987

	CDU	LDPD	NDPD
1977	115,000	75,000	85,000
1987	140,000	104,000	110,000
increase in percent	21.7	38.7	29.4

Source: Lapp, *Die 'befreundeten Parteien' der SED*, p. 143.

Table 7.4 Social Composition of Bloc Party Membership (%)

CDU			
Artisanal/Business	12	Workers	10
Cooperative Farmers	17	Clerical Employees	39
Intellectuals	13	Housewives	9

LDPD			
Artisanal/Business	24	Clerical Employees	33
Cooperative Farmers	5	Retired Persons	16
Intellectuals	18	Others	4

NDPD			
Artisanal/Business	23	Workers	4
Cooperative Farmers	2	Clerical Employees	32
Intellectuals	17	Others	22

Source: Based on Weichelt, *Der Staat im politischen System
der DDR*, pp. 301-303.

Note: Data are based on statistics compiled by individual
Bloc parties which were published in 1984. They employ
different classification schemes and are therefore not
strictly comparable.

percent of CDU membership, 23 percent of NDPD membership, and 24
percent of the LDPD membership. It has been suggested that the share of
these sectors had grown disproportionately in the LDPD.[19] In a party
document published in 1987, the LDPD reported that since 1982 about
2,500 members of handicraft cooperatives and more than 4,400 private
artisans had joined the party.[20] The LDPD further reported that from the
private and cooperative artisans who were LDPD members, more than
2,000 served as deputies (constituting 20 percent of all LDPD deputies),
1,300 participated in the private sector "working groups" of the National
Front at district, county, and municipal levels, more than 500 were on the
executive boards of the Chambers of Handicraft and the credit unions for
the private and cooperative sector, and more than 200 purchase and
delivery cooperatives (ELG) were headed by LDPD members.[21]

The Bloc parties had a full-time staff of about 2,000 each. Between 150
to 200 employees worked at the respective party headquarters in East
Berlin, with special secretaries and departments responsible for the private
sector. The CDU, for example, had permanent working groups for handicraft and trade.[22] As already mentioned, the Bloc parties were not permitted to formulate their own party programmes, but, like other mass
organizations in the GDR, were called upon to discuss and make sugges-

tions for the SED party programme. The congresses of the Bloc parties were usually held one year after a SED Party Congress and were generally uneventful, repeating and at best detailing the major resolutions and decisions of the preceding SED Party Congresses and programmes. The major speeches were tedious and sometimes appeared to outpace the orthodoxy of the Communists. Thus, Gerald Götting, Chairman of the CDU, noted at his party's 16th Congress in 1987 that "private retailers, restaurant owners and business people . . . demonstrate with their selection of goods, their industriousness and friendliness *socialist trade culture*."[23] In one sense, private entrepreneurs should have been offended by this statement. In many cases, they could take pride in exceeding the standards of comparable state shops in all three respects. On the other hand, it is quite clear that the purpose of this statement was to demonstrate the ideological, political, and professional integration of the private sector into the socialist economy and society. While according to some reports the last Bloc party Congresses in 1986 were somewhat more lively and critical than previous meetings,[24] they had, like most of the formal institutional roles of the Bloc parties discussed so far, a predominantly symbolic function. It would be mistaken, however, to dismiss this function of the Bloc parties as irrelevant for the private sector. They did contribute in this way to the general acceptability of private firms in the GDR—an important precondition for a functioning legal private sector under socialism.

The Actual Role and Influence of the Bloc Parties in Private-Sector Policy

In his address to a meeting between the Secretariat of the CDU Central Executive and party members from the private sector, published in the CDU party organ *Neue Zeit,* party Chairman Gerald Götting explained why private entrepreneurs had good political allies in the Bloc parties. Members of the Bloc parties occupied posts in the network of institutions of importance to the private sector—deputies and state functionaries, particularly those in the Standing Commissions on the local service economy in the *Volkskammer*; activists in the National Front and its working groups, particularly in the "working group" on handicraft and trade, and Bloc party members who had a position in the Chambers, the product and supply group councils, or the purchase and delivery cooperatives (ELG). He suggested that they had a significant influence at all levels on the implementation of the policy of promoting the private sector, as well as more specifically on the issuing of licenses. Further assistance, according to Götting, came from the special working groups for the private sector which each Bloc party maintained at its national headquarters.[25]

What exactly was it that these various political actors who were Bloc party members did that made them good political allies for a private entrepreneur?

The actual role and significance of the Bloc parties for the private sector in the GDR was related to three areas. (1) They played an important though somewhat unofficial and largely unrecognized role in the policy-making process. (2) In various formal and informal ways they assisted in policy implementation at local levels. (3) They fulfilled information and social functions for private entrepreneurs not unlike professional associations. After discussing these three areas, the question of special benefits that motivated private entrepreneurs to join a Bloc party will be considered (4). The formal-symbolic integration and the functional integration of the private sector into the political system are represented in Figure 7.1.

(1) Bloc parties played a significant, though officially downplayed or even unrecognized, role in the *formulation of specific policies and regulations* for the private sector. It appears that the SED had been unwilling to acknowledge in its mass publications in anything but extremely general and vague terms the large number of proposals submitted by the Bloc parties. The reason, one may surmise, is that the SED wanted to claim the positive initiatives in this area for itself. Perhaps the leading Party also did not want to give the impression that "special interests" outside the working class were effectively represented by "special interest groups." In their internal publications and meetings with private entrepreneurs, on the other hand, the Bloc parties were free to advertise their contributions in this area.[26] For example, the 1988 decree whose objective was the stimulation of the private retail and restaurant sector through, among other things, higher wages for employees and the reprivatization of state retail outlets,[27] came about on the initiative of the Bloc parties.[28]

For the 1990–1995 plan period, the Bloc parties were working out new proposals for the private and cooperative sector. In the case of the CDU, for example, they included:

- extension of the 10-employee limit for private firms
- greater activity of the county branches of the Chambers of Handicraft in order to strengthen their work for, and representation of, handicraft interests
- improving wage structures and incomes as well as more favourable tax rates, in order to stimulate higher performance
- equal wages for employees in the private sector
- greater independence for handicraft cooperatives in their disposition of funds in order to stimulate more investment.[29]

Figure 7.1 Political Integration of the GDR Private Sector

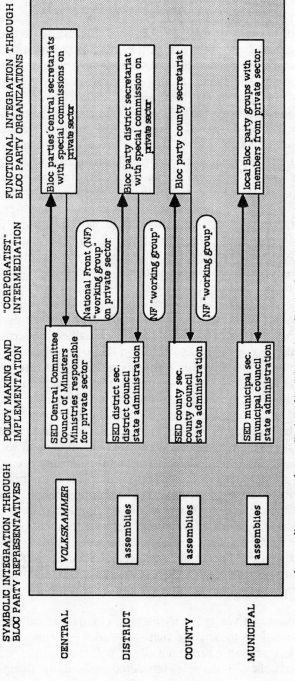

= policy proposals, monitoring of/assistance in policy implementation, interest representation

= control of Bloc parties through SED Secretariats

The main forums where these proposals were worked out and debated were the respective party headquarters in Berlin, in particular the special private-sector working groups. At this level, discussions could be frank and controversial. A proposal that in the fall of 1988 was still at the stage of preliminary debate within the CDU, for example, was the establishment of a Chamber of Handicraft at the central level as a "corporatist" or occupational organization for the private handicraft sector.[30] As a top level LDPD representative maintained, while a much more generous and far-reaching promotion of private firms in the existing branches of the economy was discussed within the party, the reprivatization of other sectors of the economy, e.g., certain manufacturing industries nationalized in 1972, was not an issue.[31] This illustrates the freedom, as well as the limitations, of policy debate within the Bloc parties. Within the general confines of the policy of promoting the private sector, they were free (and probably expected) to debate and propose new measures. Bloc party debates on fundamental policy direction, on the other hand, would not have been tolerated by the SED. Privately, Bloc party members and functionaries did discuss more fundamental questions of economic reform. As "the barrel is stretching" (as a CDU functionary put it in November 1988, describing the gradually increasing room for maneuver of his party), these discussions were expected increasingly to shift from the private to the semi-public (internal Bloc party) and eventually public realm.[32]

(2) The Bloc parties were also active in the *implementation of private-sector policy* and the economic administration of private firms. They functioned as networks of party members who held administrative positions in local state organs and governments, or who served in Chambers, product and supply group councils, and the private-sector "working groups" of the National Front. Local Bloc party executives could activate these networks to launch special territorial initiatives or to solve specific problems. Initiatives were directed at local state organs in order to incorporate private firms in the development of the state trade networks, to reopen vacant shops and restaurants, to improve cooperation between private retail trade and state wholesale and industrial enterprises,[33] to establish clearer contractual relations between purchase and delivery cooperatives (ELG) and the capital goods distributors, and to create direct relations between ELG and state producers.[34] Specific problems included soliciting commitments from private restaurants in the territory to extend their business hours and monitoring the fulfillment of such commitments.[35]

Bloc party executives at the national level regularly called upon their local representatives to activate these networks by bringing together all party members who were professionally or politically active in the area of private-sector policy.[36] This was considered particularly urgent in light of the "political narrowmindedness" and "bureaucratic attitudes" on the part of certain local councils and economic functionaries.[37] According to an analysis conducted by the CDU, many local councils were either ignoring the 1988 decree on the private sector,[38] or even boycotting it.[39] Identifying similar problems of local implementation, the Deputy Minister for District Directed Industry and the Food Industry, K. Lohsse (SED), appealed to the LDPD to support the central government in clearing away such local obstacles.[40] To what extent local Bloc party networks did in fact work together and successfully deal with these tasks is another question. As may be expected, there were significant local differences. The model local executive was to cooperate systematically with the local SED executive, the state organs, the Chambers, and the National Front on territorial tasks. Its Secretariat should produce regular and systematic analyses of private-sector problems in cooperation with its special commissions. Special party meetings with private entrepreneurs were to be held with the aim of soliciting concrete commitments to increase their output, which could then be publicized to boost the Bloc party's image.[41]

(3) In the absence of occupational or professional associations, the Bloc parties fulfilled a number of *information and social functions* for private entrepreneurs. For instance, they organized numerous meetings and conferences dealing with the concerns of specific strata or occupational groups (e.g., handicraft trades).[42] Like the SED, they organized party seminars (*Parteilehrjahre*) for their members on an annual basis. These consisted of monthly meetings and were, at least formally, designed as political instruction and propaganda courses. In some cases, these seminars were a forum for open political debate among party members, and thus represented an opportunity for politically-interested private entrepreneurs to exchange views with other party members.[43] At any rate, it was an opportunity to establish contacts. Some of the Bloc party publications, in particular their daily newspapers, addressed themselves in part to the concerns of the private sector. The LDPD daily *Der Morgen* in particular was devoted to problems of the private sector. Pages 3 to 6 regularly dealt with private-sector issues. For example, SED and LDPD functionaries wrote on special problems of the private sector, or individual LDPD party members and their businesses were introduced. Only the NDPD's daily *National-Zeitung* gave similar priority to the private sector.[44] Bloc party dailies were of course available to non-members as well.

(4) This raises the more general question of the "free-rider" problem, i.e., what *specific benefits supplied by the Bloc parties* for the private sector could only be obtained by party members? Individuals in the process of applying for a license felt most vulnerable and were therefore more likely to join a Bloc party than a private entrepreneur who was already estab-

lished. This was a time when insecurity was greatest, and when the Bloc parties were able to argue most convincingly that their support might be crucial. Under the favourable conditions of the 1980s, however, it was unlikely that an otherwise qualified applicant would need the support of a Bloc party, for the state was very much interested in removing political barriers to new licensing. Nevertheless, there were other barriers for a new entrepreneur; for example, if the applicant could not take over an existing business with an established infrastructure. In such cases, the Bloc parties' influence and connections at various local government levels could be useful for a new entrepreneur to locate and be allocated business premises and equipment. Some simply may have felt more secure politically through their membership, and considered it as a kind of insurance against arbitrary treatment by local authorities. All private entrepreneurs who did join a Bloc party expected to receive effective support in solving their problems and in dealing with state organs. Yet, as LDPD Deputy Chairman Raspe warned his local executives, "we should not give the impression that we can if necessary assist our members like a state organ responsible for the economy or that we are in a position or willing to ignore realities."[45]

Another more diffuse benefit that may have been a motivation for Bloc party membership was that many private entrepreneurs in the 1980s saw the Bloc parties as guarantors for the preservation of the positive attitude of the SED towards the private sector. The Bloc parties sought to reinforce this view when they declared that they were working for the interests of their self-employed members.[46] That private entrepreneurs, at any rate, were not lining up at the doors of the Bloc parties is evident from the months or even years of intense efforts on the part of Bloc party functionaries that frequently preceded an individual's final decision to join.[47] LDPD deputy Chairman Raspe asked his local party executives why some county organizations had managed to increase their membership from the private sector while numbers in others were stagnating. Obviously, as he stated in response to his own question, the reason was that many county executives were not closely cooperating with the executives of the Chambers and the occupational groups,[48] and they were not quick enough in approaching newly-established entrepreneurs.[49] The strongest competition for the private sector existed between the LDPD and NDPD. The Liberal Democrats and the National Democrats, in particular, made every effort to recruit members from the private sector. As West German analyst P.J. Lapp, author of a recent monograph on the Bloc parties, has noted, the LDPD had been the most successful of the three. "Today, much to the chagrin of NDPD and CDU, this party is considered *the* party of the old and young self-employed in the GDR."[50]

Finally, a special incentive for a private entrepreneur to join a Bloc party was the expansion of his or her network of informal relations. It was customary that party members at the local level helped each other by exchanging goods or services which were difficult to obtain through official channels. For instance, the private plumber in Greifswald received his supply of game from the private butcher and in return installed a bathroom heater which was difficult to get. Both were members of the NDPD and had initiated this exchange during a monthly membership meeting. Or a private cabinetmaker built a wall panel with imported wood for a party colleague who operated a private restaurant in a neighboring town. The restaurant owner returned the favour by giving him the address of a party colleague in another part of the country who had foreign polishing equipment for sale at a low price.[51]

In addition to such practical benefits of Bloc party membership for private entrepreneurs, and the largely symbolic significance of the Bloc parties' representation in more or less powerless formal political institutions, three areas of Bloc party activity with particular functional importance for the private sector have been identified. These were their role in the formulation of specific policies and measures, their involvement in policy implementation, and their information and social functions. The SED's positive private-sector policy since 1976 significantly reduced the tension between the Bloc parties' "transmission function" and their "interest representation function", for initiatives on behalf of private entrepreneurs could be justified as the faithful transmission of the SED's own goals. Nor was this contrary to the interests of the SED leadership, for the crucial obstacles to successful implementation of its private-sector policy were of a systemic and bureaucratic nature. Because the political networks of the Bloc parties spanned from central to local levels, and had a degree of independence from the local SED apparatus and the state administration, they could play an effective role in assisting in policy implementation, in monitoring local officials, and in representing the interests of private entrepreneurs.

It should be emphasized that the political integration of the private sector through the Bloc parties was a legacy from the past rather than a result of clever institutional engineering on the part of the SED. The political integration at a symbolic-ideological level gave the SED the opportunity to portray its private-sector policy as a long-standing tradition and an integral element of its general socio-economic strategy (alliance policy). The political integration of the private sector at an institutional-organizational level offered a network of experienced auxiliary agencies for policy implementation and limited interest representation. Somewhat ironically, though very much in keeping with the logic of institutional continuity stressed throughout the present study, the Bloc parties have played a leading role in shaping East Germany's new private-sector policy since the downfall of the SED regime in late 1989. Before examining this—once again unintended—consequence of past policies in the following chapter, a further aspect of the private sector's integration into socialist society will be addressed.

The Social Integration of the Private Sector

What was the social status of private entrepreneurs in GDR society, how were they perceived by their fellow citizens, how did they see themselves? Private entrepreneurs in a socialist society were potentially threatened in their existence in a number of ways. *First,* for ideological reasons, they could always expect to be subjected to restrictive policies, ranging from prohibitive tax rates all the way to full-scale expropriation. As a distinct social stratum or class, they were, after all, assumed to be ultimately obsolete. The SED alliance policy provided a kind of protection from the ideological dynamic which made private entrepreneurs almost automatically into convenient political scapegoats for Party functionaries intent on demonstrating their political resolve and ideological zeal in creating the new society. To be sure, the alliance policy had never become anything approaching a guarantee for the private sector's survival. Just like the Bloc parties, the private economy had been instrumentalized by the SED rather than having been granted some independent right to exist. After four decades of alliance policy, this instrumentalization had become a tradition and had become firmly institutionalized. At the level of politics and ideology, the alliance policy—and the social groups and political and economic organizations whose continued existence it justified—had reduced the costs for the SED of tolerating actors and institutions that were in priniciple foreign to socialist societies of the Marxist-Leninist type. Ideologically and politically, in other words, private entrepreneurs had been sufficiently integrated into socialist society so as not to trigger the ideological dynamic described above. I consider this the social integration of the private sector at a general—ideological and theoretical—level, and I will begin this section with a brief survey of recent East German sociological perspectives concerning the social status and integration of the private sector.

A *second* potential threat for private entrepreneurs under socialism derives from their objective social status (i.e., mainly their relative income), from how they are popularly perceived (e.g., as parasites or exploiters vs. fellow citizens), and from their self-image and corresponding behaviour (e.g., honorable, responsible and modest vs. marginal, irresponsible and flaunting). Later in this section I will explore these three dimensions of the GDR private entrepreneur's social status and how they interrelate. Problems of social status are very important for the success of a policy of promoting the private sector because ideological and political threats to a private economy do not necessarily originate with the communist party, but may have their source in widespread negative sentiments, such as envy of the independence and wealth of private entrepreneurs, on the part of local government officials and among the general population. In fact, an enlightened or liberal policy may evoke strong resistance within the population if, for whatever reasons, it is felt to be unfair. Furthermore, such a policy may be difficult to sustain when it antagonizes and alienates precisely those strata whose allegiance to the regime was to be strengthened through the expected positive economic results of a more liberal approach to the private economy. Nevertheless, the SED private-sector policy since 1976, as we will see, also found relatively favourable preconditions in the form of a socially-integrated stratum of private entrepreneurs in GDR society.

We begin a brief survey of the East German social-scientific perspective on the private sector with a rather conservative formulation of the state of, and prospects for, social integration of private entrepreneurs into GDR society. It is taken from the already cited *Bündnispolitik* (1981), the official statement of alliance policy in the Honecker era. It is also of interest because it refers to the role of the Bloc parties in the social integration of the private sector.

> The work of the allied parties is of great significance for another reason. Certain traditional modes of thinking, life styles and behaviors originating in the capitalist social order continue to have an effect among the allies [of the working class, i.e., members of the private sector] even under socialism. They are not eradicated once the economic transition to socialist positions is made. The aim of the ideological work of all political parties in the GDR is to exploit for socialism whatever is positive in these traditions and to enrich it. But it also means coping with the difficult task of overcoming attributes of the earlier ways of working and living that are irreconcilable with socialism, and to do so with a correct understanding of the longer periods of time required for this.[52]

Social integration through a gradual assimilation of private entrepreneurs into the working class, even with the important proviso that "a correct understanding" of the time this will require is necessary, is an outdated view according to the GDR's sociological literature of the 1980s. Leading sociologist Rudi Weidig of the Academy for Social Sciences at the Central Committee of the SED (the Party's "think tank") has summarized the new perspective and insights generated by recent sociological research. He writes that with the transition from extensive to intensive economic growth, certain socio-structural trends no longer continue. There is no longer a growth in the numerical strength of the working class. As well, the numerical decline of private entrepreneurs has stopped. The traditional view of a drawing closer of different classes and strata, based on abstract and unhistorical criteria, is no longer tenable. What is important are the social potentialities of different social strata for the development of modern productive forces.[53]

The significance of the distinction between relations of production and forces of production and their relationship in the contemporary Marxist-Leninist debate may be roughly summmarized in the following terms. The orthodox view prevalent until the 1970s was that as productive forces (the technological and economic infrastructure) developed further, differences in the living conditions of different classes and strata (workers, farmers, white-collar employees, the intelligentsia, the self-employed) in socialist society tend to be significantly reduced. This would thus constitute a step towards communism.[54] The implicit equation between economic progress and greater social equality, however, had been increasingly rejected since the late 1970s. Relations of production (e.g., economic inequality within and between social strata), as Weidig suggests, should also be judged in terms of their functionality for economic growth. This represents a rejection of the dogma of increasing equality under socialism and an attack on one the most fundamental premises of Marxist-Leninist theory, according to which the relations of production are determined by the forces of production. It is in this context that another participant in the debate, M. Brie, suggested that as a result of the heterogeneous character of the forces of production in the scientific-technical revolution, the relations of production have to be developed in a complex and differentiated fashion. An example of this, he argued, is the promotion of cooperative and private handicraft.[55]

A more far-reaching critique and reconceptualization was published by another member of the SED's "think tank" in 1988. A. Kosing, recognizing the fundamental challenges and problems confronting socialist societies today, called for a much clearer separation between the two phases of Communism, implying that the present, lower form, the socialist formation of society, must be understood on its own terms, by analyzing its real processes and conditions. He suggested that it is necessary to stop treating socialist relations of production solely in terms of ownership. Moreover, socialist society's inherent contradictions, namely, those between plan and market, had to be recognized much more clearly. Central planning, he argued, is necessary, but cannot succeed without using market mechanisms. Problems in the consumer goods sector indicate that the "objective economic mechanisms" of the market are underestimated. Social equality under socialism necessarily had to give rise to social inequality because of the principle of rewarding each individual according to his or her work performance. The problem of equality could not be solved through forcibly imposing social homogeneity or a schematic levelling, through legal changes in ownership conditions, or through fictitious definitions.[56]

The implications of the discussions and arguments advanced in the more recent sociological literature in the GDR leave little doubt that the two traditionally most sensitive issues for the existence and survival of the private sector—ownership and social inequality—had lost much of their theoretical and ideological import. The implications of this reorientation in sociological thinking for private entrepreneurs, however, have not been systematically explored. Irene Falconere, from the Institute of Sociology at the GDR Academy of Sciences, published in 1982 the last systematic attempt at reconceptualizing the role and status of the GDR's private entrepreneurs. She identified a number of fundamental theoretical problems that still awaited their solution: the prospects for small private firms, their optimal size, their ownership forms, and the question of whether or not the continued existence of the private sector was a result of the differentiated and still underdeveloped level of development of the productive forces.[57] Falconere herself proposed a solution to the ideologically-problematic question of private ownership with the following ingenuous argument. "Based on the new role in principle and the functions of this form of ownership in the economic process of reproduction, the characterization of such property as a socialist form of ownership is quite conceivable."[58] Perhaps because a further exploration of this issue was considered ideologically undesirable, Falconere's was the last contribution in the East German social-scientific literature applying the general insights of recent sociological research to the private sector.[59] We can conclude that the social integration of private entrepreneurs in the GDR was, from the perspective of East German social science in the 1980s, not an issue. Was the same true for their social integration in everyday life?

Beginning with a brief characterization of the social status of private entrepreneurs in the GDR, we can note that they were distinguished from the mass of the population by their often considerably higher income, their relative independence, and their privileged access to special exchange networks. The average net income of an East German entrepreneur in the 1980s was estimated to be about 2–2.5 times that of the average wage in the GDR. The low end of the income scale in the private sector was equal to the average wage, and maximum incomes were around twenty times the average wage.[60] While entrepreneurs on the whole did not engage in conspicuous consumption, this is not to say that their wealth was not visible. Many owned modern homes, weekend or summer cottages, new or imported cars, and some even had their own yachts.[61] Next to top-level state and Party functionaries, they represented the wealthiest stratum in the GDR. Just as important for their material well-being as their direct income was their privileged access to informal sources of goods and services. Their own line of business usually offered valuable "currency," to be exchanged for the equally valuable and scarce goods and services of fellow private artisans and shopkeepers.[62]

In spite of the numerous restrictive regulations and the ubiquitous shortages of material and equipment, the GDR private entrepreneur enjoyed a degree of independence that further added to his or her social status. It was a privileged position also in a non-material sense. Unlike most East Germans, who had resigned themselves to investing their energies in their private lives after work, they were able to apply private initiative and talents to their professional lives. They thus experienced a degree of fulfilment from work that was missed by most who were employed in large state enterprises or bureaucracies. An important contributor to, and even precondition for, enjoying their relative independence as private entrepreneurs under socialism was a positive attitude of the regime towards the private sector. By officially encouraging private economic initiative, a sense of social security and confidence in their own future was created in the private entrepreneurs. Without this, their social status would have been severely diminished.

With an eye on both the sentiments of private artisans and business operators, and the perception of its policy among the general population, the official SED press tried hard to establish the sincerity of the Party's commitment to the private sector. Not only was the private sector officially recognized as "a significant economic factor for the realization of the party's social policy,"[63] it was even held up as a model of work ethic and achievement orientation for socialist society as a whole. Thus, after reporting a net increase of over 100 private firms in the district of Erfurt during the first 7 months of 1988, the SED regional daily stressed in response to a reader inquiry that the country needs both small and large enterprises, and that small enterprises need to be promoted more vigorously. "Healthy competition" can only be good. In fact, the article continues, for some employees in state enterprises it would not hurt to develop more initiative and show more "ownership consciousness" as well. Private entrepreneurs should not be seen as people in the business for a fast buck. Good work performance should be remunerated accordingly, whether in the private or in the state sector. "In this respect the interests of the individual who wants to earn a good income and the interests of society no doubt are compatible."[64] Private entrepreneurs were even awarded high state honours for their contributions to socialism, and Honecker himself paid a symbolic visit to a private butcher shop to underline the party's commitment to its private-sector policy.[65]

While the official East German media in the 1980s bestowed upon private firms extremely favourable public attention, it is difficult to assess whether this was shared more widely in the population.[66] What responses to readers such as the one just mentioned indicate, however, is that there continued to be doubts in the minds of some people about how the promotion of private firms could be reconciled with the official socialist ideology. On the whole, however, private artisans and shopkeepers were perceived as honest and hard-working citizens rather than as profiteers or even exploiters. The elaborate framework of regulation and control already described indeed left little room for charging high prices or getting away with shoddy service or workmanship. Because East German entrepreneurs were rather conservative, fairly law-abiding, and maintained high work standards,[67] they were generally respected and valued by their fellow citizens. There may be some additional reasons why in the GDR they did not attract the kind of negative public sentiment as do private entrepreneurs in other socialist countries.[68] One very simple reason is that despite policy changes, they had always been there and people were therefore simply used to their existence. This is, as it were, the element of continuity at the grassroots level. Another reason is that strong egalitarianism and the general lack of incentive to work hard were a cause of frustration for many East Germans. They tended to respect the initiative and long working hours which most owners of private firms had to invest in order to achieve a higher income. Finally, the strong orientation towards, or even internalization of, materialist values prevalent in the Federal Republic and the much more aggressive entrepreneurialism with which they are identified made the prosperity of the East German private sector by comparison appear insignificant.

Most important for the popular conception of private artisans and shopkeepers, however, was how they appeared in the daily lives of ordinary citizens. It was a simple fact of life that private restaurants, for example, offered better service for the same or only slightly higher prices than state restaurants. The private bakery in the neighborhood with its daily supply of fresh bread, buns, and pastry, or the private butcher shop enhanced the quality of life in a way obvious to any East German. Even more highly respected were many private artisans whose services were not only valued, but also not always readily available. It was important and extremely useful, for example, to be on good terms with the owner of the local private auto repair shop, for he was often able to get that spare part quickly and do the repair job which in a state shop would involve a long waiting period. It almost goes without saying that such respected, needed, and well-paid individuals were often envied by those who found themselves in less fortunate positions.[69] The various aspects of the private entrepreneurs' social integration into GDR society discussed here explain

why any such negative feelings towards the private sector had not translated into a generally unfavourable conception, let alone a groundswell of
popular resentment that could pose a political threat to the SED's private-
sector policy.

Private entrepreneurs in East Germany were generally self-confident
and optimistic about their future. This is not to say that they did not have
many grievances, but these concerned predominantly systemic problems,
particularly the conditions of material and technical supply and the
bureaucratic red tape they were forced to struggle with. It was a sign of
their feeling of security that they talked about these problems openly.[70]
For them, the SED's private-sector policy since 1976 represented a clear
admission from the communists that "they can't do without us," and it is
this consciousness of being needed by those who not too long ago had
considered the private sector rapidly becoming obsolete which provided
a source of both personal satisfaction and confidence about the future.
Those who had not lived through the politically more difficult times, while
sharing this same source of confidence, of course did not derive their
personal satisfaction from their belated triumph over the communists.
They had, in this respect, a more pragmatic attitude. They saw their
private business as an opportunity to live a more independent and
prosperous, albeit often more difficult, life than would have been possible
if they had worked for the state.[71]

Like the economic and political integration of the private sector, the
social integration of private entrepreneurs in East German society was
largely a result of social continuity. That is, both the work ethos of private
entrepreneurs and their traditional perception in the population as respectable citizens were never undermined by the SED regime. Apart from brief
periods when the "class struggle was intensified," they were treated as
allies of the working class. Whether such values and perceptions would
have survived in the absence of effective forms of social and political
integration of the private sector is at least doubtful. Without the adaptation
and integration of an institutional framework for the private sector which
made legal and honest behaviour feasible, and to some extent necessary
and normal, for private entrepreneurs, a new type of entrepreneurial
behaviour oriented towards quick profit-making and with little regard for
high work standards may well have emerged.[72] Conversely, it is doubtful
that the East German population would have preserved favourable attitudes in the absence of corresponding behaviour on the part of private
entrepreneurs. In any event, both aspects of this social tradition should
prove a positive starting point for East Germany's transition to a market
society.

Notes

1. The history and significance of the Democratic Bloc is discussed in greater detail in Chapter 2.

2. On the DBD, see especially B. Wernet-Tietz, *Bauernverband und Bauern-partei in der DDR* (Farmers' Association and Farmers' Party in the GDR) (Cologne: Verlag Wissenschaft und Politik, 1984).

3. H. Zimmermann, "Power Distribution and opportunities for participation: aspects of the socio-political system of the GDR," in: K. von Beyme and H. Zimmermann, eds. *Policymaking in the German Democratic Republic* (Aldershot: Gower, 1984); and H. Zimmermann, "Zum Verständnis des Gegenstandsbereiches, zur Forschungslage und zur weiteren Forschung auf dem Gebiet der Blockparteien" (On the Conception of the Subject Area, on the State and on Further Research in the Area of the Bloc Parties), mimeo. MS (Berlin: Freie Universität, 1977). Prof. Zimmermann from West Berlin's Free University is one of the leading West German authorities on the GDR.

4. The major exception in the GDR, of course, were the churches, especially the Evangelical Church which in the late 1980s played an important opposition role. See, for example, T. Mechtenberg*, "Kirche im Sozialismus. Eine kritische Analyse des Staat-Kirche-Verhältnisses in der DDR" (The Church in Socialism. A Critical Analysis of the Relationship between State and Church in the GDR), *Deutschland-Archiv*, Vol. 21, No. 4 (1988), 380–389 and G. Helwig*, "'Störfälle'. Zum Dialog zwischen Staat und Kirche" ('Emergencies'. On the Dialogue between State and Church), *Deutschland-Archiv*, Vol. 21, No. 4 (1988), 340–344.

5. See Chapters 2 and 3.

6. W. Weichelt et al., *Der Staat im politischen System der DDR* (The State in the GDR's Political System) (East Berlin: Staatsverlag der DDR, 1986), p. 131.

7. *Ibid.,* pp. 158–159.

8. *National Zeitung,* 10 August 1976.

9. *Bündnispolitik im Sozialismus* (Alliance Policy under Socialism) (East Berlin: Dietz Verlag, 1981). Towards the end of the Ulbrich era in 1969, the same institute published *Gemeinsam zum Sozialismus. Zur Geschichte der Bündnispolitik der SED* (Together Towards Socialism. On the History of the SED's Alliance Policy) (East Berlin: Dietz Verlag, 1969), which was still tailored to the much larger private and semi-state sector existing at that time (see Chapter 2 above) and wedded to Ulbricht's notion of a "socialist community of man", which also included private entrepreneurs.

10. *Bündnispolitik,* p. 248.

11. *Ibid.,* pp. 239–240.

12. M. Gerlach, "Bündnispolitik und Parteizusammenarbeit unter der Führung der SED—Fundament unserer Staatsmacht," *Staat und Recht,* Vol.35, 3 (1986), 179–188; J.Herrmann, "Bündnispolitik unserer Partei gestern und heute," *Einheit,* Vol. 43, Nos. 11/12 (1988), 978–984; H. Hümmler, "Zur Bündnispolitik unserer Partei," *Einheit,* 2 (1988), 182–186, W. Kirchhoff, "Im Bündnis mit allen Kräften des Volkes," *Einheit,* Vol. 41, 6 (1986): 531–536. From a Western perspective, see

D. Staritz, "Neue Akzente in der SED-Bündnispolitik," *DDR Report*, No. 2 (1983). This was also stressed to me by a staff member of the CDU central secretariat (Engel, interview). This individual pointed out, however, that the image of the Bloc parties in the population at large would at best gradually change. As a vivid illustration of the results of decades of officially ignoring the Bloc parties, they had not only a credibility problem; in many cases, GDR citizens did not even seem to be aware of their existence.

13. The SED had a special Department "Allied Parties" at the Central Committee Secretariat which monitored the activities and personnel decisions of the Bloc parties. See P.J. Lapp*, *Die "Befreundeten Parteien" der SED. Die DDR-Blockparteien in den achtziger Jahren* (Cologne: Verlag Wissenschaft und Politik, 1988), p. 25.

14. *Ibid.*, pp. 141–143. See also W. Mleczkowski*, "Bewegung im Monolith. Das sozialistische 'Mehrparteiensystem' der DDR," *Aus Politik und Zeitgeschichte*, Vols. 16–17 (21 April 1984), 3–17.

15. This paragraph is largely based on Lapp, *Die "Befreundeten Parteien"*, pp. 78, 80–81.

16. *Ibid.*, pp. 86–88.

17. See also Chapter 2.

18. The only statistics available on the social composition of Bloc party membership are published in Weichelt, *Der Staat im politischen System*.

19. *Ibid.*, p. 302.

20. Sekretariat des Zentralvorstandes der LDPD, ed., *Die Aufgaben der LDPD bei der bedarfsgerechten Entwicklung der Dienst-, Reparatur-und unmittelbaren Versorgungsleistungen* (The Tasks of the LDPD in the Satisfactory Development of Services, Repairs, and Direct Supply) (East Berlin 1987), p. 11.

21. *Ibid.*, pp. 6–7.

22. Lapp, "Die 'Befreundeten Parteien' der SED," pp. 52–57.

23. Emphasis added. "Referat des Vorsitzenden der CDU, Gerald Götting" (Address of the CDU Chairman, Gerald Götting), in *16. Parteitag der CDU*, 14–16 October 1987, Dresden, Sekretariat des Hauptvorstandes der CDU, ed. 1987, p. 35.

24. Engel (interview). See also on the recent Bloc party congresses, P.J. Lapp*, "Blockparteien im Aufwind? Der 14. Parteitag der LDPD; Der XII. Parteitag der DBD" (Bloc Parties Moving Ahead? The 14th Party Congress of the LDPD; the XIIth Party Congress of the DBD), *Deutschland-Archiv*, Vol. 20, 7 (1987), 729–731; H. von Löwis of Menar*, "Der 13. Parteitag der NDPD" (The 13th Party Congress of the NDPD), *Deutschland-Archiv*, Vol. 20, 7 (1987), 731–732. "12. Parteitag der DBD," *Informationen*, ed. Bundesminister für innerdeutsche Beziehungen*, No. 9 (1987), 11–13; "14. Parteitag der LDPD," *Informationen* (ed. Bundesminister für innerdeutsche Beziehungen*), No. 8 (1987), 9–11; "13. Parteitag der NDPD," *Informationen* (ed. Bundesminister für innerdeutsche Beziehungen), No. 10 (1987), 9–10.

25. *Neue Zeit*, 26 November 1988, p. 3.

26. For instance, at a conference with party members from the handicraft sector in April 1987, LDPD Chairman Martin Gerlach listed the following of his party's

proposals that had been adopted by the SED: the new model statute for the purchase and delivery cooperatives (ELG) of the handicraft sector, various price subsidies for selected "problem" trades, and the establishment of a new office for the "local service economy" at the district level, with special financial responsibilities for improving the supply of the handicraft sector. M. Gerlach, "Die Aufgaben der LDPD bei der bedarfsgerechten Entwicklung der Dienst-, Reparatur- und unmittelbaren Versorgungsleistungen," in Sekretariat des Zentralvorstandes der LDPD, ed., *Die Aufgaben der LDPD bei der bedarfsgerechten Entwicklung der Dienst-, Reparatur-und unmittelbaren Versorgungsleistungen* (East Berlin 1987), p. 7. These and other measures for the private sector are further discussed in Chapter 5 above. For the CDU stressing the party's important contribution to numerous decrees for the private sector, see its news bulletin for party members, *Union teilt mit*, No. 11/12, Nov./Dec. 1987, 1–4, 6, 9, 11–13.

27. See, further on this, Chapter 5 above.

28. Engel (interview).

29. *Ibid.*

30. *Ibid.* On this question, see also section on the Chambers in Chapter 6 above.

31. Bogisch (interview). However, this issue was put on the agenda in December 1989. See, further on this, Chapter 8.

32. Engel (interview).

33. Hans-Dieter Raspe, *Ein Jahr nach dem 14. Parteitag der LDPD*, Referat des stellvertretenden Vorsitzenden der LDPD auf der Konferenz des Sekretariats des Zentralvorstandes mit den Kreis-und Stadtbezirkssekretären am 13./14. April 1988 in Weimar (One Year After the 14th Party Congress of the LDPD, Address of the Deputy Chairman of the LDPD at the Conference of the Secretariat of the Central Board with County and City District Secretaries) (East Berlin: Sekretariat des Zentralvorstands der LDPD, 1988), pp. 33–35.

34. M. Gerlach, "Bündnispolitik und Parteizusammenarbeit," p. 10.

35. Raspe, "Ein Jahr nach dem 14," pp. 33–34.

36. *Ibid.* The LDPD central executive, for instance, in a resolution of 10 November 1987 published as an internal party communication for the local party unit executives, gives specific guidelines for how to solve problems of the retail trade (*Information 10/87 für die Vorstände der Grundeinheiten*).

37. Raspe, "Ein Jahr nach dem 14," p. 35.

38. See Chapter 5.

39. Engel (interview).

40. K. Lohsse, "Alle Reserven mobilisieren im Interesse zufriedener Kunden" (Mobilizing all Reserves in the Interest of Satisfied Customers), in *Die Aufgaben der LDPD*, p. 19.

41. This is the job description of the successful local executive as presented by LDPD Deputy Chairman Raspe, "Ein Jahr nach dem 14," pp. 33–35 at a conference of the central executive with county secretaries. Raspe identified a number of local Bloc party executives by name, strongly urging them to fulfil their responsibilities with respect to the private sector more faithfully.

42. Lapp, "Die 'Befreundeten Parteien' der SED," pp. 67–68.

43. Personal information from private entrepreneur. The openness and attractiveness of such meetings varied from one basic organization to the next.

44. Lapp, "Die 'Befreundeten Parteien' der SED," pp. 116–117.

45. Raspe, "Ein Jahr nach dem 14," p. 32.

46. Lapp, "Die 'Befreundeten Parteien' der SED," p. 77.

47. Ibid., pp. 139–140.

48. The occupational groups are local-level groups of artisans with the same trade. See also Chapter 6.

49. Raspe, "Ein Jahr nach dem 14," p. 57.

50. Ibid., p. 37.

51. Examples taken from ibid., p. 140.

52. Bündnispolitik im Sozialismus, p. 248.

53. Rudi Weidig, "Soziologische Forschung in der DDR—eine Bilanz" (Sociological Research in the GDR—a Resume), Deutsche Zeitschrift für Philosophie, Vol. 34, No. 7 (1986), 577–587.

54. See, for example, Kleines politisches Wörterbuch, 6th ed. (East Berlin: Dietz Verlag, 1983), p. 467.

55. M. Brie, "Die Gestaltung der sozialistischen Produktionsverhältnisse als Entwicklungsform der Produktivekräfte der wissenschaftlich-technischen Revolution" (The Shaping of Socialist Relations of Production as a Developmental Form of the Forces of Production of the Scientific-Technical Revolution), Deutsche Zeitschrift für Philosophie, Vol. 35, Nos. 10/11 (1987), 977–86.

56. Alfred Kosing, "Zur Dialektik der weiteren Gestaltung der entwickelten sozialistischen Gesellschaft" (On the Dialectic of the Further Shaping of Developed Socialist Society), Deutsche Zeitschrift für Philosophie, Vol. 36, No. 7 (1988), 577–587.

57. I. Falconere, "Zur Rolle der Handwerker und Gewerbetreibenden im gesellschaftlichen Reproduktionsprozeß der DDR unter den veränderten Reproduktionsbedingungen der 80er Jahre" (Concerning the Role of Artisans and Business Operators in the Process of Social Reproduction of the GDR under the Changed Conditions of Reproduction in the 1980s), Wirtschaftswissenschaft, Vol. XXX, No. 9 (1982), p. 1339.

58. Ibid., p. 1341.

59. Confirmed by personal information from the author.

60. See Chapter 4.

61. See also Lapp, "Die 'Befreundeten Parteien' der SED," p. 77.

62. See for a more detailed discussion and specific examples the comments on Bloc parties as informal exchange networks in this chapter.

63. "Zur Sozialpolitik der SED" (On the SED's Social Policy), in Neues Deutschland, 29 January 1987.

64. Response to a letter to the editor, in: Das Volk (SED), 24 August 1988.

65. See K.C. Thalheim, and M. Haendcke-Hoppe, "Das Handwerk in der DDR und Ost-Berlin," Beilage zum Jahresbericht der Handwerkskammer Berlin (1984), pp. 4–5.

66. My conjectural account in this and the following paragraphs is based on numerous conversations with East Germans, both inside and outside the private sector.

67. See Aslund, *Private Enterprise,* p. 208; H. Brezinski, "The Second Economy in the GDR—Pragmatism is Gaining Ground," *Studies in Comparative Communism,* 20, 1 (1987), 85–101.

68. See on this Chapter 1.

69. Interestingly, private entrepreneurs I interviewed considered personal envy rather than ideological motives the main reason for problems with local state officials.

70. With very rare exceptions, I found the private entrepreneurs I interviewed most forthcoming, even eager to talk about their problems.

71. Some differences between the old and the new generation of private entrepreneurs in the GDR are discussed at the end of Chapter 4.

72. On this behavioural type, and the reasons for its emergence in Communist countries, see especially A. Hegedüs and M. Markus. "The Small Entrepreneur and Socialism," *Acta Oeconomica,* Vol. 22, 3–4 (1979), 267–289.

8

Institutional Continuity Revisited: The Private Sector in the Early Transition Period, 1989–1990

The Significance of Institutional Integration and Continuity for the Early Transition Period

The present study has attempted to resolve two explanatory problems that are posed by the peculiar development of the private economy in the GDR. First, until the advent of *perestroika,* the GDR, widely considered Moscow's staunchest ally under the rule of an ideologically-orthodox Communist party, deviated from other Soviet-bloc countries by preserving a mixed-ownership economy throughout the 1950s and 1960s. I have argued that the emergence of a mixed ownership structure was an *unintended consequence* of what the Communists regarded as temporary compromises between their orthodox ideological goals and political and economic constraints. These compromises led to the gradual "organic" integration of the private sector into the socialist economy, and to its increasing ideological assimilation (*institutional integration thesis*). Second, Poland, Hungary, and the Soviet Union, which at various points during the 1980s began reintroducing forms of private enterprise, exacerbated the problems of corruption and illegality in their economies, as well as keeping private entrepreneurs in a state of existential insecurity. Contrary to the policy-makers' intentions, the newly established private firms were rejected by the official socialist system. None of these problems were characteristic for the East German private sector during the same period. The surprising legality, stability, and security in the GDR's private economy, I have argued, is a result of its historical evolution as an integral component of the official socialist system (*institutional continuity thesis*).

At first glance, it may appear that with the radical political changes in the GDR since October 1989 that brought a sudden end to Communist rule and led to the unification of Germany in less than one year, the central questions to which this study has sought to offer answers remain only of historical interest. For with the end of Communist hegemony, the ideological claims and goals that clashed with private property and entrepreneurship have lost their political influence. As a result, the explanatory problem in the specific form in which it has been posed in the present analysis has, for the future, been resolved by the political changes since the fall of 1989.

At a more fundamental level, however, this study was inspired by the question of the relationship between ideas and actions, between ideology and policy-making. The major finding—i.e., the importance of existing institutional structures and unintended consequences in shaping the realization of ideological goals, and in providing constraints and opportunities for policy-making—should still have validity, even if ideological goals and the general framework for policy-making change. With the monetary, economic and social union between the Federal Republic and the GDR established on 1 July 1990 and the unification treaty, East Germany's political, economic and legal framework was indeed radically changed. The goal has been rapidly to transform East Germany into a social market economy. The means adopted has been a wholesale imposition by decree of the Federal Republic's socio-economic and political-administrative order. This ambitious strategy of fundamental transformation bears a striking resemblance to the socialist transformation of the GDR pursued by East German Communists after World War II. The common assumption underlying both transformation projects is that a transition from one socio-economic order to another can be engineered by policy-makers who presumably know how to create the crucial preconditions to bring about the transition. The Communists placed primary emphasis on establishing political hegemony and on nationalizing the means of production. The social engineers of the 1990s, who were given political control by a large majority of East Germans, are employing the reverse strategy of de-nationalizing the state economy and extending the Federal Republic's social and political system to the former GDR.

To be sure, there are important differences between the two transformation projects. The Soviet model, imported and slightly modified by East Germany's Communists, has in crucial respects proved to be inferior to the West German model. Moreover, whereas the SED had to contend with formidable political and economic obstacles, the government of the new Germany is acting from a position of political and economic strength. Nevertheless, the theoretical argument of the present analysis suggests that the more ambitious and radical the attempts at socio-economic transformation, the greater the likelihood of producing unintended consequences that will work against realization of the original political and ideological goals. The survival and integration of a private sector in the GDR, I have argued, was a result of the unintended consequences of radical policies aimed at eliminating the private economy—consequences that forced the SED to make compromises that became gradually accepted, institutionalized, and ideologically innocuous. If the theoretical argument presented here is correct, then the current radical de-nationalization strategy for the East German state economy can be expected to produce unintended consequences (large-scale unemployment, de-industrializa-tion) that will force the German government to compromise its present goals—compromises that will become gradually accepted, institutional-ized, and ideologically unobjectionable. The outcome would be an eco-nomic structure significantly deviating from the West German model that provided the original goal.

While there are some initial indications that seem to support such a hypothesis, it is too early in the transition process to arrive at any substantive conclusion; it is also beyond the scope of the present analysis to do more than suggest some implications of the theoretical argument advanced here. This will be the task of the following chapter. The main purpose of this chapter is to trace the fate of the private sector and its organizations in the early transition period. The discussion is divided into two sections. The first will describe the "democratic awakening" of the private sector and its institutional infrastructure between October 1989 and January 1990. The significance of this process is that it illustrates the emergence of the private sector and its organizations as a functioning subsystem of the old order that, freed from the political constraints of Communist orthodoxy, could immediately play a constructive part in the beginning reform process. It demonstrates the importance of institutional continuity that we have followed throughout this analysis.

By January 1990, a broad consensus had emerged in the GDR that unification with the FRG was to be the central pillar of any reform strategy. This farewell to socialism and the GDR was the crucial message endorsed by East German voters in the country's first free parliamentary elections on 18 March 1990. In the months following the election, the East German state and economy basically collapsed, leading to the earlier-than-anticipated unification with the FRG on 3 October 1990. From the perspective of the present analysis, this collapse has meant the rapid disintegration of the institutional infrastructure of the private sector. It might seem that the free-market conditions established by the monetary, economic and social union of July and the unification treaty would have greatly benefited the GDR's private entrepreneurs. The initial evidence, however, is much more equivocal. The main reason, as I will argue at greater length in the next chapter, is that rather than gradually reforming the existing system in which the private sector was integrated, a new economic, political and legal-administrative system was introduced vir-tually overnight. While this institutional revolution has provided most favorable conditions for private enterprise in principle, it has in fact produced a whole range of negative unintended consequences that have also seriously affected the East German private sector. This illustrates the dangers of institutional discontinuity and disintegration.

I will preface my discussion of the "democratic awakening" of the GDR private economy with some considerations relating to the potential contribution that could have been expected from the old institutional infrastructure of the private economy under conditions of more gradual reform. Politically, these considerations are now irrelevant. The majority of East Germans did not see a more gradual reform approach and a slower unification process as a realistic or desirable alternative. From a theoretical point of view, however, these conjectures may offer a context within which to understand and assess the problems emerging from the radical transformation strategy chosen by a majority of East Germans and masterminded by the new German government.

Democratic Awakening: The Institutional Infrastructure of the Private Sector in the Fall of 1989 and Its Potential Contribution to Gradual Reform

When this study was conceived and while the bulk of the research was carried out, my assumption was that political and economic reform would, if at all, proceed at a slower pace and in a gradual fashion. I would have concluded that for the 1990s the SED would find itself in a relatively favourable position from which to embark on further liberalization of the private economy. The existing framework of private firms, economic and political organizations, regulations, and ideological conceptions and justifications—in short, the institutional infrastructure—offered fertile ground from which to undertake a reform of socialism in the GDR, including its private sector.

What might have been true had the SED had the opportunity to restructure socialism, however, may have been equally true for a non-Communist GDR government.[1] The following contributions from the old institutional infrastructure integrating the private sector would have been conceivable if it had been allowed to survive and had been changed in a less radical and wholesale fashion than has actually occurred. (I will return to these potential contributions in the next chapter to contrast them with the effects of the radical transformation strategy.)

For any post-Communist GDR government, the strengthening and expansion of the private economy would have been a central objective of economic reform. While the future of the state sector was more difficult to predict, there was a consensus among all political forces in the GDR at the end of 1989 that small and medium-sized private firms must be strongly promoted. The institutional continuity provided very favourable conditions for implementing such a new private-sector policy. The "institutional engineering" necessary to transform the private sector as it existed under socialism was minimal compared to the enormous task of reforming the entire state economy. First, and obviously, institutional continuity refers to the 140,000 self-employed who operated private firms in the GDR in 1989. They constituted a reservoir of entrepreneurial skills and attitudes that could be immediately further activated. In addition to the core sectors of the East German private economy, i.e., trade and handicraft, some of the "marginal" private economic activities (see Chapter 4), such as professional services that were permitted only on a part-time basis and private property in rental housing, could have come to play a more central role in the GDR's new private economy simply by lifting some of the excessively restrictive regulations. This points to the second element of institutional continuity offering favourable preconditions for economic reform.

In the four decades of the GDR's existence, an elaborate regulatory framework for the private sector had been established (see Chapter 5). Taxation, investment, subsidization, pricing, licensing, occupational training, wages, patterns and practices of cooperation between responsible state organs, and supervision and control were the major elements of this legal framework for the private economy. Many specific regulations were quite restrictive, such as a very steep tax progression, lower wages for employees in the private sector, and the range of occupations for which private firms could be licensed. From the perspective of institutional continuity, however, an existing regulatory framework, even if inadequate in many respects, overly complex, and in need of revision, constitutes an asset rather than a liability for economic reform. The reason is that it forms part of an already functioning system. This means that the participants in this system—administrators and private entrepreneurs—already possess valuable knowledge, skills, and habits integral to its functioning. It also means that they know where the weak points of the system are and what changes should be made to improve it. This contrasts sharply with a situation in which a legal framework must be newly created (such as in the Soviet Union), or a degenerate and corrupt system must be fundamentally changed (as, for example, in Poland). For such a new framework will give rise to many negative consequences unforeseen by policy makers.

A similar argument can be made with respect to the private sector's integration into, and subordination to, the state economy which was analyzed in Chapter 6. Again, there are a host of restrictions that have been placed on private firms, such as confining private firms to providing predominantly repairs and services for the population, state enterprises deciding on the division of labour between state and private enterprises in a specific sector of the economy, the preferential supply of state enterprises, or the political barriers to innovation by private firms imposed by state enterprises. At the same time, however, the economic forms of integration of the past might have been beneficial in the reform process in a number of respects. First, until a workable market allocation system had replaced the administrative allocation of supplies, private firms would have been guaranteed access to scarce supplies through the traditional channels (e.g., the purchase and delivery cooperatives for private handicraft firms). Second, the Chambers as the major organizations for the economic integration and subordination of the private sector—with their curious double function of representing both the state and private firms— would have quickly developed into genuine interest representatives of and for the private economy. Third, existing ties between private and state enterprises might have become beneficial for private firms as they gained greater freedom to choose business partners in the state sector.

Finally, the political mobilization and representation of private entrepreneurs through the GDR's former Bloc parties discussed in Chapter 7 proved to be the most dynamic element of institutional continuity in late 1989. Freed from their dependent status as subordinate allies of the leading Communist party, the LDPD and the CDU had seized the growing opportunities since October 1989 to formulate as public demands for private-sector reform what in the past they had only been able to discuss internally and to submit as proposals to the SED Central Committee. Their knowledge of the economic problems and their consistent work for and with private entrepreneurs put them in a position to play a leading role, both programmatically and politically, in the shaping of a new private-sector policy and in the adoption of immediate reform measures. The main purpose of the remainder of this chapter is to describe the "democratic awakening" of the institutional infrastructure of the East German private sector.

In just three months, there was a fundamental break with past political structures in the GDR. The SED was transformed from a party with a virtual monopoly of power into an organization struggling for its sheer political survival. Erich Honecker stepped down as the SED's General Secretary on 18 October 1989. On 20 January 1990, public demands for the dissolution of the reconstituted SED/PDS[2] under the leadership of Gregor Gysi—an attorney who had defended dissidents in the past— received added force by the appeal of forty prominent party members from Dresden for the party's dissolution after returning their own membership cards. Until the March elections, the PDS and its Prime Minister Hans Modrow still formally led the new coalition government formed on 18 November 1989. However, it depended for legislative action on the consent not only of the other coalition parties (the former Bloc parties

CDU, DBD, LDPD, and NDPD which threatened to leave the coalition). It also required the approval of the new opposition parties and organizations represented at the Round Table,[3] which had the power of the street behind them. On 22 January 1990, Modrow recognized the precarious political position of his government by inviting the opposition to join the existing government in a grand coalition until the general elections on March 18. On 8 February 1990, eight ministers were sworn in from the new opposition parties. The old power centre of SED Politburo and Central Committee Secretariat had been eliminated. In the realm of politics, it was not institutional continuity but rather revolutionary institutional change that was shaping developments and events in the GDR.

The ambitious economic reform plans that were being prepared pointed to a similarly fundamental break with the institutional past. It was becoming increasingly clear that the goal of economic reform could not be a "third way" between the East German planned economy and the West German market economy. Rather, the majority of the East German population and of political parties and organizations had decided that the model for a "third way" between capitalism and socialism was represented by the West German "social market economy" (*soziale Marktwirtschaft*), which was widely viewed as the most successful compromise between the imperatives of economic efficiency and social justice. The real question was how to get there from here. There were many as yet unforeseen difficulties and problems involved in restructuring a highly-centralized state economy. The transition was seen to be necessarily gradual and piecemeal, even if the envisaged economic structure was radically different from the existing one.

The situation was quite different with respect to the GDR's private sector. Institutional continuity, as I have argued above, is not a burdensome liability but a fortunate asset for post-Communist economic reform in East Germany. An existing base of private firms and entrepreneurial skills, a regulatory framework, occupational organizations, and political parties representing their interests have had a long history in the GDR. Until the fall of 1989, the SED's political hegemony concealed from public view the fact that the former Bloc parties played a central role in the design and implementation of private-sector policy. The SED claimed the successes of private-sector policy for itself, while barely acknowledging the contributions of the other parties and organizations in the process. The "democratic awakening" of this institutional infrastructure that is the subject of this section may therefore easily be misunderstood as the formulation of new demands by and for the private sector. In fact, however, what is new is only the formulation in public as demands of what in the past could only be submitted as internal proposals to the SED.

In order to illustrate this important element of institutional continuity with respect to private-sector policy in the GDR after the "revolution", I will begin my account of "democratic awakening" in the private sector with a short summary of a document for private-sector reform submitted by the LDPD to the SED Central Committee in May 1989.[4] This will serve as a reference point for the subsequent more detailed account of reform proposals and demands as they emerged after the resignation of Honecker on 18 October 1989.

LDPD Proposals to the SED
for Private-Sector Reform of May 1989

(1) More consistent implementation of existing measures for promoting the private sector at the local level. The document points out that many problems in the private sector are due to local administrators' inadequate knowledge of existing regulations. In order to redress this situation, it is proposed that central guidelines be formulated and published for local state organs to facilitate a uniform implementation of private-sector policy in all territories.[5]

(2) Revision of existing regulations in order to stimulate private economic activity. The LDPD proposes that local state organs be issued specific guidelines on when it is permissible to exceed the 10-employee limit for private firms.[6] The scope of private-sector activity should be widened by instructing local state organs to issue licences for private firms in the areas of manufacturing tools and rationalization equipment, providing architectural, engineering, software, and accounting services, and municipal road construction,[7] as well as the creation of new, flexible private wholesale firms.[8] The private sector should be offered greater investment opportunities, and receive significantly more material and technical supplies.[9] For the more efficient supply of private retailers, a system of travelling salespersons should be reintroduced, greater opportunities for direct purchases from producers be created, and seasonal sales be permitted.[10]

(3) Financial autonomy for handicraft cooperatives (PGH). The model statute for PGHs of 21 February 1973, designed in the wake of the 1972 nationalization to curtail the cooperatives' financial autonomy, should be revised giving them full responsibility over the use of funds. In order to ensure greater continuity in PGH management, the term of office of the elected boards should be extended from 2 years to at least 3 years.[11]

(4) Reform of financial regulations. Price subsidies should be provided to selected handicraft trades[12] and flexible pricing allowed in retail trade for new, improved, and outdated products.[13] Private firms involved in export trade should receive a share of export earnings. Tax regulations

should be relaxed (higher triggers for application of additional profit charges; more favourable income tax rates; tax breaks for selected firms; higher tax exemptions for assisting spouses). Private-sector employees should receive the same wages as their colleagues in corresponding sectors of the state economy, and private firms and purchase and delivery cooperatives (ELG) should be allowed to pay their employees tax-deductible annual bonuses.[14]

(5) Redefinition of the role of the Chambers. The Chambers, which have predominantly political-ideological tasks and are subordinated to the district councils, should become independent occupational organizations rather than organs of economic administration. They should represent their members vis-à-vis state organs, the economic administration, and other organizations in all respects. A Chamber of Handicraft and a Chamber of Trade and Commerce should be established at the central level. The governing boards of Chambers should be elected rather than appointed. They should have co-determination (*Mitbestimmung*) in the design and implementation of private-sector policy and in the economic administration, planning, and promotion of private firms. They should establish counselling centres for applicants seeking a license.[15] In private retail trade, sectoral groups at county and district levels should be established corresponding to the occupational groups in handicraft.[16]

It should be stressed again that these LDPD proposals were not publicized at the time. Rather, they were submitted to the SED Central Committee to be taken into account in its preparation of the new five-year plan. The LDPD, like the other Bloc parties responsible for private entrepreneurs, thus had no opportunity to bring to bear political pressure on the SED to adopt these measures by mobilizing public support for its suggestions.[17] Rather, they were framed as "alliance contributions to economic growth" based on more than 65,000 individual contributions from LDPD members.[18] This unpublicized LDPD document well illustrates a salient characteristic of private-sector policy in the GDR until October 1989. While the Bloc parties played an important and constructive role in the design, implementation, and evaluation of measures for promoting private economic activity, their political effectiveness was severely limited by the very restrictive standards of public discourse enforced by the SED. With the onset of large demonstrations in October 1989, the power of the SED rapidly diminished and the new leadership was forced to enter into a public dialogue.

In the short period from mid-October to mid-December 1989, three phases of democratization may be distinguished. The first phase, beginning with the ascendancy of Egon Krenz to the position of SED General Secretary, was that of "*dialogue*" between the ruling Communist party and the people. The assumption, at least on the part of the SED, was that reforms could be worked out within the existing power structure. The second phase, roughly beginning with the resignation of the old government on November 7 and the formation of the new coalition government under Prime Minister Hans Modrow between November 13–17 and lasting until mid-December, was one of growing political *radicalization*. While the continued survival of a socialist GDR was generally not questioned, the "leading role" of the SED was increasingly challenged. Finally, the third phase starting in early-to mid-December after the resignation and dissolution of the Politburo and the Central Committee, saw the growing *renunciation of socialism and the affirmation of German unity*. A far-reaching consensus quickly emerged on the need to create a market economy and to prepare the confederation of the two German states. Each phase was reflected in the level of demands for reform of the private sector.[19]

Dialogue

In its edition of 21/22 October 1989, the LDPD's central daily, *Der Morgen*, reported on a meeting of the political executive of the LDPD which had taken place on 17 October 1989, one day before Honecker's resignation. The LDPD leadership demanded "essential changes of economic strategy and policy" in order to strengthen the "unity of economic and social policy" (the general policy slogan of the Honecker era). "Socialism", it was argued, "must be an achievement society." Referring to its proposals submitted to the SED Central Committee summarized above, the article listed some of the changes suggested by the LDPD for private and cooperative firms. The goal was "to use fully private initiative for socialism." Similarly, Christian Renatus, member of the LDPD political executive, in an article published on 24 October in *Der Morgen*, presented a number of proposals for political reform—a greater role for Parliament, secret ballots, and a new electoral law—after reaffirming the "leading role of the working class and its party." He concluded that one should always search for "feasible and realizable, and at the same time always socialist, avenues for participation in the process of change. There is no better alternative to socialism!" This was to be the basic pattern for the presentation of reform demands during the dialogue phase. Specific, often far-reaching, proposals were presented in the framework of ritual references to traditional political concepts.

The LDPD proposals for the reform of private-sector policy listed above were finally published in various newspaper articles in late October.[20] Even the SED, in its central organ *Neues Deutschland* of 28 October 1989, endorsed the suggestions of the Bloc parties in a discussion of private-sector policy—albeit in the traditional alliance policy fashion of

not acknowledging their source.[21] The first, more far-reaching, proposals
for economic reform thus surfaced. They included a reduction in the scope
of state plan targets, the transformation of service and repair cooperatives
into manufacturing enterprises, and the formation of new private enterprises for consumer goods production.[22] Nevertheless, even one of the
leading early advocates of reform in October, LDPD Chairman Manfred
Gerlach, was not yet prepared to break with the fundamental taboos of
the old system. Asked in an interview published on 1 November about
his view on the leading role of the SED and socialist property, he
responded:

> I am for the preservation of these principles for historical reasons . . . the
> leading role of the working class and its party is an objective necessity . . . .
> Equally indispensable for us is socialist property . . . . My belief and my
> firm conviction is that socialism is the sole, the better alternative to capital-
> ism. The LDPD is . . . for a socialism that is fun.[23]

Private entrepreneurs now also began joining the public debate. In an
open letter to the Council of Ministers of 1 November, private and
cooperative artisans formulated their demands for immediate measures
in the area of taxes and wage rates, as well as for financial incentives, the
creation of an economic ministry with a special secretariat for handicraft,
an elected Chamber at the central level, and a fundamental reform of the
planning system.[24] Chairmen of handicraft cooperatives (PGHs) identified
the lack of individual incentive as the major obstacle for better performance in their enterprises, and severely criticized state industry for being
in many cases years behind schedule in delivering new machinery. They
charged that in the past PGHs had been treated like state enterprises.[25] A
local state administrator, member of the LDPD and committed to the
promotion of private firms, pointed out that the major dilemma in trying
to stimulate the expansion of the private sector at the local level was
shrinking material allocations. More private service enterprises could
start up in the city if only the equipment was available that had long been
promised as part of the SED's measures for promoting the private sector.[26]

Radicalization

The phase of dialogue of the rulers with the ruled ended as the SED's
political hegemony was publicly called into question in November. LDPD
Chairman Manfred Gerlach, in an interview with the West German news
magazine, *Der Spiegel,* published on 6 November, stated that a discussion
concerning the leading role of the SED should be possible. As to his own
party, he declared: "We are no longer a Bloc party in the traditional
sense." This, indeed, constituted a radical break with the political past.

As Gerlach put it, "we believe it is a revolution, a new revolution."²⁷ The new political horizons that were emerging were also reflected in bolder thinking about the future of the private economy. Gerlach maintained that much could be done in the private sector, not only in its existing forms, but also by leasing state enterprises to private individuals.²⁸

In an open letter by members of the Berlin Chamber of Trade and Commerce to the GDR Parliament (*Volkskammer*), the proposals for private-sector reform of the past were now submitted as political demands.²⁹ Private trade firms should also be licensed in new areas, and all private enterprises should have access to capital and be able to cooperate directly with foreign partners. In a declaration by the chairmen of the district Chambers of Handicraft drafted in early November, it was requested that the government promptly begin work on new handicraft legislation. The declaration noted that the transformation of the Chambers into democratically-elected and independent occupational organizations was to be completed by 30 June 1990. The Ministry of District Directed Industry and the Food Industry was reproached for having formed a working group on new handicraft legislation without incorporating representatives of the handicraft sector.³⁰

In his inaugural speech as head of the new coalition government on 18 November 1989, Prime Minister Hans Modrow (SED) sent less radical, though nevertheless clear signals for a new approach to private-sector policy. "We declare ourselves to [be committed to] socialist entrepreneurial spirit." More concretely, he stated that it was possible for the "takeover of small enterprises by private entrepreneurs in consumer goods production" and elsewhere to occur. He promised that the new government would take immediate measures to promote this. "For a long time there have been suggestions from private entrepreneurs concerning obstacles to their initiative. Together with the Chambers and the parties of our government coalition it should be examined what changes could be made very soon, and decisions will not be long in coming."³¹

Meanwhile, at the local level, heads of the district administration responsible for the private sector and representatives of the district Chamber of Handicraft met in a spirit of "open and constructive discussion as has never taken place before." Not only were questions of private-sector policy discussed, but there was agreement that "general, free, democratic elections are the precondition for a functioning democracy, and that the constitutional article laying down the leading role of a party must be eliminated."³² In addition to specific reform demands concerning private and cooperative handicraft firms, the Dresden district Chamber of Handicraft, in a letter to Prime Minister Modrow, called for the strict enforcement of the rule of law (*Rechtsstaatlichkeit*), fundamental changes in administration, planning, and the material allocation system for the private sector, as well as the elimination of the SED's constitutionally-guaranteed leading role.[33]

By late November, the SED was under siege. LDPD Chairman Gerlach asserted that with respect to the SED, "I no longer use the phrase 'primus inter pares' . . . . We are free to leave the coalition (government)." With the *de facto* loss of its leading role, the SED was also being deprived of its power to set the agenda, though socialism itself was still accepted, if only as a shell to be filled with new content. We want, said Gerlach, "to make socialism into that pluralistic, democratic, new socialism that we desire, that would also be our socialism."[34]

The LDPD put forth its specific demands for the fundamental economic reform of socialism with respect to the private sector in early December. Included were:

- full development of private initiative, including the formation of private firms and admission of other—in addition to national and cooperative ownership—forms, e.g., limited commercial partnerships (*Kommanditgesellschaften*),[35] limited liability companies (*GmbH*), and share companies in all sectors of the economy;
- new priorities in the construction industry, giving greater scope for cooperative and private firms;
- pervasive reform of wholesale trade, including the possibility for a private wholesale trade;
- new handicraft and trade legislation, as well as fundamental reforms of price, tax, credit, and wage policy in the non-state sector;
- equal economic relations for private entrepreneurs in the economy;
- self-administration of the cooperatives, and permission for manufacturing cooperatives to be established;
- the right freely to establish a business (*Gewerbefreiheit*) on the basis of evidence of formal qualifications provided by applicant;
- development of the Chambers into independent occupational organizations;
- formation of a Chamber of Industry and Trade after formation of private forms of industrial enterprise.[36]

As promised, the Modrow government moved quickly on reform measures for the private sector, passing a set of new regulations on December 4. The following immediate measures were adopted:

- suspension of a decree of 14 August 1989 prohibiting private firms from purchasing any materials and equipment through retail outlets;
- liberalization of cooperatives' (PGH and ELG) use of employee funds;

- upper limits for "free" investment extended (PGH: from 100,000 to 200,000 Marks; private firms: from 20,000 to 50,000 Marks) to stimulate modernization;
- county and municipal councils authorized to extend 10-employee limit for private firms;
- tax deduction for assisting spouses doubled to 4,000 Marks per year;
- price regulations that have negative incentive effect to be revised by 1 July 1990;
- price subsidies for cooperative and private automobile repair firms.

In addition, a number of intermediate measures to be adopted in 1990 were announced:

- liberalization in cooperatives' use of funds;
- creation of a simplified regulatory framework;
- Chambers to present a new draft statute to the government for ratification within first quarter of 1990;
- provisions in 1990 plan for better supply of private and cooperative firms.

Moreover, the government made a commitment to work out more fundamental changes in private-sector policy in the course of the economic reform process.[37]

The steps taken by the government as it moved to implement many of the changes long proposed by the former Bloc parties and the Chambers appeared quite modest in light of the rising level of demands that were being formulated in this radicalization phase. They were modest even for a fundamentally restructured *socialist* economy—still the common goal of all political parties until early December—which could not simply be created with a set of short and medium-term measures. It is important to note, however, that the improvements for the private sector under the existing system had been worked out and were already available at the time the rapid political changes began in the GDR. Thus, the preconditions had been created for their public formulation as demands and for their swift adoption by the government. However, the more far-reaching reform demands and goals—such as those formulated by the LDPD in their "Principles" cited above—required for their realization a much more comprehensive legal reform and extensive institutional engineering. Moreover, as LDPD Chairman Gerlach himself recognized, it was not only a question of time, but also of knowledge. "There is nothing at the moment that could be characterized as an economic strategy that would be politically practicable."[38]

Toward Reunification and a Market Economy

During the phase of radicalization, the gap was visibly widening between the level of demands for private-sector reform and what could possibly be achieved in the foreseeable future. From early December, the goals of economic reform became ever more ambitious. Four core goals for economic reform crystallized:

- an unequivocally market-oriented economy;
- deconcentration of the highly-centralized state economy;
- opening up of the economy for private initiative in all ownership forms (i.e., both the formation of new private firms and cooperatives and private financial participation in state enterprises);
- foreign capital investment and joint ventures.[39]

Particularly interesting from the perspective of institutional continuity is the fact that a number of former part-owners of semi-state enterprises[40] and their children expressed an interest in buying themselves back into their former enterprises.[41] Wolfgang Doss, LDPD member since 1948, a former private entrepreneur in the consumer goods industry who after the conversion of his firm into a semi-state enterprise became a part-owner and director until its nationalization in 1972, expressed his bitterness about the role of the LDPD in the 1972 nationalization.[42] While recognizing that the LDPD had been used by the SED to carry out its nationalization campaign, he was deeply disappointed that they had only criticized the procedure, rather than the policy itself.[43] If today the experiences gained with small and medium-sized private enterprises until 1972 are pulled out of the drawer again, he hoped that the term "transitional period" with respect to their future prospects would once and for all be dropped.[44] East German economic historian, Jörg Roesler, who has recently interviewed former part-owners, reports that they considered the 1960s their "golden age".[45] Under the New Economic System (1962–1971) when the SED pioneered what Aslund has described as "functional socialism"—the integration of different ownership forms in a profit-oriented socialist economy—private part-owners remained the managers of their enterprises, had good profit opportunities, and received most of their investment capital from the state.[46]

By mid-December 1989, a clear differentiation of reform goals was taking shape. Both LDPD and CDU, as well as most opposition parties and groups, were bidding farewell to socialism. The LDPD leadership stated that socialism had nowhere lived up to its promises. "The majority of Liberal Democrats rejects a 'third way with a socialist character' as is now advocated by the SED. Article 1 of the Constitution—'The GDR is a socialist state'—represents for the LDPD only a description of what is and a challenge to develop more ambitious political goals."[47] It was becoming increasingly clear that the question of economic reform was directly linked to the question of the future of the GDR as a separate state. Only a socialist GDR, however defined, could justify separate statehood for East Germany. East Germans in their great majority, however, were not prepared to participate in another socialist experiment. Indeed, the term socialism itself had become utterly discredited in the GDR, and with it the major element of the country's political identity. Unification with the Federal Republic was the formula for rapid economic improvement. In keeping with its new economic reform goals, the LDPD leadership declared that a "confederated political structure and a possible unification (of Germany) within the borders of 1989 is a national process which should not only be tolerated but actively promoted."[48]

With the growing consensus on the GDR's departure from socialism and its gradual integration with the West German economy and the EC, new and very difficult problems arose in connection with the "transition period." Rising popular expectations for a rapid and significant improvement in living standards sharply contrasted with the unavoidable social costs of fundamental reform. Despite the liberation from a regime that was in many respects very oppressive, a large number of East Germans grew more and more despondent that their expectations for economic improvement would remain unfulfilled for some time to come. This was reflected in the unabated East-West migration. From 1-25 January 1990 alone, 41,500 East Germans arrived in West Germany to settle permanently.

In early December, the GDR coalition government under Hans Modrow (SED) had attempted to broaden its basis of legitimacy by closely working with a Round Table, composed of representatives from both the old political parties forming the coalition government and the newly established opposition parties and groups. But the crisis of legitimacy of the regime, even under a reformist leadership and with the informal participation of opposition forces, was progressing rapidly. Demonstrations continued throughout January, animosities against the SED/PDS, and indeed against most everything associated with the old regime, grew, and popular demands called for the immediate unification of Germany. In late January, the government coalition was broadened by formally incorporating representatives of opposition groups as cabinet ministers, and elections were rescheduled for mid-March. This marks the end of the indigenous democratic revolution in the GDR and the beginning of "unification politics."

Unification Politics: The Emergence of
the Radical Transformation Strategy

The young and inexperienced democratic organizations in the GDR were ill-prepared to fight an effective election campaign at this early date. They had barely established themselves, were only beginning to work out political programmes, and were lacking basic financial and human resources. With the popular mood fixed on unification as the cure for East Germany's economic problems, West German political parties had a field day in the GDR in the weeks leading up to the election. East German political parties quickly formed alliances corresponding to the West German party system, received logistical and programmatic assistance, as well as the political authority from West German party leaders who campaigned on their behalf, promising East German voters a bright future in a unified Germany. The former GDR Bloc party, CDU, emerged as the winner of the election, thus receiving a mandate to negotiate with the Bonn government under CDU Chancellor Helmut Kohl steps towards quick unification.

Until that time, the institutional infrastructure of existing private firms, regulatory frameworks, and organizations representing the private sector had proved to be a dynamic and positive element in the economic reform process aimed at creating a vigorous and expanding private economy. It underscores the importance of institutional continuity, even under the new conditions of moving away from socialism. What under the old political system often appeared as organizations utterly compromised by their apparent role as mere instruments of the SED regime turned out to be effective interest representatives from the moment that opportunities emerged for independent political action. The reason for this is, as I have argued, that they had been able to function to a considerable extent as separate, "independent" organizations in the past. By permitting their survival and giving them limited functional tasks, the SED unwittingly preserved an institutional infrastructure that worked not only with the private sector, as was its official mission, but also understood its work as promoting the specific interests of the private sector. As a result, it could emerge as a functioning subsystem of socialist society with its own diverging goals and solutions to existing problems as soon as the SED had been deprived of its political hegemony.

At the same time, however, the history of the East German private economy, its political organizations and legal structure, to a large extent also determined its limitations under conditions of rapid political change and fundamental economic reform. The thinking, habits, and aspirations of private entrepreneurs and their representatives were, until very recently, conditioned by and adapted to a life and a future under socialism. The new opportunities, challenges, and problems that emerged in early 1990 far exceeded what until December 1989 seemed realistically conceivable. To the extent that completely new structures for the private sector were demanded and put on the government's agenda, institutional continuity at best constituted a valuable starting capital. Undoubtedly, democratic conditions would bring the collective demands of the private sector in conflict with other interests in society. They would also lead to a growing differentiation of interests within the private sector, now that the common "enemy" no longer produced a common private-sector identity and as competitive conditions arose. The ambitiousness of the economic reform program, moreover, put the future of the existing private sector in the GDR in the hands of more or less able social engineers, who would to some extent determine the success of the reform project. Clearly, economic reform might also spell social *déclassement* and economic ruin for some of East Germany's private entrepreneurs who under socialism had no easy, though nonetheless a secure, respected, and relatively prosperous existence. The initiative for economic reform increasingly moved to Bonn as the East German government tried unsuccessfully to deal with what was perceived as a growing economic crisis. More important, East Germans wanted to see positive results quickly, and it was West German politicians, in particular Chancellor Helmut Kohl, who understood how to respond to these hopes. Economic reform became part of his government's political calculus to mobilize GDR voters for the CDU. With his promise to introduce the Deutsche mark into the GDR as soon as possible, Kohl commanded a powerful symbol embodying East Germans' hopes to finally share in the Federal Republic's prosperity. Not surprisingly, economic prudence did not figure prominently in what was essentially an electoral strategy.

The Ministry for the Economy and the Finance Ministry, the FRG's central bank (*Bundesbank*), the economic Council of Experts (*Sachver-ständigenrat*), and most economists in West Germany had cautioned the federal government not to proceed too hastily in establishing a monetary and economic union with the GDR. The logic of the election campaign in the GDR in February and March, and the continuing massive outflow of East Germans to the West during the first two months of 1990, led the Kohl government to assure the GDR population that a monetary union with the FRG would be introduced in the summer. After a grand-coalition government under Christian Democrat Lothar de Maizière had been formed in the GDR, negotiations between Bonn and East Berlin on a comprehensive agreement for an economic union between the two German states began. In the space of only a few weeks during April and early May, a *Staatsvertrag* was hammered out that set the GDR on a course of radical economic, social, and political transformation.

With the introduction of the Deutsche mark as the GDR's official currency on July 1, East Germany took the plunge into the cold waters of capitalism. The foreseeable costs of monetary and economic union alone were to be massive. In order to finance the GDR's estimated budget deficit in 1990 and 1991, as well as the start-up costs for pension and unemployment funds, a "German Unity Fund" (*Fond "Deutsche Einheit"*) was set up, containing 75 billion dollars. In return, the GDR had to agree to Bonn's terms and conditions. The monetary authority over East Germany passed to the *Bundesbank's* central council, with no representation from East Berlin. The implications of the *Staatsvertrag* for the sovereignty of the GDR government are summed up in the provision that with respect to decisions "affecting the principles of economic policy, [the GDR government] must reach an agreement with the government of the FRG . . . ."[49] The GDR, by contrast, would only be informed of legislative changes and altered legal regulations. Yet, according to the *Staatsvertrag,* the GDR had the responsibility for the modernization of its economy.

The policy instruments at the disposal of the East German government to carry out the task of radical marketization, however, were extremely limited. Apart from protective tariffs on the import of agricultural products, which was to facilitate the restructuring of its own food industries, the GDR was expected to leave the transition process to market forces and to the wisdom of the Bonn government. Initial plans in the GDR to restrict the purchase of real estate for a ten-year period in order to permit the development of an East German real estate industry had to be abandoned during the negotiations. The same goes for the plan to give East Germans a share in state-owned industries. Nationally-owned assets are to be used primarily to finance the structural adjustment of the GDR economy.

It appeared as the logical conclusion of "unification politics" when the GDR coalition government, after having abdicated control over the reform process, decided to absolve itself also of all responsibility for its consequences. Two months earlier than originally scheduled, the GDR ceased to exist when its barely reconstituted six *Länder* joined the Federal Republic on 3 October 1990. With the demise of the GDR, the country's formal state institutions at the central and district levels disappeared, the new *Länder* came under the rule of the Basic Law (*Grundgesetz*), and East Germans became full and formally equal citizens of the Federal Republic of Germany. Discontinuity—at least at the level of state institutions—could hardly be more absolute. The same is of course not true for the private entrepreneurs and some of their organizations that have been the subject of this study. How has the radical break with the past affected them? What relevance, if any, does the theoretical argument guiding the present analysis retain under conditions of rapid political and socio-economic transformation?

Notes

1. It is evident that one of the most important preconditions for the success of such a restructuring effort would have been the political legitimacy of the GDR as a separate state. In 1990, most East Germans had no faith in the capacity of their state to implement far-reaching reforms successfully. It is also clear, however, that the standards for success were derived from living conditions in the Federal Republic and the assumption that unification would guarantee successful reforms.

2. The acronym PDS stands for Party of Democratic Socialism (*Partei des Demokratischen Sozialismus*).

3. The Round Table included representatives from all East German political parties and major organizations. Up to the March 18 elections, it met frequently to debate, and create a consensus, on major political measures to be taken by the government.

4. I received a copy of this internal document from a member of the LDPD economic committee. It is entitled "Proposals to the Central Committee of the SED for the further realization of the main task in the unity of economic and social policy" (*Vorschläge an das Zentralkomitee der SED zur weiteren Verwirklichung der Hauptaufgabe in der Einheit von Wirtschafts-und Sozialpolitik*), n.d. In addition to proposals for the reform of private handicraft and trade, it contains sections on "Economic and social policy as well as industry", "Construction and housing," and "Agriculture." Similar documents containing proposals for private sector reform have been submitted to the SED in the past, and by the other two Bloc parties, CDU and NDPD, that represent the private sector (interview with CDU economic expert Eberhard Engel, East Berlin, 21 December 1989).

5. "Vorschläge," pp. 19–20, 23, 25–26.

6. *Ibid.*, pp. 19–20.

7. *Ibid.*, p. 25.

8. *Ibid.*, p. 33.

9. *Ibid.*, pp. 21–22.

10. *Ibid.*, pp. 33–34.

11. *Ibid.*, 23–25.

12. *Ibid.*, p. 27.

13. *Ibid.*, p. 32.

14. *Ibid.*, pp. 27–28.

15. *Ibid.*, pp. 29–30, 36.

16. *Ibid.*, p. 37.

17. One specific proposal on raising the permitted investment by private firms was in fact adopted on 15 September 1989 by the Council of Ministers before the beginning of political reforms. See "Anordnung Nr. 2 über die Leitung und Planung der Investitionen in Handwerk-und Gewerbebetrieben vom 15.9.1989," *GBl. I*, No. 18, p. 217.

18. "Vorschläge," p. 1.

19. My reconstruction of events in the period from October to December is based on a systematic evaluation of the LDPD central daily organ, *Der Morgen,* supplemented with selected relevant material from other newspapers published by the CDU as well as the SED. In addition, it draws on interviews conducted in East Berlin and Dresden with academic specialists, leading representatives of the LDPD and CDU, the Chamber of Handicraft and the Chamber of Trade and Commerce (East Berlin) and others between December 17 and 23, 1989.

20. See, for example, *Der Morgen,* No. 251, 25 October 1989, p. 5; No. 253, 27 October 1989, p. 3.

21. This was specifically criticized by CDU economic expert Eberhard Engel. See *Neue Zeit,* 4 November 1989.

22. See *Der Morgen,* No. 256, 31 October 1989, p. 3.

23. *Der Morgen,* No. 257, 1 November 1989, p. 5.

24. Printed in *Der Morgen,* No. 262, 7 November 1989, p. 5.

25. *Der Morgen,* No. 258, 2 November 1989, p. 3.

26. *Der Morgen,* No. 262, 7 November 1989, p. 3.

27. Interview reprinted in *Der Morgen,* No. 265, 10 November 1989.

28. *Ibid.*

29. Reprinted in *Der Morgen,* No. 266, 11/12 November 1989, p. 3.

30. Published in *Das Neue Handwerk,* Vol. 43, No. 11 (November 1989), p. 1.

31. *Neues Deutschland,* 18/19 November 1989, p. 3.

32. Reported in *Union* (CDU), 22 November 1989, p. 3.

33. *Ibid.*

34. Address by Manfred Gerlach to the 7th Meeting of the Central Executive of the LDPD, 24 November 1989, reprinted in *Der Morgen,* No. 279, 27 November 1989, p. 3.

35. Laws for limited commercial partnerships as well as for open commerical partnerships (*offene Handelsgesellschaften*) have always been in force in the GDR. This was pointed out to the author by Ernst Happach, Chamber of Trade and Commerce, East Berlin, in an interview on 22 December 1989.

36. Excerpts from "Principles of Liberal-Democratic Politics Today", published in *Der Morgen,* No. 286, 5 December 1989, p. 4.

37. See *Neue Zeit,* 8 December 1989, p. 3.

38. "Address".

39. See, for example, *Der Morgen,* No. 287, 6 December 1989, p. 3.

40. See on semi-state enterprises Chapters 2 and 3.

41. *Der Morgen,* No. 287, 6 December 1989, p. 3.

42. On the 1972 nationalization, see Chapter 3.

43. The LDPD has publicly admitted its responsibility for the 1972 nationalization. "The LDPD considers the 1972 nationalization to have been a mistake. The party is aware of the fact that it is partly responsible for this mistake." *Der Morgen,* No. 293, 13 December 1989, p. 1.

44. *Der Morgen,* no. 292, 12 December 1989, p. 3.

45. Interview with Prof. Jörg Roesler, Institute for Economic History, Academy of Sciences of the GDR, East Berlin, 19 December 1989.

46. The New Economic System and its implications for the private sector is discussed in greater detail in Chapter 3.

47. *Der Morgen*, No. 293, 13 December 1989, p. 1.

48. *Der Morgen*, No. 293, 13 December 1989, p. 1.

49. "Staatsvertrag", Article 11, Section (4), Deutscher Bundestag, Drucksache 11/7350, 7 June 1990, p. 57.

9

Institutional Continuity Rejected: East Germany's Second Radical Transition

Free at Last? The Fate of the East German Private Economy in the New Germany

The introduction of a liberal market order and the GDR's monetary and economic integration with the Federal Republic in July 1990 freed East German private entrepreneurs from the many restrictions imposed upon them by the Communist system. For example, limitations on the size of private firms, on the type of products or services offered, or on access to technology and supplies no longer exist. Optimistic projections estimated that, as a result, established and new small and medium-sized private enterprises in the GDR would create hundreds of thousands of jobs by the end of the year. These hopeful—and, in the summer of 1990, widely held—views were based on the assumption that the elimination of restrictions would be sufficient to stimulate rapid expansion of the East German private sector. The more radical the break with the Communist past and the more rapid the introduction of the West German economic system, the greater the success of economic restructuring.

By contrast, the theoretical argument of the present analysis suggests that the more ambitious and radical the attempts at socio-economic transformation, the greater the likelihood of producing unintended consequences that will work against the realization of the original political and ideological goals. The virtual collapse of the GDR's state sector in the wake of the monetary and economic union, while clearly not anticipated, can perhaps be explained and justified as a necessary price to be paid for the introduction of an ultimately healthy market order—though I will dispute this argument below. But what came as a surprise even to

---

This chapter was completed in April 1991.

East German private entrepreneurs were the negative consequences of rapid transformation for the private sector. I will now examine to what extent these consequences are due to the rapid dismantling of the existing institutional infrastructure in the GDR. The discussion will follow the same lines laid out in Chapter 8 where the potential contribution of this institutional infrastructure under conditions of more gradual reform was explored.

The 140,000 private businesses operating in the GDR in 1989 seemed well-positioned to take advantage of the market conditions created with the monetary, economic, and social union between the two German states in July 1990. Freed from the numerous restrictions imposed upon them by the socialist state, they were widely regarded as the nucleus of a dynamic East German private sector of small and medium-sized enterprises. This optimism was shared by many GDR entrepreneurs, who in the summer of 1990 prepared for modernization and expansion of their businesses. Monetary union meant that they were now able to purchase Western products—cars, machines, supplies, etc.—and to secure bank loans for investment. Two basic problems of the GDR private sector had thus disappeared virtually overnight: scarcity of materials and political limitations on expansion. The entrepreneurial and professional skills that had been preserved under socialism constituted the foundation for the expansion of the existing private sector, to be complemented by new private firms and privatized state enterprises.

By the end of 1990, it had become evident that the high hopes for dynamic economic development in East Germany initiated and sustained by the private sector would be disappointed. True, almost 200,000 new commercial licenses were issued in 1990, thus roughly doubling the number of self-employed in the former GDR. Yet about half of this growth is accounted for by small service enterprises (mainly in the retail and restaurant sectors). By contrast, in the traditionally dominant handicraft sector only about 30,000 new licenses were issued, while many established handicraft firms were forced to lay off employees. Less than 2,000 new manufacturing enterprises were established, while the privatization of the old state sector was proceeding very slowly. These general trends in private sector growth have been extremely disappointing given the expectations connected with the marketization of the GDR economy. They point to a set of fundamental problems that have adversely affected both the existing private sector and the growth of a new private sector. These problems are directly related to the speed and radical character of socio-economic transformation.

First, the introduction of the Deutsche mark on July 1 was accompanied by a 50 percent *devaluation* of liquid assets. Due to the SED's restrictive investment policy for the private sector, most private entrepreneurs held a large share of their accumulated capital in liquid assets. At a time when their opportunity and need for investment was greatly increased, they were deprived of funds. At the same time, *costs* of resources and technology rose drastically as the price system quickly adapted to West German levels. Moreover, the East German private sector was exposed to *competition* as West German firms (especially in retail trade) expanded into the GDR market, and East Germans increasingly bought products and services in West Germany. GDR entrepreneurs were caught in a double-bind. On the one hand, they had to learn very quickly how to produce and market their services according to West German standards in order to be competitive. On the other hand, they were undercapitalized, and access to capital was difficult for reasons discussed below.

Second, *property rights* have not been secure. The West German government in its negotiations with the GDR insisted that all private property nationalized or otherwise expropriated since 1949 must be returned to its original owners, many of whom live in West Germany. This has created a flurry of applications for restitution (over 1 million by the end of 1990) bogging down East German registration offices and courts. As a result, some private entrepreneurs have lost, or are in danger of losing, title to their commercial property. More important, the fact that title to a large number of potential industrial sites and commercial properties is still contested or may become so in the future means that new investors hesitate to make financial commitments. In addition, it is difficult or impossible to secure bank loans on the basis of questionable property rights.

Third, the GDR *state sector* has all but collapsed. The funds made available to the *Treuhand-Anstalt,* the newly created institution responsible for the management and privatization of East Germany's approximately 8,000 state enterprises, proved insufficient. As a result, a large number of state enterprises became illiquid and/or failed to pay their suppliers. Combined with East German consumers' almost wholesale rejection of products made in GDR after the monetary union and the drastic cutbacks of orders by other former CMEA countries, the GDR's state sector saw a steep decline in output in 1990. This has also affected existing private firms that relied on the state sector as both supplier of materials and buyer of services. Moreover, the uncertain fate of many state enterprises, massive layoffs, and the profound insecurity among East Germany's workforce have sharply reduced the demand for products and services supplied by East Germany's "old" private entrepreneurs.

The discontinuity in the institutional infrastructure integrating the GDR private sector into state and economy has been most pronounced and radical in the area of public administration. As already mentioned, with unification state bureaucracies at central and district levels were eliminated, and a new administrative structure in the five East German *Länder* is being established. While at county and municipal levels, which were the most important for the private sector under socialism (see Chapter 5), there has been a formal continuity of state bureaucracies, they have to adapt to the administrative code of the Federal Republic. Thus, local state bureaucrats are faced with the enormous task of learning to operate in an entirely new framework of rules and regulations that assigns considerably greater powers and responsibilities to local levels of government than was the case in the GDR's highly centralized political system.

At the same time, the functions of economic administration that the state apparatus fulfilled in the centrally planned economy—allocation of supplies, investment goods and capital, commercial space, manpower, price-setting, etc.—have been significantly reduced or entirely eliminated in the new system. In these respects, the private sector has been freed from a restrictive set of rules, regulations, and practices. Nevertheless, the unintended consequences of the radical restructuring of the administrative system have affected the private sector as well.

First, despite large infusions of capital from Bonn, the collapse of the state economy and the introduction of a new revenue collection system have created a pervasive fiscal crisis of the state. This has required cancellation of service contracts and public projects particularly at the local level, in which GDR handicraft firms participated. On the other hand, most of the large-scale public investment projects that have been launched, such as the replacement or upgrading of the telecommunications system, can only be carried out by large West German firms. Second, the predominant share of commercial space is still state-owned. Private entrepreneurs in the GDR have always confronted the problem of securing scarce business space from the state administration. While scarcity continues to be a problem, East German entrepreneurs now have to compete with West German investors for space. In their scramble for financial resources, local governments give preference to the highest bidders, which in most cases are the economically stronger and more experienced West German firms. Third, as pointed out above, the task of determining title to property is hopelessly overloading the capacity of local bureaucracies. This is slowing down private sector expansion and maintaining an atmosphere of insecurity. Finally, East German entrepreneurs are at a distinct disadvantage compared to West German investors, who are familiar with the legal and regulatory system governing the private economy that now also applies in the former GDR.

In the socialist GDR, the private sector was institutionally integrated with the state economy, albeit in a subordinate position (see Chapter 6). State enterprises were given preference in the allocation of supplies, commercial space, and market shares. Again, institutional discontinuity would seem to be a blessing for East Germany's private firms. Yet the speed and radical character of transformation has, also in this respect, produced unintended consequences that are negatively affecting the "old" private sector. The virtual collapse of the state economy in the wake of the monetary and economic union has disrupted traditional supply channels for East German private firms and reduced the demand for their services by state enterprises. Of course, GDR entrepreneurs at the same time have gained access to Western suppliers. But the integration into Western supply networks is in many cases more difficult than it might appear at first glance. Such networks have evolved in West Germany over a long period of time, and they are adapted to Western markets and firms. Quite apart from the learning process required on the part of an East German entrepreneur, such supply channels may not be suitable for the specific needs of the underdeveloped East German market. In addition, the "old" East German private sector is undercapitalized, and East German markets are highly volatile.

In one sense, there is an ironic institutional "continuity" creating serious problems for East German private firms. Particularly in retail trade, West German chains have purchased GDR state enterprises which traditionally had a dominant market position (e.g. supermarkets). With their aggressive and well-tried marketing strategies, they are formidable, if not deadly, competitors for the independent East German retailers that are still in the early stages of learning to operate in the new market environment. The East German entrepreneur's new freedom has been obtained at the price of losing a restricted though secure market share—with practically no time for adapting to new conditions.

The Chambers of Handicraft and the Chambers of Trade, under socialism the organizational link between the state and the private sector, quickly emerged as genuine interest representatives of the private sector in the period of "democratic awakening," as described in Chapter 8. Moreover, in early 1990, numerous independent business associations emerged in the GDR. Both the Chambers and other associations were quickly integrated into the established structures of Chambers and industrial associations of the Federal Republic. Since the fall of 1989, particularly the West German Chambers of Handicraft have provided extensive logistical and financial support to their East German counterparts. Clearly, the political, economic, and administrative discontinuity I have discussed has not weakened or destroyed this particular element of the private sector's institutional infrastructure. Rather, it has strengthened the organizational structure of existing Chambers, as well as extended the system of industrial and business associations to East Germany.

However, it is questionable whether this organizational strengthening of organizations for the private sector has also increased their effectiveness. First, like any other surviving institution, the Chambers face the enormous challenge of quickly adapting to the new environment. At the same time, the problems of their old members have changed fundamentally. Thus, organizational continuity has not translated into functional continuity, as the Chambers' functions under the new system have been redefined, again with very little time for adaptation. Second, while West German Chambers have offered invaluable assistance and contributed their own experience as organizations representing the private sector, this experience is of limited relevance for the different conditions existing in a process of rapid transformation. Third, even to the extent that the reconstituted Chamber system does effectively represent the concerns of the East German private sector, their input into the decision-making process is very limited. For the relevant state agencies to which these concerns have to be addressed are still in the process of reestablishing themselves, and they are in any case hopelessly overloaded by the vast range of new tasks they have to deal with. This means that regular channels of communication need to be established, and practices of interest mediation developed before the Chambers can begin to represent the interests of the private sector in the policy-making process. Thus, despite a significant degree of institutional continuity in this aspect of the private sector's infrastructure, the discontinuity in most other social and economic institutions—at least for the time being—seriously hampers their work as effective interest representatives.

This brings us to the final element to be considered in this discussion of the effects of rapid and wholesale change for the private sector. Under socialism, the Bloc parties CDU, LDPD, and NDPD had the official task of representing the non-working class groups in society, in particular the self-employed (see Chapter 7). Like the Chambers, they had in fact a curious double function. On the one hand, they were enjoined by the state to assist in the implementation of public policy, and their work was monitored and controlled by the SED. On the other hand, they articulated the concerns, grievances, and demands of private entrepreneurs and communicated them to state and party officials. In the period of "democratic awakening", particularly the CDU and the LDPD blossomed into genuine political representatives of and for the East German private sector (see Chapter 8).

From January 1990, there was a groundswell of popular sentiment in the GDR for rapid unification with the Federal Republic. The first free parliamentary elections in the GDR in March were dominated by the unification issue. The West German Christian Democrats adopted the former East German Bloc party CDU, designed and stage-managed its election campaign, and, with the promises of Chancellor Helmut Kohl for early monetary and economic union between FRG and GDR, led the party to victory. The two other former Bloc parties representing the private sector, LDPD and NDPD, had not found West German partners to provide political, financial, and logistical support. The LDPD, in alliance with two newly founded liberal parties, managed to secure just over 5 percent of the vote, while the NDPD with less than 0.4 percent dwindled into political insignificance. The NDPD was dissolved in the summer of 1990, and the LDPD was united with the new East German Free Democrats (FDP) prior to the *Land* elections in October. New party apparatuses were set up at the *Land* level. With unification in October, the East German CDU and FDP at the central level have been incorporated into the national party organizations of the Federal Republic.

Thus there has been very little institutional continuity as these former Bloc parties, if not simply disbanded (NDPD), were fundamentally reorganized (CDU) or amalgamated with other parties (LDPD), ultimately to become small and politically insignificant components of much larger, more powerful, and firmly established West German party apparatuses. While East German entrepreneurs, like the GDR population at large, have looked towards the West German party system for new orientations and identifications, it remains questionable whether the imported political approaches and programs correspond to the realities and problems of the East German private sector. At the national level, ideological exhortations of the merits of a liberal market order have been a poor substitute for policies based on a sober assessment of the specific problems of East Germany's private entrepreneurs. At the level of the new East German *Länder,* the problem load is so enormous and the administrative capacity still so underdeveloped that little attention can be given to the specific concerns of the old and new private entrepreneurs. In part, the lack of effective representation is simply due to the growing size and diversity of the private economy. In addition to the established entrepreneurs and the significant number of new small businesses that have started up, political priority is given to the privatization of the crisis-ridden state enterprises that employed the bulk of the GDR workforce. But the basic problem is of a more general nature. The East German *Länder* do not necessarily speak with one voice, and in the *Bundesrat,* the Chamber representing the *Länder* at the national level, they are in a minority. With the demise of their state, East Germans as a whole, and private entrepreneurs in particular, have lost their political institutions and thus to a large extent any collective capacity to deal with the problems of transition.

The "Old" Private Sector as a Test Case
for the Radical Transition Strategy

The fate of the private sector in East Germany is obviously only a small facet of the radical and rapid restructuring of the entire socioeconomic and political system. But, from a theoretical point of view, it is of particular interest. The transformation of a socialist society should provide very favorable conditions for the private economy. Successes and failures in this respect are therefore particularly sensitive indicators of more fundamental problems inherent in a strategy of wholesale socio-economic change. They point to deeper structures and institutional relationships that play a crucial role in maintaining the stability and functioning of an economy and society and in shaping processes of change.

Our knowledge of these deep structures of society is limited. Our knowledge of how to successfully engineer institutional change is even more superficial. The political collapse of Communism and the comparatively poor record of centrally planned economies have fed the illusion that parliamentary democracy and a market economy are the natural order of things for industrial societies in the late 20th century. It is widely assumed that there is a basic set of formal institutions that makes this order work. Hence the task of bringing about the transition from Communist autocracy to capitalist democracy is reduced to establishing these basic political and economic institutions in as rapid and comprehensive a fashion as possible. The immense difficulties encountered in all former Communist countries are widely seen as a consequence of their failure to create this new institutional infrastructure with sufficient speed and resolve.

It may be noted in passing that the basic structure of this argument bears a strong resemblance to arguments relating to the Communist transformation project and the response of Communist regimes to problems—especially economic crises—in their early phases of building socialism. These problems were usually explained in terms of the resistance put up by old structures, institutions, and classes to the establishment of the new socialist order. And the speeding up of the process of transition and the intensification of the class struggle were seen as the solutions. The survival of the private sector in the GDR and its integration into socialism (discussed in Chapters 2 and 3) were a result of pragmatic compromises and their unintended consequences in the face of overwhelming difficulties emerging in the pursuit of this radical strategy of transition. It is quite probable that such compromises, with similarly lasting consequences for the type of socio-economic order that will ultimately emerge, will have to be made in all post-Communist societies where radical strategies of transformation are pursued.

Now the crucial question is whether such compromises are to be regretted, or whether they represent more realistic and less socially costly ways of changing Communist societies in principle. This question is of the utmost importance because the answer determines whether a radical strategy or a gradualist strategy of change should be endorsed. According to the radical view, it is preferable to forcefully push ahead with the fundamental restructuring of society towards the goal of capitalist democracy because short-term costs will be outweighed by the long-term benefits of approaching the goal more closely. According to the gradualist view, it is preferable to make compromises an integral part of the strategy of transformation. The reason is that short-term costs may prove so enormous that they will pose powerful obstacles on the way to reaching the goal.

Both views are based on assumptions concerning the process and manageability of change, the relative validity of which is difficult to establish. The radical strategy of the Communists was justified by the presumed knowledge of objective historical laws that made the transition policies appear much less arbitrary and voluntaristic than they actually were. The radical strategy of the 1990s is justified by the presumed knowledge of what are the essential political and economic institutions that fulfil the systemic requirements of late 20th century industrial society and the needs and aspirations of its citizens. There are two significant asymmetries between these two radical views. First, today's radicals can justify their position with reference to the fact that the socio-economic and political order they seek to create actually exists, rather than being a mere ideological construct. Second, whereas Communists confidently relied on historical forces to propel the process of transition to socialism, today's radicals have no explicit theory of transition. Implicitly, however, the assumption is that the key to a successful transition is the speedy and comprehensive establishment of what are seen as the basic economic and political institutions of Western industrial society.

It is important to distinguish these two asymmetries. For while the first asymmetry does indeed lend considerable support to today's radical view, the second points to its major weakness. The feasibility of a transition strategy cannot be justified in terms of the realism and viability of its goals. The Communists' radicalism failed on account of the utopianism of its goals, which by implication doomed any transition strategy. Today's radicalism may fail not on account of the utopianism of its goal (it is, in fact, quite realistic as such), but on account of its utopian transition strategy. The central problem of any radical transition strategy is, as I have argued throughout this analysis, that wholesale institutional change will produce a range of unintended consequences that may undermine the realization of the original goal.

The former GDR provides an ideal testing ground for the relative strength of the radical position and of my critique, which supports a more gradualist strategy. The two treaties concluded between the FRG and the GDR—on monetary, economic, and social union and on unification—established the conditions that, according to the radical view, need to be fulfilled in order to make a successful transition to parliamentary democracy and a social market economy: the speedy creation of what are considered the essential political and economic institutions and rules of capitalist democracy. Two further conditions are favorable for the transformation project in East Germany: the virtually complete elimination of political resistance to change by old vested interests in the state bureaucracy as a result of the comprehensive reorganization of the political and administrative system; and massive financial, logistical, and personnel support from West Germany in setting up and operating the new institutions.

The situation in East Germany in early 1991 was characterized by skyrocketing rates of unemployment, serious problems with the privatization of state enterprises, and a widespread sense of hopelessness and first manifestations of social unrest among East Germans. Compared to the contraction of the state sector, expansion in the private sector was very modest. A snapshot of transition problems at any one point in time, particularly in this early phase, is of course not sufficient to reject the radical transformation strategy as a whole as inadequate. It is fair to say, however, that the scale of economic and social problems that emerged in 1990 was not anticipated by proponents of the radical position. In this sense, they were unintended consequences. Nevertheless, these transitional problems may be of a temporary nature, and they may be corrigible by new measures and policies that had not been considered necessary before. Unintended consequences obviously are unavoidable in any attempt to bring about fundamental changes in a socio-economic order. The crucial question for the purposes of the present argument is whether there are unintended consequences of a lasting nature—consequences that cannot be corrected and ultimately subvert basic goals of the transformation.

Any systematic and balanced assessment will have to await future developments. I will offer here some speculations and conjectures about unintended consequences of radical transformation that seem to point to the emergence of problems, political responses, measures, and ultimately the emergence of new structures and institutions that will represent at the very least significant deviations from, if not subversions of, the original objectives and expectations. Clearly, these considerations can offer only indirect support for a gradualist strategy of change. They do however underline the need for discussing the viability of a gradualist approach to economic reform.

The main problems encountered by East German private firms in the first year of the transition period can be directly attributed to the speed and radical character of reform. They were all unintended consequences of an approach that aimed to create the most favorable conditions for the private sector. The single most devastating factor affecting private firms was the collapse of the state economy. The simplistic assumptions guiding the marketization of the East German economy encouraged faith in the automaticity and self-healing forces of a jumpstarted liberal market order. When economic activity went on a course of sharp and continuous decline, policy-makers were caught by surprise. Without the massive infusion of capital since the summer of 1990 designed to facilitate currency conversion, postpone layoffs in the state economy, and provide financial guarantees to fulfil export contracts with CMEA countries, the collapse of the East German economy would have been immediate. But clearly the expectation was that this large-scale capital transfer would provide a boost to the East German economy which under market conditions would quickly generate its own growth dynamic.

It was further assumed that while some non-competitive state enterprises would be reorganized or shut down, the bulk of the state sector could be sold off to private investors who, together with East Germany's small and medium-sized private firms, would manage the country's economic transition to capitalism. The role of the federal government was to be limited to providing "initial-push financing" (*Anschubfinanzierung*) for state enterprises, local state budgets, and social insurance funds. By early 1991, it had become evident that this *laissez-faire* policy approach had failed. By April, the Bonn government was moving towards a more activist policy approach. In particular, the *Treuhand* agency in charge of the East German state enterprises was instructed to give higher priority to preserving state enterprises over privatizing them at all cost in order to save jobs; additional funds were committed to this and other policy measures; and more flexible regulations governing the restitution of property were adopted in order to expedite the process of settling pending claims. At the political level, this policy reorientation has found expression in a greater willingness on the part of the ruling Christian Democrats to consult with the Social Democratic opposition in the formulation of specific policies and measures for the East German economy.

The current phase of the restructuring process (spring 1991) bears an astonishing resemblance to the periods of pragmatism in the SED's private sector policy that followed the party's "socialist offensives" of 1948/49, 1952/53 and 1958-60 (see Chapters 1 and 2). In each case, ideologically inspired radical measures aimed at speeding up the transition to the new order resulted in economically disastrous consequences that prompted the Communist policy-makers to reverse some of their policies. However, if one compares the scope and speed of Communist transition policies with those of the current transition, it is evident that the present transformation is considerably more rapid and radical than anything East German Communists ever attempted to do. There are several reasons for this. First, today's (West) German decision-makers can feel politically much more secure than East German leaders ever could. An overwhelming majority of East Germans endorsed unification; the CDU/CSU-FDP coalition received a strong mandate from German voters in the elections of December 1990; and the German government is acting in a rather favourable international environment. Moreover, the current transition is occurring in the framework of a very strong West German economy that can provide huge amounts of capital for the integration and development of a relatively small East German economy.]

Are the Unintended Consequences of the Radical Transition Strategy Reversible?

Favourable conditions give policy-makers a sense of confidence in the realizability of their ambitious ideological goals that may not be justified if the enormity of the task is assessed in more realistic terms. It is only when serious unintended consequences become visible that ambitions are tempered, goals scaled down, and policies reversed. The problem is, however, that some changes may be irreversible by the time it is recognized that they should not have been attempted. Let us briefly review the most important policies and their unintended consequences from this perspective.

The single most important and consequential set of policies was introduced with the monetary and economic union of the two German states in July 1990.[This strategy of instant marketization through currency reform, full economic integration, and privatization produced the most disastrous unintended consequences. First, East German consumers spent their newly gained purchasing power almost exclusively on West German products. Second, as a result of this and because of the disruption of the East German economic system, the state sector all but collapsed. Third, this strongly affected both the existing private economy in the GDR and the enthusiasm of new investors, who were expected to create a large number of jobs to absorb the workforce released from state enterprises. The most devastating consequence is an unemployment rate projected to be anywhere between 30 and 50 percent or more by the end of 1991.]

There is an additional set of unintended consequences that have been generated by the political unification of Germany. Its relative contribution to the current crisis is more difficult to assess, though there can be no doubt that it has been significant.[First, the ideologically motivated policy of returning all property to its original owners (restitution), rather than giving higher priority to compensation, has created a degree of insecurity and a bureaucratic nightmare that have acted as powerful deterrents to investment. Second, the complete administrative restructuring of the East German state (re-creation of five *Länder* under FRG law) has added fundamental disruption in the state bureaucracy to the disintegration of the state economy.

The rapid move towards monetary and economic union in 1990 was to a considerable extent motivated by a desire to stem the flow of East Germans migrating to the West in search of better career opportunities. But this strategy has backfired. The unintended consequence of very high and rising levels of unemployment is now forcing many East Germans to move to the West to find any work at all. The economic boom in the "old" Federal Republic, again largely an unintended consequence of the unification process, has increased the demand for skilled labour. While the existence of employment opportunities in the West is a blessing for qualified East Germans, it may at the same time permanently deplete the former GDR of substantial portions of its skilled workforce, thus contributing to a vicious circle of economic decline, outmigration, and further de-industrialization.

There is a host of less tangible consequences that are beginning to emerge. Just as the economic union of Germany has left, and indeed even created, a growing disparity between the haves in the West and the have-nots in the East, so political unification has left a body politic deeply divided between the West German "ins" and the East German "outs" who feel more and more like second-class citizens in their new state. The absence of a strong sense of national solidarity, as well as the often arrogant and at times even "colonial" mentality of West Germans vis-à-vis their new fellow citizens, will do nothing to alleviate an already well-established sense of inferiority among many East Germans. In the minds of most West Germans, they will be collectively held responsible for their failure to adapt quickly to the new conditions, while the credit for any successes will be claimed by the economically and organizationally superior West. This is not to say that, as individuals, East Germans do not have a wide range of opportunities for personal advancement and integration in the new Germany. But, from a social-psychological point of view, East Germans with their own identity, history, and culture will not gain the self-respect and sense of collective achievement that may well be a crucial condition for a successful transition. This lack of a positive sense of collective self-identity in East Germany will be all the more painful the greater the number of those who as individuals are left behind in the rapid transition process.

Which of these unintended consequences are merely of a transitory nature and at least in principle reversible; which are causing irreversible damage to the project of reconstructing East Germany? And which of those potentially irreversible consequences could have been avoided if a more gradual strategy of transformation had been followed? I have identified the following set of unintended consequences of the radical transformation strategy: (1) the collapse of the state sector, resulting in massive unemployment, and serious problems in the existing private sector; (2) the restitution of pre-Communist property rights and titles, which has produced hundreds of thousands of claims and created an atmosphere of insecurity for investors; (3) the uninterrupted migration of labour from East to West; and (4) the socio-psychological and political disempowerment of large sectors of the East German population ("colonization", creation of a *de facto* group of second-class citizens).

(1) The unexpected collapse of the East German economy was a direct result of the crash program of economic liberalization introduced by the monetary and economic union of July 1990. It deprived the GDR government of any policy instruments for the temporary protection of its industries, such as exchange rate and tariff policies, which could have facilitated the adaptation of enterprises to the new market environment. To a large extent, this most serious unintended consequence is irreversible. What is to some extent reversible under present economic conditions is the scope of bankruptcies and unemployment. Thus the shift underway since the spring of 1991 from an ideologically orthodox non-interventionist to a pragmatic interventionist policy approach—subsidizing many state enterprises rather than privatizing them, massive government spending on public investment projects—will buy much-needed time for adaptation and reduce lay-offs in some enterprises, albeit at great cost. However, this pragmatic reorientation cannot reverse the structural effects of quick marketization, nor can it induce private investment on a scale sufficient to offset the decline of the state sector. These structural effects are the de-industrialization of East Germany and the emergence of regions with permanent large-scale unemployment.

(2) The initial policy on the property issue has been to give preference in principle to the restitution of real estate to its former owners over the payment of compensation. Like the approach to marketization just discussed, it has been motivated primarily by ideological rather than functional considerations. Its ostensible goal has been to redress the injustice inflicted upon property owners by the Communist regime by restoring the *status quo ante.* The practical difficulties involved in clearly ascertaining rightful title in many cases is creating lengthy legal disputes which hold up the use of such properties for commercial purposes. In addition, this policy frequently is inflicting new injustice upon those who have owned and/or used such property under the Communist regime. While minor modifications have been made to expedite the process of settling contested properties, it is unlikely that a fundamental policy reversal will occur that would give primacy to the principle of compensation. The problem is not that such a reversal would come too late to remove the obstacles to investment and commercial use posed by the policy of

restitution. Rather, the problem is political. The commitment of the Bonn government to this policy has created an interest group in the West of those who stand to gain from restitution. Perhaps equally important, the commitment carries considerable symbolic significance in that it represents the refusal by the West to regard as legitimate any of the political and economic changes instituted by the Communist regime, even if such a view might be justified for functional reasons as facilitating the task of transformation. The policy on property is therefore unlikely to change in principle, though further pragmatic modifications can be expected to occur in the operationalization of this general policy.

(3) The continued flow of labour from East to West is one of the unintended consequences that would seem to be most easily reversible. If and when job opportunities significantly improve in East Germany, many people will decide to migrate from West to East. For this reason, one may assume that this trend will be reversed as soon as the problems discussed above (1) come to be gradually resolved. Yet the very process of East-West migration may negatively affect the economic recovery of East Germany. The still-booming West German economy will continue to absorb especially skilled and highly skilled labour from the former GDR. It is obviously easier to relocate labour than it is to relocate production facilities. A saturation point on the West German labour market will be reached when the West German economy enters a period of recession. But it is difficult to conceive of a situation in which the much larger and more dynamic industrial core of Germany's economy in the West goes into recession while the underdeveloped and depressed East German regions experience a period of dynamic growth. The implication is that unless economic growth in East Germany can outpace economic growth in the West, the trend towards the draining of qualified labour from the East will continue. Individual firms as a rule will give preference to locations that offer an existing pool of qualified labour, as well as the industrial and service infrastructure of established, dynamic industrial growth regions. The unintended consequence of continued East-West migration is thus one factor in the chain of economic collapse and de-industrialization. While to some extent it simply reflects more general economic conditions and prospects, it also further undermines the attractiveness of East Germany as an investment site. As such, it may well become another element in the vicious circle of economic decline in the former GDR.

(4) Whether and to what extent the unintended consequences of rapid transformation that I have labelled earlier as disempowerment, "colonization", and the permanent division between "ins" and "outs" in the Federal Republic is reversible will depend, above all, on the economic opportunities for social mobility available to East Germans in the coming

years. I have argued that any successes in the transition to the new order will be claimed by the West as the representative of this order. Nevertheless, the psychological wounds many East Germans have suffered at the hands of the old regime and the superior new regime will heal to the extent that the economic, social, and political integration process succeeds. On the other hand, however, the collective state of mind of East Germans is so vulnerable that failures will reinforce a pervasive sense of inferiority and marginality that will form the socio-psychological complement to, and perhaps even constitute a powerful causal factor in, the continuing division of Germany.

Between Ideology and Pragmatism: The Failure of the Radical Strategy and the Return to Gradualism

According to conventional wisdom, a *gradualist strategy* of political unification and economic restructuring was not a politically feasible option. While it is undeniable that political pressures for rapid change were great, particularly in the GDR, it is simply not true that a more piecemeal approach could not have become a realistic alternative. The basic preconditions that would have made such an alternative feasible can be easily identified. The West German government would have had to, and certainly could have, insisted on a slower timetable for unification, working out with the new GDR government a schedule of stages for economic reform leading towards monetary and economic union and ultimately full political unification. It is true that such an approach by the West German government would not have been received with great enthusiasm by East Germans whose impatience was only outpaced by their unrealistic expectations of the results that quick unification would produce.

A firm schedule would have given East Germans a guarantee that national unity would be achieved within the foreseeable future. Admittedly, it would not have debunked the idea that more rapid unification represented the best solution. It is quite probable that the inevitable problems of a more gradual transition strategy would have tended to discredit this strategy in the eyes of many East Germans who continued to regard rapid unification as a panacea. The West German government, on the other hand, would not have faced any comparable degree of pressure from its voters in favour of quick unification. To be sure, a variety of factors would have made a gradual strategy vulnerable to political opposition in the West. For example, the in any case immense costs of economic restructuring would have been blamed on an incompetent GDR government, the migration of labour from East to West would have been interpreted as a result of inadequate economic reforms, etc. But it is conceivable that a West German government might have succeeded in defending a gradual strategy as preferable.

Indeed, the Social Democratic opposition seemed to be in favour of a more piecemeal approach, but it was defeated both programmatically and electorally by the Christian Democrats' surprisingly successful mixture of appeals to patriotism and necessity. As I have argued earlier, economic prudence lost out in the political calculus of the Kohl government. While the majority of East Germans quite understandably succumbed to the lure of the quick-fix solution, the West German government was at least aware of some of the potential risks and costs involved. Nevertheless, even more skeptical economic advisers to the government did not predict the serious consequences of rapid and wholesale restructuring that are now emerging. Politically motivated optimism combined with a state of blissful ignorance about possibly disastrous consequences. This disqualified a cautious approach as an expression of a lack of political will and courage to seize a historic opportunity. Could a more gradual strategy of economic transformation and political unification actually have been more successful?

Perhaps the most powerful argument against a piecemeal approach is that it delays what are at any rate necessary and painful adjustments, i.e. that it only postpones the "day of reckoning". In the meantime, it allows "reactionary" or "conservative" forces opposed to fundamental change to preserve their positions, and to slow down or even sabotage the reform process. In short, it wastes valuable time and resources. Admittedly, these may be some of the negative unintended consequences of more gradual reform. However, they can be easily overrated. In my view, they represent the negative side-effects of a strategy that has the great potential benefit of allowing time for adaptation. It should be remembered that even such a more gradual strategy of reform—say, one planned for a five to ten-year period—would still be much more radical and profound than any reform program ever implemented in Western democracies. There is, of course, no guarantee that this opportunity for adaptation will always be successfully used. But it should be clear that without such a period for adjustments and reorientation, social and economic institutions may simply collapse under the strain of radically altered conditions.

Thus, the collapse of the East German economy may have been avoidable if the competitive pressures introduced by the monetary and economic union had been phased in over a period of several years. While undoubtedly many state enterprises would still not have survived and unemployment would have grown to substantial levels, individual enterprises and employees would have had a better chance to adapt to new conditions. Exchange rate and tariff policies, for example, could have preserved a larger market for East German products. Similarly, there would have been more time to assess the implications of different approaches to the property issue, and to give a greater number of East Germans an opportunity to acquire property. Whether a more gradual strategy would have significantly reduced the outflow of labour is doubtful, but fewer people would have been forced to seek employment in the West.

Perhaps most important, East Germans would have been spared the shock of facing the conditions of a competitive market society "overnight". The *de facto* exclusion from substantive citizenship of those who have been put out of work—whether actually unemployed or as idle "short-time workers"—with little prospect for a new career would, at the very least, have been postponed for several years. Psychologically, this time for adjustment might have proved invaluable. There can be little question that a feeling of inferiority vis-à-vis West German society would have prevailed even under conditions of gradual transition. But the gap between expectations connected with unification and the reality of life in a united Germany may have been less stark than it is now. Moreover, time for adaptation would have provided an opportunity for a new social consciousness to arise, as well as for GDR political organizations to define the collective interests of East Germans in a united Germany. This might have reduced the sense of disempowerment currently felt by many East Germans, and it might have created the social and political power to fight the condition of "second-class citizenship", which is now an individual fate at the mercy of market forces and, once again, a powerful and distant state.

The failures of the radical strategy will require pragmatic, piecemeal responses in an attempt to deal with its most serious unintended consequences. It is because radical strategies of change never work out as anticipated that the adoption of a gradualist approach ultimately becomes inevitable. To the extent that unwanted consequences are reversible by abandoning or modifiying a particular policy (e.g. on the property question), such "belated" gradualism may well be able to undo the damage caused by earlier radical measures. However, to the extent that these consequences are irreversible because particular policies cannot be abandoned or effectively modified (e.g. the monetary and economic union leading to the collapse of the East German state sector), "belated" gradualism tends to take the form of reactive, unplanned measures—in short, trouble-shooting. Thus the failure of the East German economy to quickly generate its own growth dynamic after the introduction of comprehensive liberal market conditions in July 1990, as had been expected, has forced the German government to react by pumping more and more money into East Germany. Clearly, this can hardly be called a "strategy" of reform, but rather represents a sequence of haphazard measures designed to stave off the accelerating decline of the East German economy.

In the spring of 1991, the dominant assumption continues to be that before long East Germany will take off into self-sustained growth. But this official ideology is no longer a useful guide for policy-making, and it is increasingly becoming an empty rhetorical shell as the government begins to embark on a course of interventionism and structural policy-making that flatly contradicts basic assumptions of the original radical strategy. Take the following example. The *Treuhand* agency which manages East German state enterprises was set up as a temporary body to oversee and organize the privatization of the old state sector. Its original mandate was premised on the expectation that a large part of the state sector would be taken over by private investors, while a smaller number of enterprises would receive temporary subsidies to become competitive, financed largely from the sale of state-owned assets; the rest would be closed down.

The scope and speed of privatization has remained far below these optimistic expectations. Too few private investors have been interested in purchasing state enterprises, while only a very small number of old state enterprises have managed to reach a level of productivity that would make them competitive. Surreptitiously, the *Treuhand* agency's mandate is being redefined, although lip service continues to be paid to privatization as the overriding goal. In fact, however, the agency is evolving into a permanent institution for the management of state enterprises that cannot (yet) be privatized, but that at the same time cannot simply be closed down since this would add to an already enormous unemployment problem. The agency's bureaucratic apparatus is growing quickly, with several branches set up in each of the new *Länder*. Not surprisingly, the *Treuhand* is far from self-financing, requiring large infusions of capital from the federal government.

The example of the *Treuhand* agency illustrates a more general point. A radical and wholesale strategy of change not only generates a host of serious unintended consequences. It also gives rise to the emergence of hybrid institutions that had no place in the original plan for the new order. They emerge as a result of pragmatic compromises that policy-makers are forced to make when faced with the unintended consequences of their ideological program for change. As I have shown earlier in this study, this is precisely how a sizable private sector came to survive and was integrated into GDR socialism. Such pragmatic compromises and their institution-alization, while representing deviations from the ideological program, may represent positive and constructive adaptations to a social reality that proves much more resistant to conscious transformation than radical ideological conceptions lead us to believe. Just like the gradual integration of the private sector into the East German socialist order generally proved beneficial, so the survival and institutionalization of the *Treuhand* agency may come to play a very positive role in East Germany's transition to a new order. It may provide an institutional framework for policies that can give many state enterprises the necessary time for adaptation, which was ruled out by the radical strategy of marketization.

As these benefits become more evident, there is increasing pressure to make the corresponding adjustments and revisions in the official ideology. The East German Communists developed an elaborate new political economy and philosophy in the 1960s to account for the hybrid institutions that had evolved in the 1950s (see Chapter 3). The need for, as well as the possibility of maintaining, a fairly consistent official ideology is clearly not the same in liberal democracies as it is in Communist regimes. Moreover, given the reality of a mixed economy in West Germany, as well as the existence of sizable state sectors in countries such as Italy and France, the partial revision of the ideology of radical transformation is unlikely to pose a major political problem.

In 1991, the institutional consequences of the transition process in East Germany are only just beginning to emerge. The official optimism is based on false premises, and large-scale unemployment and de-industrialization provide strong support for a pessimistic view of the future. My own view of the future is vague. It maintains that East Germany will be different from both the optimistic and pessimistic scenarios. It will be neither a carbon copy of West Germany nor a permanently depressed and underdeveloped hinterland. Forty-five years of separate development make the carbon copy view too unlikely for anything but the distant future. In this sense, there will be yet another "lost generation" of East Germans whose hopes will be disappointed. At the same time, the hinterland view underestimates the economic strength, political resolve, organizational ingenuity, and cultural discipline of German society. But when the question will arise, why did East Germany not become the fully integrated region of the Federal Republic that the ideology of the policy makers in the early 1990s promised, then part of the answer may be found in the same fundamental problems posed by the tension between ideology and pragmatism that explained the peculiar history of the private sector in the GDR.

Bibliography

East German Sources

Ackermann, Anton. "Gibt es einen besonderen deutschen Weg zum Sozialismus," *Einheit,* 1 (1946), 22–32.

――――. "Produktions-und Eigentumsverhältnisse in der sowjetischen Besatzungszone Deutschlands," *Einheit,* 2, 9 (1947), 844–857.

Appelt, R. "Wesen und Ziele der Blockpolitik," *Einheit,* 9 (1947), 825ff.

Bauernfeind, Alfred, Heinz Buske and Heinz Hümmler. "Die Bündnispolitik der SED mit Komplementären, privaten Unternehmern, Handwerkern und Gewerbetreibenden (1968–1973)," *Jahrbuch für Wirtschaftsgeschichte,* II (1978), 7—27.

――――. "Die Umwandlung der Betriebe mit staatlicher Beteiligung und Privatbetriebe in Volkseigene Betriebe," *Zeitschrift für Geschichtswissenschaft,* Vol. 23, 1 (1975), 5–16.

Beer, Willi. *Kollektive Beratungen—demokratisch, rationell, effektiv.* East Berlin: Staatsverlag, 1982.

Behrens, Fritz. "Zum Problem der Ausnutzung ökonomischer Gesetze in der Übergangsperiode," *Wirtschaftswissenschaft,* 5 Sonderheft 3 (1957), 105—140.

Benary, Arne. "Zu Grundproblemen der politischen Ökonomie des Sozialismus in der Übergangsperiode," *Wirtschaftswissenschaft,* 5, Sonderheft 3 (1957), 62—94.

Berufsberatung zum gesellschaftlichen und persönlichen Nutzen. Kommunalpolitik aktuell. Schriften für Abgeordnete und Mitarbeiter der Staatsorgane. East Berlin: Staatsverlag, 1988.

"Beschluß über das Musterstatut der Einkaufs-und Liefergenossenschaften des Handwerks vom 6. Februar 1986," *Gesetzblatt der DDR,* Sonderdruck 1265. East Berlin 1986.

Bielig, Walter. "Zur Rolle der Steuern im Prozeß der sozialistischen Umgestaltung in der DDR," in *Währung und Finanzen im Reproduktionsprozeß.* East Berlin: Humbold Universität, 1983, pp. 192–195.

――――. "Zu Grundfragen und zur Ausnutzung der Steuern bei der Gestaltung der entwickelten sozialistischen Gesellschaft in der Deutschen Demokratischen Republik." Diss., Humboldt-Universität, East Berlin 1981.

Bielig, Walter and Waltraud Falk. "Die Rolle der Steuerpolitik für die Entstehung und Entwicklung sozialistischer Machtverhältnisse," *Beiträge zur Geschichte der Arbeiterbewegung,* 17, 6 (1975), 990–1002.

Bogisch, Manfred. *Handwerk und Gewerbe in der Politik der LDPD.* East Berlin: Buchverlag Der Morgen, 1979.

Börner, Rolf. *Die Bestrebungen der CDU zur Einbeziehung der Mittelschichten in den sozialistischen Aufbau (1956–1958).* East Berlin: Sekretariat des Hauptvorstandes der CDU, 1967.

Im Bündnis vereint. Beiträge zur Theorie und Praxis der Bündnispolitik. East Berlin: Sekretariat des Zentralvorstandes der LDPD, 1971.

Buske, Heinz, Werner Gahrig, Janine Haschker et al. *Bündnispolitik im Sozialimus.* East Berlin: Dietz Verlag, 1981.

Büttner, Gudrun. "Die historische Entwicklung des sozialistischen Staatshaushaltes in der DDR und seine Rolle beim sozialistischen Aufbau." Diss. A, Humbold-Universität, East Berlin 1982.

Cramer, Werner. "Über den privaten Einzelhandel in unserer Volkswirtschaft," *Einheit,* Vol. 43, No. 10 (1988), 951–954.

Dittmann, Roswitha, Hans Pomerenke and Kurt Schubert. *Die Verantwortung und Arbeitsweise der örtlichen Staatsorgane bei der Leitung der Wirtschaft.* Potsdam-Babelsberg: Akademie für Staats-und Rechtswissenschaft der DDR, 1984.

"Zur Direktive des XI. Parteitages der SED zum Fünfjahrplan für die Entwicklung der Volkswirtschaft der DDR in den Jahren 1986 bis 1990," Berichterstatter: Genosse Willi Stoph. East Berlin: Dietz Verlag, 1986.

Dörschel, Erhard. "Das System der sozialistischen Produktionverhältnisse und seine Vervollkommnung beim Aufbau der entwickelten sozialistischen Gesellschaft in der DDR," *Wirtschaftswissenschaft,* 23, 12 (1975), 1761–1780.

Dorner, Axel and Otto Rennert. "Zur Entwicklung des Binnenhandels während der antifaschistisch-demokratischen Umwälzung auf dem Gebiet der heutigen DDR," *Jahrbuch für Wirtschaftsgeschichte,* 2 (1977), 9–26.

Falconere, Irene. "Zur Rolle der Handwerker und Gewerbetreibenden im gesellschaftlichen Reproduktionsprozeß der DDR unter den veränderten Reproduktionsbedingungen der 80er Jahre," *Wirtschaftswissenschaft,* Vol. XXX, No. 9 (1982), 1337–1352.

Falk, Waltraud. "Allgemeines und Besonderes beim Übergang vom Kapitalismus zum Sozialismus als Ausgangspunkt einer vergleichenden Wirtschaftsgeschichte des Sozialismus," *Jahrbuch für Wirtschaftsgeschichte,* II (1980), 9—30.

_____. "Der Beginn des planmäßigen Aufbaus des Sozialismus in der DDR— Bestandteil des revolutionären Weltprozesses," *Beiträge zur Geschichte der Arbeiterbewegung,* Vol. 14, No. 6 (1972), 956–969.

_____. "Zur Dialektik von Politik, Ökonomie und Ideologie in der Wirtschaftspolitik der SED," *Beiträge zur Geschichte der Arbeiterbewegung,* Vol. 13, special issue (1971), 79–96.

_____. "Die politische, organisatorische und ökonomische Konstituierung des volkseigenen Sektors der Wirtschaft und seine Entwicklung in der ersten Etappe der volksdemokratischen Revolution in der DDR 1945 bis 1950," *Wissenschaftliche Zeitschrift der Humboldt-Universität zu Berlin* (Gesellschafts-und sprachwissenschaftliche Reihe), Vol. XVI, No.1 (1967), 19–32.

Falk, Waltraud and Otto Schröder. "Der Beginn des Übergangs vom Kapitalismus zum Sozialismus in der antifaschistisch-demokratischen Umwälzung, die Ausgangsbedingungen und die Wiederherstellung der Volkswirtschaft der DDR," *Wirtschaftswissenschaft,* Vol. 26, 2 (1978), 193–205.

Falk, Waltraud, Hans Müller and Karl Reißig. "Die historische Bedeutung der II. Parteikonferenz der SED. Die Übergansperiode vom Kapitalismus zum Sozialismus in der DDR— Bestandteil des revolutionären Weltprozesses," *Jahrbuch für Wirtschaftsgeschichte*, II (1972), 11–42.

Finzelberg, Sigtraut. "Die Stärkung der sozialistischen Produktionsverhältnisse und der führenden Rolle der Arbeiterklasse durch die Neubildung volkseigener Betriebe im ersten Halbjahr 1972," *Jahrbuch für Wirtschaftsgeschichte*, I (1975), 13–33.

Frühauf, Erika. "Die Aufgaben der Räte und Bezirke und ihrer Fachorgane bei der Leitung, Planung und Bilanzierung zur Sicherung der bedarfsgerechten Versorgung der Bevölkerung (dargestellt am Beispiel der Getränkeversorgung)," in *Innere und äußere Aspekte der Verwirklichung der Wirtschaftsstrategie in den 80er Jahren*, ed. Akademie für Staats-und Rechtswissenschaft der DDR, 1982, pp. 37–44.

Der Fünfjahrplan 1986–1990. Ed. Sekretariat der Volkskammer der DDR. No. 1, 9th election period (1987).

Gambke, Heinz and Rolf Stöckigt. "Die Bündnispolitik der SED beim Aufbau der entwickelten sozialistischen Gesellschaft," *Zeitschrift für Geschichtswissenschaft*, Vol. 24, No. 4 (1976), 400–414.

Gemeinsam zum Sozialismus. Zur Geschichte der Bündnispolitik der SED. East Berlin: Dietz Verlag, 1969.

Gerlach, Horst. "Die Förderung des Handwerks durch Kredit und Zins" in *Rechtsnormen für das Handwerk. Gesetze, Kommentare, Verordnungen*, ed. Das Neue Handwerk. East Berlin: Verlag Die Wirtschaft, 1978, pp. 182–184.

Gerlach, Manfred. "Bündnispolitik und Parteizusammenarbeit unter der Führung der SED—Fundament unserer Staatsmacht," *Staat und Recht*, Vol.35, 3 (1986), 179–188.

Geschichte der SED. Abriss. East Berlin: Dietz Verlag, 1978.

Ein Gesetz wird Praxis. Kommunalpolitik aktuell. Schriften für Abgeordnete und Mitarbeiter der Staatsorgane. East Berlin, Staatsverlag, 1987.

Gesetz über die örtlichen Volksvertretungen. 3rd ed. East Berlin: Staatsverlag der DDR, 1986.

Gläss, Klaus and Evamaria Krey. "Fragen der staatlichen Leitung auf dem Gebiet der halbstaatlichen Betriebe und der Produktionsgenossenschaften des Handwerks," *Staat und Recht*, 1 (1964), 106–125.

Gläss, Klaus. "Die Zusammenarbeit der Stadtverordnetenversammlung und ihrer Organe mit den Stadtbezirksversammlungen und ihren Organen auf dem Gebiet des Handwerks in der Stadt Leipzig." Diss. A, Leipzig 1962.

Görne, Wolfgang. "Der Beitrag der LDPD zur Einbeziehung von kleinen und mittleren Unternehmen in den sozialistischen Aufbau." Diss. A, Humboldt-Universität Berlin, 1979.

Grabarse, Kurt. "Die Aus-und Weiterbildung im Handwerk", in *Rechtsnormen für das Handwerk. Gesetze, Kommentare, Verordnungen*, ed. Das Neue Handwerk. East Berlin: Verlag Die Wirtschaft, 1978, pp. 118–129.

Handwerk im Sozialismus. Bericht über die Tagung des Präsidiums des Hauptvorstandes der CDU mit Handwerkern am 25. Mai 1973 in der Lutherstadt Wittenberg. Ed. Sekretariat des Hauptvorstandes der CDU. East Berlin 1973.

Handwerker—Bündnispartner. Höhere Leistungen für die sozialistische Gesellschaft. Bericht über die Tagung des Präsidiums des Hauptvorstandes der CDU mit Unionsfreunden aus dem Handwerk am 8. Juli 1977 in Burgscheidungen. Ed. Sekretariat des Hauptvorstandes der CDU. East Berlin 1977.

Hanke, Erich. "Zur Lösung des Widerspruchs zwischen der Bourgeoisie und der Arbeiterklasse in der DDR," *Wirtschaftswissenschaft,* Vol. 9, 5 (1961), 678–694.

Harder, Friedel. "Unser bewährtes Zusammenwirken mit den befreundeten Parteien," *Einheit,* Vol. 43, No. 10 (1988), 889–893.

Harder, Friedel, Rolf Schönefeld and Manfred Zinssler. "Die Rolle der mit der SED befreundeten Parteien im politischen System der DDR," *Staat und Recht,* Vol. 35, 4 (1986), 275–295.

Hartmann, Ulrich. "Die Industrie der DDR in der sozialistischen Revolution. Zu Stand und Problemen industriegeschichtlicher Forschungen," *Jahrbuch für Wirtschaftsgeschichte,* 3 (1984).

Haschker, Janine. "Zur Bündnispolitik der SED gegenüber den Handwerkern und Gewerbetreibenden nach dem VIII. Parteitag der SED," *Zeitschrift für Geschichtswissenschaft,* Vol. 29, 2 (1981), 987–95.

Heinrichs, Wolfgang. "Zur Einbeziehung des privaten Einzelhandels in den sozialistischen Aufbau der DDR," *Wirtschaftswissenschaft,* 5, 6 (1957), 835–847.

Hensel, Dieter and Günter Kuciak. "Zum Einfluß der Reprodukionsbedingungen auf die Rolle kleiner und mittlerer Betriebe und Betriebsteile in Kombinaten der verarbeitenden Industrie," *Wirtschaftswissenschaft,* 32, 3 (1984), 363–380.

Herrmann, Joachim. "Bündnispolitik unserer Partei gestern und heute," *Einheit,* Vol. 43, Nos. 11/12 (1988), 978—984.

Heuer, Uwe-Jens et al. *Wirtschaftsrecht.* East Berlin: Staatsverlag der DDR, 1985.

Heuer, Uwe-Jens. *Recht und Wirtschaftsleitung im Sozialismus. Von den Möglichkeiten und von der Wirklichkeit des Rechts.* East Berlin: Staatsverlag der DDR, 1982.

Horn, Werner. "Der Prozess der Entwicklung der Kommissions- und privaten Einzelhändler zu sozialistischen Werktätigen in der Etappe des umfassenden Aufbaus des Sozialismus in der DDR." Diss. B, Leipzig 1968.

Hoyer, Lutz. "Ideologiegeschichtliche Probleme der LDPD in der Übergangsperiode vom Kapitalismus zum Sozialismus," *Deutsche Zeitschrift für Philosophie,* Vol. 33, No. 11 (1985), 961–970.

Hümmler, Heinz. "Zur Bündnispolitik unserer Partei," *Einheit,* 2 (1988), 182–186.

Industriekombinate und Vergesellschaftung von Produktion und Arbeit. Autorenkollektiv, Ltg.: Werner Maiwald. East Berlin: Verlag Die Wirtschaft, 1981.

Kästner, Hartmut. "Die Überwindung des Privatkapitals in der Großindustrie Sowjetrußlands bzw. der UdSSR (1917 bis Ende der 20er Jahre)," *Jahrbuch für Wirtschaftsgeschichte,* 3 (1984).

Kaiser, Monika, Christel Klose and Ursula Münch. "Zur Blockpolitik der Sozialistischen Einheitspartei Deutschlands von 1955 bis 1961," *Zeitschrift für Geschichtswissenschaft,* Vol. 30, 12 (1982), 1059–1071.

Keßler, Ruth. *Ausgewählte Probleme der Leitung einer Stadt.* East Berlin: Staatsverlag, 1981.

Kinze, Hans Heinrich, Hans Knop and Eberhard Seifert, eds. *Sozialistische Volkswirtschaft*. East Berlin: Verlag Die Wirtschaft, 1983.

Kirchhoff, Werner. "Im Bündnis mit allen Kräften des Volkes," *Einheit*, Vol. 41, 6 (1986), 531–536.

Klatke, Heinz. "Die weitere Einbeziehung des privaten Einzelhandels in den sozialistischen Aufbau der DDR". Diss. A, Humboldt Universität, East Berlin 1963.

Kleines Politisches Wörterbuch. 6th ed. East Berlin: Dietz Verlag, 1986.

Körner, Gustav. "Die Perspektive des Handwerks und ihre planmäßige Festlegung beim Aufbau des Sozialismus in der DDR." Diss. A, Dresden 1961.

Kratsch, Ottomar. "Entwicklungstendenzen der sozialistischen Produktionsverhältnisse," *Wirtschaftswissenschaft*, Vol.23, No.12 (1975), 1781–1797.

Krubke, Erwin. *Wirtschaftspolitik zwischen Gestern und Morgen. Die Stellungnahme der CDU zur Herausbildung der sozialistischen Planwirtschaft in der DDR in Gestalt des Zweijahrplanes 1949/50 und des ersten Fünfjahrplanes 1951/1955*. East Berlin: Christlich-Demokratische Union, 1977.

Kross, Herbert. "Bank fördert Leistungen des Handwerks," *Sozialistische Finanzwirtschaft*, 27, 4 (1973), 20–22.

Lehmann, Horst. "Der Beitrag des Handwerks zur Erfüllung der Hauptaufgabe," *Einheit*, Vol. 32, 7 (1977), 877–880.

Leistungen vergleichen—Erfahrungen auswerten. Kommunalpolitik aktuell. Schriften für Abgeordnete und Mitarbeiter der Staatsorgane. East Berlin: Staatsverlag, 1988.

Lemm, Joachim. "Zu Wesen und Merkmalen der Versorgungsgruppenarbeit auf dem Gebiete der hauswirtschaftlichen Dienstleistungen und Reparaturen," *Wirtschaftswissenschaft*, Vol. 7, 2 (1969), 1678–1691.

Lohse, Eberhard and Siegfried Voigtsberger. "Zur Einbeziehung der halbstaatlichen und privaten Industriebetriebe sowie des allgemeinproduzierenden Handwerks in die perspektivische Entwicklung," *Wissenschaftliche Zeitschrift der Hochschule für Ökonomie*, 8, 3 (1963), 257–274.

Luck, Herbert. "Bemerkungen zum Artikel von Behrens, 'Zum Problem der Ausnutzung ökonomischer Gesetze in der Übergangsperiode," *Wirtschaftswissenschaft*, Vol. 5, special issue 3 (1957).

Mand, Richard, Kurt Schneider and Carola Schultze, "Parteienbündnis und sozialistischer Staat," *Staat und Recht*, Vol. 34, 7 (1985), 546–555.

Mehr handwerkliche Versorgungsleistungen für die Bevölkerung—Ziel unserer Arbeit. Bericht über die Tagung des Sekretariats des Hauptvorstandes der CDU mit Unionsfreunden aus der Versorgungswirtschaft am 26. April 1976 in Burgscheidungen. Ed. Sekretariat des Hauptvorstandes der CDU. East Berlin 1976.

Meister entscheide dich. Handwerker beraten den Siebenjahrplan. Ed. Parteileitung der CDU. East Berlin 1959.

Ministerium für Bezirksgeleitete Industrie und Lebensmittelindustrie, ed. *Rechtsvorschriften für das Handwerk*. East Berlin: Staatsverlag der DDR, 1989.

Ministerium für Handel und Versorgung, ed. *Zur Gewerbetätigkeit privater Einzelhändler und Gastwirte. Erläuterung gesetzlicher Bestimmungen*. East Berlin: Verlag Die Wirtschaft, 1986.

Mittag, Günther. *Die Bedeutung des Buches "Politische Ökonomie des Sozialismus und ihre Anwendung in der DDR" für die weitere Gestaltung des ökonomischen Systems des Sozialismus in der DDR und die Entwicklung des ökonomischen Denkens der Werktätigen.* East Berlin: Dietz Verlag, 1970.

Mühlfriedel, Wolfgang. "Die Wirtschaftsplanung in der sowjetischen Besatzungs-zone von den Anfängen bis zur Bildung der Deutschen Wirtschaftskommis-sion," *Jahrbuch für Wirtschaftsgeschichte,* 2 (1985), 9–30.

_____. "Die Entwicklung der privatkapitalistischen Industrie im Prozeß der antifaschistisch-demokratischen Umgestaltung," *Jahrbuch für Wirtschaftsge-schichte,* 3 (1984).

Müller, Wolfgang. "Bedeutung und Formen der Integration des Handwerks der DDR in die Gestaltung der entwickelten sozialistischen Gesellschaft zwischen 1961 und der Gegenwart." Diss. B, Humboldt-Universität, East Berlin 1978.

_____. "Grundfragen der Planung und Leitung des Handwerks während der Periode des Übergangs vom Kapitalismus zum Sozialismus in der DDR." Diss. A, Humboldt-Universität, East Berlin 1968.

Mussler, Werner. *Der kapitalistische Sektor der Industrie als Problem der Über-gangsperiode zum Sozialismus in der Deutschen Demokratischen Republik.* East Berlin: Verlag Die Wirtschaft, 1959.

_____. "Die privatkapitalistische Industrie und die ökonomische Politik der Arbeiter-und-Bauernmacht," *Einheit,* Vol. 11, 5 (1956), 530–537.

Nagel, Hans-Jürgen. "Die Einbeziehung der Betriebe mit staatlicher Beteiligung in die sozialistische Planwirtschaft beim Aufbau der entwickelten sozialis-tischen Gesellschaft in der DDR," *Jahrbuch für Wirtschaftsgeschichte,* II (1972), 229–240.

Nippert, Erwin. "Die Bündnispolitik der SED zur Einbeziehung der Komplemen-täre, Handwerker und Gewerbetreibenden in die entwickelte sozialistische Gesellschaft in der DDR (Dezember 1965–April 1968)." Diss. A, Humboldt-Universität, East Berlin 1971.

Oelssner, Fred. *20 Jahre Wirtschaftspolitik der SED.* East Berlin: Akademie-Verlag, 1966.

_____. "Staat und Ökonomie in der Übergangsperiode," *Wirtschaftswissenschaft,* Vol. 5, 3 (1957), 321–331.

_____. *Die Übergangsperiode vom Kapitalismus zum Sozialismus in der Deutschen Demokratischen Republik.* East Berlin: Akademie-Verlag, 1955.

_____. "Zu einigen ökonomischen Problemen der Übergangsperiode vom Ka-pitalismus zum Sozialismus in der Deutschen Demokratischen Republik," *Wirtschaftswissenschaft,* Vol. 3, 3 (1955), 299–321.

Örtliche Baukapazitäten schaffen bessere Wohnbedingungen. Kommunalpolitik aktuell. Schriften für Abgeordnete und Mitarbeiter der Staatsorgane. East Berlin: Staatsverlag, 1987.

Parteileitung der Christlich-Demokratischen Union. *Wir arbeiten mit staatlicher Beteiligung.* East Berlin: VOB Union, 1957.

Peter, Willy. "Zum historischen Prozeß der Herausbildung der theoretischen und strategischen Schlußfolgerungen über das Wesen und die Gestaltung der ent-wickelten sozialistischen Gesellschaft in der DDR in den sechziger Jahren bis Anfang der siebziger Jahre," in *Inhaltliche und methodologische Probleme einer vergleichenden Wirtschaftsgeschichte des Sozialismus.* East Berlin: Humboldt-Universität, 1978, pp. 38–57.

Peters, H. and U. Hädrich. "An-und Verkauf mit wachsenden Leistungen und hohem Niveau," *Der Handel,* 35, 6 (1985).

Pilz, Walter and Michael Schulz. *Erläuterungen zur Besteuerung privater Handwerker.* East Berlin: Verlag Die Wirtschaft, 1989.

Pohl, Heidrun and Gerhard Schulze. *Anliegen der Bürger—wie werden sie bearbeitet?* East Berlin: Staatsverlag der Deutschen Demokratischen Republik, 1984.

Politische Ökonomie des Sozialismus und ihre Anwendung in der DDR (Foreword by W. Ulbricht). East Berlin: Dietz Verlag, 1969.

"Rechtsnormen für das Handwerk. Gesetze, Verordnungen, Kommentare," ed. *Das neue Handwerk,* special issue, 2nd ed. (1978).

Reinhold, Otto. "Zur marxistisch-leninistischen Gesellschaftspolitik unserer Partei," *Einheit,* 10/11 (1987), 947–953.

———. "Ökonomische Gesetze des Sozialismus und Wirtschaftspolitik," *Wirtschaftswissenschaft,* Vol. 20, 10 (1972), 1441–1456.

———. "Probleme der Übergangsperiode vom Kapitalismus zum Sozialismus in der DDR," *Einheit,* Vol.25, 4 (1970), 428–437.

———. "Das 35. Plenum und die Wirtschaftswissenschaftler," *Wirtschaftswissenschaft,* Vol. 6, 2 (1958), 161–171.

Richter, Helmut. "Wertgesetz und Spontaneität in der Übergangsperiode," *Wirtschaftswissenschaft,* 5, special issue 3 (1957), 44–61.

Röder, Gerhard. "Zu einigen Aufgaben der Einkaufs-und Liefergenossenschaften des Handwerks," in *Rechtsnormen für das Handwerk. Gesetze, Kommentare, Verordnungen,* ed. Das Neue Handwerk. East Berlin: Verlag Die Wirtschaft, 1978.

Roesler, Jörg. "Strategies and their realisation involving private industrial capital in the socialist construction of the GDR between 1949 and 1959," *Economic Quarterly* (Hochschule für Ökonomie, East-Berlin), No. 4 (1988), 34– 45.

———. "Von der Generalperspektive zum Neuen Ökonomischen System. Wirtschaftspolitische Weichenstellungen in der DDR Ende der 50er/Anfang der 60er Jahre," *Mannheimer Berichte,* Vol. 33 (August 1988), 9–20.

———. "Die Rolle der Leitung und Planung bei der Zurückdrängung des privatkapitalistischen Sektors in der Industrie der Sowjetunion und einiger europäischer Volksdemokratien (zwanziger und vierziger Jahre)", *Jahrbuch für Geschichte der sozialistischen Länder Europas,* Vol. 22, No. 1 (1978), 87–95.

———. "Inhalt und Methodologie des Vergleichs der Herausbildung und Entwicklung sozialistischer Planwirtschaft in allen sozialistischen Ländern," in *Inhaltliche und methodologische Problem einer vergleichenden Wirtschaftsgeschichte des Sozialismus.* East Berlin: Humboldt-Universität, 1978, 128–139.

———. "Die Rolle der Planung und Leitung bei der Umgestaltung der privaten Industrie und des Handwerks in der Übergangsperiode," *Jahrbuch für Wirtschaftsgeschichte,* II (1972), 213–227.

Rumpf, Willi. "Probleme der Finanzpolitik," *Einheit,* Vol.5, 2 (1950), 132–137.

Sandig, Helmut. "Zur Problematik der staatlichen Beteiligung an privatkapitalistischen Betrieben," *Einheit,* 12, 3 (1957), 308–317.

Schenker, Sonja. "Die Einbeziehung der Handwerker, Gewerbetreibenden und privaten Unternehmer in den sozialistischen Aufbau im Bezirk Karl-Marx-Stadt (1956–1961)." Diss. A, Technische Hochschule Karl-Marx-Stadt, 1983.

Schmalfuß, Kurt. "Einige Fragen der Rolle des Bankwesens in der DDR in der Periode der Schaffung der Grundlagen des Sozialismus," in *Währung und Finanzen im Reproduktionsprozeß*. East Berlin: Humbold Universität, 1983, pp. 187–191.

Schmidt, Peter. "Zur Rolle der Finanzen bei der Schaffung der Grundlagen des Sozialismus in den volksdemokratischen Ländern Europas," in *Währung und Finanzen im Reproduktionsprozeß*. East Berlin: Humbold Universität, 1983, pp. 112–120.

————. "Einige Probleme der Untersuchung der Rolle des Finanzwesens—insbesondere der Banken und des Geldes—in der Übergangsperiode," in *Inhaltliche und methodologische Problem einer vergleichenden Wirtschaftsgeschichte des Sozialismus*. East Berlin: Humboldt-Universität, 1978, pp. 152–156.

Schütze, Horst. "Handwerk und Gewerbe—Zwischenbilanz einer Initiative," *Einheit*, Vol. 34, 6 (1979), 651—654.

Schützenmeister, H.-O. "Haushalts-und Finanzwirtschaft und sozialistische Kommunalpolitik," *Staat und Recht*, Vol.37, 2 (1988), 152–163.

Schultze, Renate. "Die Ausarbeitung des Fünfjahrplanes der DDR 1951 bis 1955. Die Reaktion der Werktätigen und der Klassengegner auf seine Verkündigung," *Jahrbuch für Wirtschaftsgeschichte*, 2 (1980), 31–54.

————. "Der verschärfte Klassenkampf auf wirtschaftspolitischem Gebiet in der DDR unmittelbar nach ihrer Gründung," *Jahrbuch für Wirtschaftsgeschichte*, 2 (1977), 45–63.

Schwehm, Dieter. "Die Mitwirkung des Kommissionshandels an der Lösung der Versorgungsaufgaben bei der weiteren Gestaltung der entwickelten sozialistischen Gesellschaft (dargestellt am Beispiel des Bezirkes Karl-Marx-Stadt)." Diss. A, Handelshochschule Leipzig 1973.

Sekretariat des Hauptvorstandes der CDU. "Referat des Parteivorsitzenden der CDU, Gerald Götting, 16. Parteitag der CDU, 14–16 October 1987, Dresden," *Bulletin* (1987).

————. "Referat des Parteivorsitzenden der CDU, Gerald Götting, 13. Parteitag der CDU, 11–14 October 1972, Erfurt," *Bulletin* (1972).

————. "Referat des Parteivorsitzenden der CDU, Gerald Götting, 12. Parteitag der CDU, 2–5 October 1968, Erfurt," *Bulletin* (1968).

Siegmund, Klaus. "Über Entwicklungen im Dienstleistungsbereich," *Einheit*, Vol. 43, 6 (1988), 565–568.

Sorgenicht, Klaus. "Die kameradschaftliche Zusammenarbeit der SED mit den befreundeten Parteien im Demokratischen Block und in der Nationalen Front der DDR—ein wichtiger Faktor zur allseitigen Stärkung der Arbeiter-und-Bauern-Macht," *Probleme des Friedens und des Sozialismus*, Vol. 21, 10 (1978), 1334–1340.

Statistisches Jahrbuch der DDR, annually, ed. Staatliche Zentralverwaltung für Statistik. East Berlin: Staatsverlag der Deutschen Demokratischen Republik.

Steinitz, Klaus. "Zur Entwicklung des Verhältnisses von Produktions- und Dienstleistungssektor in der DDR," in H. Timmermann, ed. *Sozialstruktur und sozialer Wandel in der DDR.* Saarbrücken-Scheidt: Dadder, 1988.

————. "Probleme der sozialistischen Umgestaltung des Handwerks in der DDR," *Wirtschaftswissenschaft,* Vol.7, 8 (1959), 1121–1139.

Stöckigt, Rolf. "Probleme der Bündnispolitik der SED in der Übergangsperiode vom Kapitalismus zum Sozialismus in der DDR," *Beiträge zur Geschichte der Arbeiterbewegung,* Vol. 25, 3 (1983), 340–346.

Stoph, Willi. "Die Rolle der Privatindustrie in der Ostzone," *Einheit,* Vol. 4, 3 (1949), 243–255.

Täglich frische Waren niveauvoll angeboten. Kommunalpolitik aktuell. Schriften für Abgeordnete und Mitarbeiter der Staatsorgane. East Berlin: Staatsverlag, 1987.

Tatzkow, Monika. "Die Entwicklung der Industrie-und Handelskammer der DDR und ihre Rolle bei der Einbeziehung bürgerlicher Schichten in den Aufbau der Grundlagen des Sozialismus, 1953–1958." Diss. A, Akademie der Wissenschaften, East Berlin 1985.

Tomaszewski, Jerzy. "Die Nationalisierung in den europäischen sozialistischen Ländern—Voraussetzungen und Realisierung," in *Inhaltliche und methodologische Problem einer vergleichenden Wirtschaftsgeschichte des Sozialismus.* Berlin: Humboldt-Universität, 1978, pp. 86–102.

Ulbricht, Walter. "Die Bedeutung der marxistisch-leninistischen Theorie für die Entwicklung der Politik der SED," *Einheit,* No.2 (1966).

————. "Fragen der politischen Ökonomie in der Deutschen Demokratischen Republik," *Wirtschaftswissenschaft,* 2, 6 (1954), 593–614.

Unser Weg ist richtig. Veröffentlichung zum 10. Jahrestag der staatlichen Beteiligung am 20. Februar 1966. East Berlin: Sekretariat des Hauptvorstandes der CDU, 1966.

Vom Ich zum Wir. Ed. Parteileitung der CDU. East Berlin 1958.

Wachner, Günter. "Die Sozialversicherung für Genossenschafts-und private Handwerker", in *Rechtsnormen für das Handwerk. Gesetze, Kommentare, Verordnungen,* ed. Das Neue Handwerk. East Berlin: Verlag Die Wirtschaft, 1978, pp. 129–135.

Wachsendes Vertrauen verpflichtet zu steigenden Leistungen. Bericht über die Tagung des Präsidiums des Hauptvorstandes der CDU mit Unionsfreunden aus dem Handwerk am 19. März 1979 in Burgscheidungen. Ed. Sekretariat des Hauptvorstandes der CDU. East Berlin 1979.

Weichelt, Wolfgang et al. *Der Staat im politischen System der DDR.* East Berlin: Staatsverlag der DDR, 1986.

Wieczorek, Evelyn. "Die Politik der SED zur Förderung von Handwerk und Gewerbe in Berlin von 1976 bis 1984," *Beiträge zur Geschichte der Arbeiterbewegung,* Vol. 29, 3 (1987), 391–398.

Wietstruk, Siegfried. *Entwicklung des Arbeiter-und Bauernstaates der DDR 1949–1961.* East Berlin: Staatsverlag, 1987.

Zentralvorstand des Verbandes der Kleingärtner, Siedler und Kleintierzüchter, ed. *Kleingartenwesen, Kleintierzucht, Kleintierhaltung.* East Berlin: Staatsverlag der DDR, 1987.

West German Sources

Brandt, Hans-Jürgen and Martin Dinges. *Kaderpolitik und Kaderarbeit in den "bürgerlichen" Parteien und den Massenorganisationen der DDR.* Mimeographed. West Berlin 1983.

Bundesministerium für Gesamtdeutsche Fragen, ed. *Fünfter Tätigkeitsbericht 1965/69 des Forschungsbeirates für Fragen der Wiedervereinigung Deutschlands.* Bonn und Berlin: Bundesdruckerei, 1969.

_____, ed. *Vierter Tätigkeitsbericht 1961/65 des Forschungsbeirates für Fragen der Wiedervereinigung Deutschlands.* Bonn and West Berlin: Bundesdruckerei, 1965.

Bundesminister für Innerdeutsche Beziehungen, ed. *DDR-Handbuch.* 2 Vols. 3rd rev. ed. Cologne: Verlag Wissenschaft und Politik, 1985.

Burrichter, Clemens. "Zur Kontingenz ideologischer Reformation im wissenschaftlichen Zeitalter. Die Funktionen der Wissenschaften bei der Reparatur des beschädigten marxistisch-leninistischen Orientierungssystems in der DDR," in: *Ideologische und gesellschaftliche Entwicklung in der DDR* (18. Tagung zum Stand der DDR-Forschung in der Bundesrepublik Deutschland, 28. bis 31. Mai 1985), pp. 50–65.

Cassel, D. "Funktionen der Schattenwirtschaft im Koordinationsmechanismus von Markt-und Planwirtschaft," *Ordo,* 37 (1986).

Cornelsen, Doris. "Das Wirtschaftssystem in der DDR— Handlungsbedarf für Reformen?" *Gegenwartskunde,* 1 (1988), 33–44.

Deppe, R. and D. Hoss. "Probleme der Leistungspolitik in der DDR und Ungarn," in ed. Deutschland Archiv, *Die DDR vor den Herausforderungen der achtziger Jahre.* Cologne: Wissenschaft und Politik, 1983).

Deutsches Institut für Wirtschaftsforschung. "Das Gaststättengewerbe in der DDR," *DIW Wochenbericht,* 55, 22 (2 June 1988), 295–300.

_____. "Die Lage der DDR-Wirtschaft zur Jahreswende 1987/88," *DIW-Wochenbericht,* 55, 5 (1988), 59–67.

_____, ed. *Handbuch DDR-Wirtschaft.* 4th rev. ed. Hamburg: Rowohlt, 1984.

Dobias, P. *Die Wirtschaftssysteme Osteuropas.* Darmstadt: Wissenschaftliche Buchgesellschaft, 1986.

Eckart, K. "Die Bedeutung der privaten Anbauflächen für die Versorgung der Bevölkerung der DDR," *Deutschland Archiv,* 16, 3 (1983).

Frenzel, Paul. "Das sozialistische Geldsystem in der DDR: Entstehung und Probleme," *Deutschland-Archiv,* Vol. 21, 7 (1988), 765–777.

Fricke, Karl Wilhelm. "'So liberal wie eigenständig.' Der 13. Parteitag der LDPD in Weimar," *Deutschland-Archiv,* Vol. 15, 5 (1982), 464–466.

Grasemann, Hans-Jürgen. "Das Blocksystem und die Nationale Front im Verfassungsrecht der DDR." Diss., Universität Göttingen, 1973.

Grunenberg, Antonia. "Sinnverlust oder Funktionalisierung? Chancen und Grenzen ideologischen Wandels am Beispiel der Bewußtseinsdebatte," *Ideologische und gesellschaftliche Entwicklung in der DDR* (18. Tagung zum Stand der DDR-Forschung in der Bundesrepublik Deutschland, 28. bis 31. Mai 1985), pp. 3–14.

Haase, Herwig E. "Aktuelle Fragen der Steuerpolitik in der DDR," *Deutschland Archiv*, 10, 6 (1977), 625–635.

Haendcke-Hoppe, Maria. "Struktureffekte der SED-Handwerkspolitik seit 1976", *FS-Analysen* (1988).

──── . "Das private Handwerk in der DDR," *Deutschland Archiv*, Vol. 20, 8 (1987), 843–851.

──── . "Das DDR-Handwerk am Beginn einer neuen Fünfjahrplanperiode 1986–1990," *FS-Analysen*, 3 (1986).

──── . "Möglichkeiten und Grenzen privatwirtschaftlicher Betätigung in der DDR," in Göttinger Arbeitskreis, ed., *Wirtschaftsverfassung und Wirtschaftspolitik in der DDR*. West Berlin: Duncker & Humblot, 1984.

──── . "Neueste Entwicklungen im privaten und genossenschaftlichen Handwerk der DDR sowie in der sonstigen Privatwirtschaft," *FS-Analysen*, 2 (1984).

──── . "Kurskorrekturen in der Handwerkspolitik der DDR," *Deutschland-Archiv*, Vol. 16, 12 (1983), 1276–1284.

──── . "Privatwirtschaft in der DDR. Geschichte—Struktur—Bedeutung," *FS-Analysen*, 1 (1982).

──── . "Das Gaststättenwesen in der DDR". *FS-Analysen*, 4 (1979).

──── . "Handwerkspolitik der SED 1976—ökonomische und ideologische Aspekte der Förderungsmaßnahmen," *FS-Analysen*, 9 (1976).

──── . "Die Vergesellschaftungsaktion im Frühjahr 1972," *Deutschland-Archiv*, Vol. 6, 1 (1973), 37–41.

Haendcke-Hoppe, Maria and K.C. Thalheim. "Wechselwirkungen zwischen Dienstleistungen und Handwerk in der DDR," *FS-Analysen*, 2 (1983).

Haffner, Friedrich. "Die Bedeutung der politischen Ökonomie für die Wirtschaftstheorie und wissenschaftliche Praxis in der DDR," in: *Ideologische und gesellschaftliche Entwicklung in der DDR* (18. Tagung zum Stand der DDR-Forschung in der Bundesrepublik Deutschland, 28. bis 31. Mai 1985), pp. 158–174.

Handwerk und Gewerbe in beiden deutschen Staaten. Ed. Friedrich-Ebert-Stiftung. Bonn: Verlag Neue Gesellschaft, 1976.

Helwig, Gisela. "'Störfälle'. Zum Dialog zwischen Staat und Kirche," *Deutschland-Archiv*. Vol. 21, No. 4 (1988), 340–344.

──── . "Von der Orientierung zur Identifizierung. 14. Parteitag der DDR-CDU," *Deutschland-Archiv*, Vol. 10, 11 (1977), 1121–1124.

Hilgenberg, Dorothea. *Bedarfs-und Marktforschung in der DDR. Anspruch und Wirklichkeit*. Köln: Verlag Wissenschaft und Politik, 1979.

Hofmann, Heinz. *Mehrparteiensystem ohne Opposition. Die nichtkommunistischen Parteien in der DDR, Polen, der Tschechoslowakei und Bulgarien*. Frankfurt: Peter Lang, 1976.

Hohmann, K. "Entwicklung und Bedeutung der privaten Agrarproduktion in der DDR," *FS-Analysen*, 3 (1984).

Krieg, Harald. *LDP und NDP in der "DDR" 1949–1958*. Cologne: Westdeutscher Verlag, 1965.

Krippendorff, Ekkehart. *Die Liberal-Demokratische Partei Deutschlands in der Sowjetischen Besatzungszone 1945/48*. Düsseldorf: Droste Verlag, 1961.

Kulbach, Roderich and Helmut Weber in cooperation with Eckart Förtsch. *Parteien im Blocksystem der DDR. Funktion und Aufbau der LDPD und der NDPD.* Cologne: Verlag Wissenschaft und Politik, 1969.

Kuppe, Johannes. "Ideologie und Außenpolitik der DDR," in: *Ideologische und gesellschaftliche Entwicklung in der DDR* (18. Tagung zum Stand der DDR-Forschung in der Bundesrepublik Deutschland, 28. bis 31. Mai 1985), pp. 111–121.

Lapp, Peter Joachim. *Die "Befreundeten Parteien" der SED. Die DDR-Blockparteien in den achtziger Jahren.* Köln: Verlag Wissenschaft und Politik, 1988.

──────. "Blockparteien im Aufwind? Der 14. Parteitag der LDPD; Der XII. Parteitag der DBD" *Deutschland-Archiv,* Vol. 20, 7 (1987), 729–731.

──────. "Soziale Zusammensetzung der DDR-Blockparteien," *Deutschland-Archiv,* Vol. 20, 4 (1987), 339–341.

──────. *Wahlen in der DDR.* West Berlin: Verlag Gebr. Holzapfel, 1982.

──────. "Die NDPD—eine Partei ohne Zukunft?" *Deutschland-Archiv,* Vol. 15, 6 (1982), 572–575.

──────. "11. Parteitag der NDPD in Leipzig," *Deutschland-Archiv,* Vol. 10, 6 (1977), 577–579.

──────. *Die Volkskammer der DDR.* Opladen: Westdeutscher Verlag, 1975.

──────. *Der Staatsrat im politischen System der DDR (1960–1971).* Opladen: Westdeutscher Verlag, 1972.

Löwis of Menar, Henning von. "Der 13. Parteitag der NDPD," *Deutschland-Archiv,* Vol. 20, 7 (1987), 731–732.

Ludz, Peter Christian. *Mechanismen der Herrschaftssicherung. Eine sprachpolitische Analyse.* Munich 1980.

──────. "Das Innovationspotential des Marxismus-Leninismus in der DDR. Eine sprachpolitische und ideologiekritische Analyse," *Deutschland-Archiv,* 12, 6 (1979), 593–625.

──────. *Ideologiebegriff und marxistische Theorie.* Opladen: Westdeutscher Verlag, 1976.

──────. "Politische Ziele der SED und gesellschaftlicher Wandel in der DDR," in B. Gleitze, P.C. Ludz et al., *Die DDR nach 25 Jahren.* Berlin: Duncker und Humblot, 1975.

Lühmann, Annegret. "Die 'Blockparteien' in der DDR von 1945–1986." M.A. Thesis, Universität Köln 1987.

Mechtenberg, Theo. "Kirche im Sozialismus. Eine kritische Analyse des Staat-Kirche-Verhältnisses in der DDR." *Deutschland-Archiv,* Vol. 21, No. 4 (1988), 380–389.

Meissner, Boris. *Rußland, die Westmächte und Deutschland. Die sowjetische Deutschlandpolitik 1943–1953* Hamburg: Nölke, 1953.

Mleczkowski, Wolfgang. "Bewegung im Monolith. Das sozialistische 'Mehrparteiensystem' der DDR," *Aus Politik und Zeitgeschichte,* Vol. 16–17 (21 April 1984), 3–17.

──────. "Um die Jugend darf nicht geworben werden. Die Liberaldemokraten in der DDR: Stärkeres Selbstbewußtsein durch Zuwachs an Mitgliedern," *Frankfurter Rundschau,* 25 April 1987.

Neugebauer, Gero. *Partei und Staatsapparat in der DDR. Aspekte der Instrumentalisierung des Staatsapparats durch die SED.* Opladen: Westdeutscher Verlag, 1978.

_____. "Die Volkskammer der DDR," *Zeitschrift für Parlamentsfragen,* Vol. 5, 3 (1974).

"12. Parteitag der DBD," *Informationen,* ed. Bundesminister für innerdeutsche Beziehungen, No. 9 (1987), 11–13.

"14. Parteitag der LDPD," *Informationen,* ed. Bundesminister für innerdeutsche Beziehungen, No. 8 (1987), 9–11.

"13. Parteitag der NDPD," *Informationen,* ed. Bundesminister für innerdeutsche Beziehungen, No. 10 (1987), 9–10.

"Privates Handwerk in der DDR soll noch besser gefördert werden," *Informationen,* ed. Bundesminister für innerdeutsche Beziehungen, No. 13 (1987), 11–13.

Richert, Ernst. "Zur Funktion der Ideologie in der DDR seit 1971," *Deutschland Archiv,* No. 7 (1974).

_____. *Macht ohne Mandat. Der Staatsapparat in der sowjetischen Besatzungszone Deutschlands.* 2nd ed. rev. Opladen: Westdeutscher Verlag, 1963.

Roggemann, Herwig. *Kommunalrecht und Regionalverwaltung in der DDR. Einführung in das Recht der Gemeinden, Städte, Kreise und Bezirke.* West Berlin: Arno Spitz, 1987.

_____. *Die DDR-Verfassungen.* 3rd rev. ed. West Berlin: Berlin Verlag, 1980.

Schlenk, Hans. *Der Binnenhandel der DDR.* Cologne: Verlag Wissenschaft und Politik, 1970.

Schlüter, Rolf, ed. *Wirtschaftsreformen im Ostblock in den 80er Jahren.* Paderborn: Schöningh, 1988.

Schütze, Gisela. "Das neue Selbstbewußtsein reicht nicht aus. Die DDR-CDU auf ihrem 15. Parteitag in Dresden," *Deutschland-Archiv,* Vol. 15, 12 (1982), 1248–1251.

_____. "12. LDPD-Parteitag in Weimar," *Deutschland-Archiv,* Vol. 10, 4 (1977), 360–364.

Schwarzenbach, Rudolf. *Die Kaderpolitik der SED in der Staatsverwaltung.* Cologne: Verlag Wissenschaft und Politik, 1976.

Spittmann, Ilse, ed. *Die SED in Geschichte und Gegenwart.* Cologne: Verlag Wissenschaft und Politik, 1987.

Staritz, Dietrich. *Geschichte der DDR 1949–1985.* (Frankfurt: Suhrkamp, 1985).

_____. "Neue Akzente in der SED-Bündnispolitik," *DDR Report,* No. 2 (1983).

Suckut, Siegfried. "Die CDU in der SBZ und die Gründung der SED," *Deutschland-Archiv,* Vol. 20, 6 (1987), 612–623.

_____. *Blockpolitik in der SBZ/DDR 1945–1949.* Cologne: Verlag Wissenschaft und Politik, 1986.

_____. "40 Jahre CDU. Anmerkungen zu einem poitischen Jubiläum," *Kirche im Sozialismus,* No. 4 (1985).

_____. "Die CDU in der DDR," *Association for the Study of German Politics-Journal,* Special Issue, London (1985).

_____. "Die CDU in der DDR. Zu Funktion und Funktionswandel einer christlichen Partei im Sozialismus," *DDR Report,* No. 11 (1982).

———. "Der Konflikt um die Bodenreform in der Ost-CDU: Versuch einer Neubewertung der ersten Führungskrise der Union," *Deutschland-Archiv,* Vol. 15, 10 (1982), 1080ff.

Süss, Walter. "Widerspruchsdebatte und Systemstabilisierung. Zur sozialwissenschaftlichen Verarbeitung der 'politischen Krise' in the UdSSR und DDR," in: *Ideologische und gesellschaftliche Entwicklung in der DDR* (18. Tagung zum Stand der DDR-Forschung in der Bundesrepublik Deutschland, 28. bis 31. Mai 1985), pp. 30–49.

Thalheim , Karl C. and Maria Haendcke-Hoppe. "Das Handwerk in der DDR und Ost-Berlin," *Beilage zum Jahresbericht der Handwerkskammer Berlin* (annually, 1963-1988).

———. "Neue Schwerpunkte in der Handwerkspolitik der DDR," *FS-Analysen,* 2 (1982).

———. "Das Handwerk der DDR zwischen zwei Fünfjahrplanperioden," *FS-Analysen,* 2 (1981).

———. "Das Handwerk in der DDR 1978/1979—Handwerkspolitik und Entwicklung des Handwerks," *FS-Analysen,* 2 (1980).

———. "Das Handwerk in der DDR—Handwerkspolitik und Entwicklung des Handwerks," *FS-Analysen,* 2 (1979).

———. "Das Handwerk in der DDR und Ost-Berlin," *FS-Analysen,* 2 (1978).

van Thiel, Isolde. *Entstehung und Entwicklung des Parteiensystems der DDR 1945-1949 im Spiegel der Pravda.* Frankfurt: Peter Lang, 1981.

Voigt, Dieter, Werner Voss and Sabine Meck. *Sozialstruktur der DDR. Eine Einführung.* Darmstadt: Wissenschaftliche Buchgesellschaft, 1987.

Voigt, Dieter, ed. *Die Gesellschaft der DDR.* Berlin: Duncker & Humblot, 1985.

Vortmann, H. *Geldeinkommen in der DDR von 1955 bis zu Beginn der achtziger Jahre, DIW-Beiträge zur Strukturforschung,* no. 85 (Berlin: Duncker & Humblot, 1985).

Waldrich, Hans-Peter. *Der Demokratiebegriff der SED. Ein Vergleich der älteren deutschen Sozialdemokratie und der sozialistischen Einheitspartei Deutschlands.* Stuttgart: Klett, 1980.

Weber, Hermann. "Geschichte der SED," in Spittmann, Ilse, ed. *Die SED in Geschichte und Gegenwart.* Cologne: Verlag Wissenschaft und Politik, 1987, pp. 6–42.

———. *Geschichte der DDR.* München: dtv, 1985.

Wernet-Tietz, Bernhard. *Bauernverband und Bauernpartei in der DDR.* Cologne: Verlag Wissenschaft und Politik, 1984.

Zieger, Gottfried. *Die Haltung von SED und DDR zur Einheit Deutschlands 1949–1987.* Köln: Verlag Wissenschaft und Politik, 1988.

Ziegler, Uwe. "Die 'bürgerlichen' Parteien der DDR," *DDR Report,* Vol. 20, 5 (1987), 261–262.

Other Sources

Almond, Gabriel A. "Communism and Political Culture Theory," *Comparative Politics,* Vol. 15, No. 1 (1983).

Aron, Raymond. *18 Lectures on Industrial Society*. London: Weidenfeld and Nicolson, 1967.

Aslund, Anders. *Gorbachev's Struggle for Economic Reform*. Ithaca, N.Y.: Cornell University Press, 1989.

_____. *Private Enterprise in Eastern Europe. The Non-Agricultural Private Sector in Poland and the GDR, 1945–83*. New York: St. Martin's Press, 1985.

_____. "Private Enterprise in Poland, the GDR and Hungary," *Bidrag Till Öststatsforskningen*, Vol. 11, No. 1 (1983), 26–33.

Bates, Robert H. "Contra Contractarianism: Some Reflections on the New Institutionalism," *Politics and Society*, Vol. 16, Nos. 2 & 3 (1988), 387–401.

Baylis, Thomas A. "Agitprop as a Vocation: The East German Ideological Elite," *Polity*, Vol. 18, 1 (Fall 1985), 25–46.

_____. A. *The Technical Intelligentsia and the East German Elite*. Berkeley: University of California Press, 1974.

Bell, Daniel. "Ideology and Soviet Politics," *Slavic Review*, 24 (1965), 591–603.

von Beyme, Klaus, and Hartmut Zimmermann, *Policymaking in the German Democratic Republic*. Aldershot: Gower, 1984.

Bielasiak, Jack. "Party Leadership and Mass Participation in Developed Socialism," in *Developed Socialism in the Soviet Bloc: Political Theory and Political Reality*. Boulder, Colo.: Westview Press, 1982.

Bigler, Robert M. "The Role of Bureaucracies and Experts in the Planning and Implementation of Hungary's New Economic Mechanism," *East European Quarterly*, 18, 1 (1984), 93–112.

Breslauer, George. "The Nature of Soviet Politics and the Gorbachev Leadership," in A. Dallin and C. Rice, eds., *The Gorbachev Era*. Stanford, Cal.: Stanford Alumni Assoc., 1986.

Brezinski, Horst. "The Second Economy in the GDR—Pragmatism is Gaining Ground," *Studies in Comparative Communism*, 20, 1 (1987), 85–101.

Brown, A.H. "Policymaking in Communist States," *Studies in Comparative Communism*, Vol. 11, 4 (1978), 424–436.

_____. *Soviet Politics and Political Science*. London: Macmillan, 1974.

Bryson, P.J. *The Consumer under Socialist Planning*. New York: Praeger, 1984.

Bunce, Valerie and John Echols, "Soviet Politics in the Brezhnev Era: Pluralism or Corporatism?" in Donald Kelly, ed. *Soviet Politics in the Brezhnev Era*. New York: Praeger, 1980, pp. 1–26.

Bunce, Valerie. "The Political Economy of the Brezhnev Era: The Rise and Fall of Corporatism," *British Journal of Political Science*, Vol. 13 (April 1983).

Clarke, Roger A. "The Study of Soviet-Type Economies: Some Trends and Conclusions," *Soviet Studies*, 35, 4 (1983), 525–532.

Cohen, Stephen F. *Bukharin and the Bolshevik Revolution*. New York: Knopf, 1973.

_____. *Rethinking the Soviet Experience. Politics and History since 1917*. New York: Oxford University Press, 1985.

Cornelsen, Doris. "The GDR Economy in the Eighties: Economic Strategy and Structural Adjustments," *Studies in Comparative Communism*, Vol. XX, 1 (1987), 39–53.

Dallin, Alexander. "Biases and Blunders in American Studies on the USSR," *Slavic Review,* 32, 3 (1973).

————. "Comment" on P. Hoffman, "The Soviet Union: Consensus or Debate?", *Studies in Comparative Communism,* VIII, 3 (1975), 230–47.

DeBardeleben, Joan. *The Environment and Marxism-Leninism: The Soviet and East German Experience.* Boulder, Colo.: Westview Press, 1985.

Denitch, Bogdan, ed. *Legitimation of Regimes. International Frameworks for Analysis.* London: Sage, 1979.

Eidlin, Fred H. "Soviet Studies and 'Scientific' Political Science," *Studies in Comparative Communism,* Vol. XII, 2&3 (1979).

————. *The Logic of "Normalization".* New York: Columbia University Press, 1980.

————. "Area Studies and/or Social Science: Contextually-Limited Generalizations versus General Laws," in F.H. Eidlin, ed. *Constitutional Democracy: Essays in Comparative Politics.* Boulder, Colo.: Westview Press, 1983.

Elster, Jon. *Making Sense of Marx.* New York: Cambridge University Press, 1985

Fainsod, Merle. *How Russia is Ruled,* rev. ed. Cambridge, Mass.: Harvard University Press, 1963.

Fleron, F.J. "Soviet Area Studies and the Social Sciences: Some Methodological Problems in Communist Studies," *Soviet Studies,* Vol. XIX, 3 (January 1968).

Friedrich, Carl J., ed. *Totalitarianism.* Cambridge, Mass., 1954.

————. "Totalitarianism: Recent Trends," *Problems of Communism* (May–June 1968).

Friedrich, Carl J. and Zbigniew Brzesinski, *Totalitarian Dictatorship and Autocracy.* Cambridge, Mass., 1956.

Gerschenkron, Alexander. "Review" of Part I: Realism and Utopia in Russian Economic Thought, in E.J. Simmons, *Continuity and Change in Russian and Soviet Thought.* New York: Russel and Russell, 1967.

Grote, Manfred. "The SED under Honecker," *East European Quarterly,* 21, 1 (1987), 67–78.

Hewitt, Ed A. *Reforming the Soviet Economy. Equality versus Efficiency.* Washington, D.C.: The Brookings Institution, 1988.

Hollander, Paul. "Observations on Bureaucracy, Totalitarianism, and the Comparative Study of Communism," in Richard Cornell, ed., *The Soviet Political System.* Englewood Cliffs, N.J.: Prentice Hall, 1970.

Holmes, Leslie. *Politics in the Communist World.* Oxford: Clarendon Press, 1986.

Hough, Jerry and M. Fainsod. *How the Soviet Union is Governed.* Cambridge, MA: Harvard University Press, 1979.

Hough, Jerry. *The Soviet Prefects: The Local Party Organs in Industrial Decision-Making.* Cambridge, Mass.: Harvard University Press, 1969.

Jowitt, Kenneth. "Inclusion and Mobilization in European Leninist Regimes," *World Politics* (October 1975), 69–96.

Kanet, Roger E., ed. *The Behavioral Revolution and Communist Studies.* New York: The Free Press, 1971.

Kautsky, John. "Communism and the Comparative Study of Communist Political Systems," in Richard Cornell, ed., *The Soviet Political System.* Englewood Cliffs, N.J.: Prentice Hall, 1970, pp. 54–59.

Krisch, Henry. "Changing Political Culture and Political Stability in the German Democratic Republic," *Studies in Comparative Communism*, Vol. 19, 1 (Spring 1986), 41–53.

_____. *The German Democratic Republic. The Search for Identity.* Boulder, Col.: Westview Press, 1985.

Lane, David. *Politics and Society in the U.S.S.R.* (London: Weidenfeld & Nicolson, 1970).

LaPalombara, Joseph. "Monoliths or Plural Systems: Through Conceptual Lenses Darkly," *Studies in Comparative Communism*, Vol. VIII, 3 (1975).

Lewin, Moshe. *Political Undercurrents in Soviet Economic Debates: From Bukharin to the Modern Reformers.* Princeton: Princeton University Press, 1974.

Ludz, Peter Christian. "Legitimacy in a Divided Nation: The Case of the German Democratic Republic," in: Bogdan Denitch, ed. *Legitimation of Regimes. International Frameworks for Analysis.* Beverly Hills: Sage, 1979.

_____. *The Changing Party Elite in East Germany.* Cambridge, Mass.: MIT Press, 1972

_____. *The German Democratic Republic from the Sixties to the Seventies.* Center for International Affairs, Harvard University, Occasional Paper in International Affairs No. 26, Nov. 1970.

McCauley, Martin. "Power and Authority in East Germany: The Socialist Unity Party (SED)," *Conflict Studies*, 132 (July 1981), 1–28.

_____. *Marxism-Leninism in the German Democratic Republic.* London: Macmillan, 1979.

_____. "Liberal Democrats in the Soviet Zone of Germany, 1945–47," *Journal of Contemporary History*, 12 (1977), 779–789.

McIntyre, Robert J. "Economic Changes without Conventional Reform: Small-scale Industrial and Service Development in Bulgaria and the GDR," in NATO Economics Directorate, *The Economies of Eastern Europe under Gorbachev's Influence.* Brussels: NATO, 1988.

Meyer, Alfred G. "Cultural Revolutions: The Uses of the Concept of Culture in the Comparative Study of Communist Systems," *Studies in Comparative Communism*, Vol. XVI, Nos. 1 & 2 (1983).

_____. "Authority in Communist Political Systems," in Lewis J. Edinger, ed., *Political Leadership in Industrialized Societies* (New York: Wiley, 1967), pp. 84–101.

_____. *The Soviet Political System: An Interpretation.* New York: Random House, 1965.

Moore, Barrington, Jr. *Soviet Politics—The Dilemma of Power.* New York: Harper & Row, 1965.

O'Neill, John, ed., *Modes of Individualism and Collectivism.* London: Heimann, 1976.

Popper, Karl R. *The Open Society and Its Enemies*, 2 Vols., 5th ed., rev. Princeton: Princeton University Press, 1966.

_____. *Conjectures and Refutations.* New York: Harper & Row, 1968.

_____. "The Rationality Principle," in David Miller, ed. *Popper Selections.* Princeton: Princeton University Press, 1985.

Przeworkski, Adam. "Marxism and Rational Choice," *Politics and Society,* Vol. 14, No. 4 (1985), 379–410.

Rigby, T.H. and Ferenc Feher, eds. *Political Legitimation in Communist States.* New York: St. Martin's Press, 1982.

Scharf, C. Bradley. *Politics and Change in East Germany. An Evaluation of Socialist Democracy.* Boulder, Colo.: Westview Press, 1984.

Schmitter, Philippe C. "Still the Century of Corporatism?," in Frederick B. Pike and Thomas Stritch, eds., *The New Corporatism.* Notre Dame: University of Notre Dame Press, 1974.

Schmitter, Philippe C. and Gerhard Lehmbruch, eds., *Trends Towards Corporatist Intermediation.* Beverly Hills: Sage, 1979.

Shlapentokh, Vladimir. "The XXVII Congress—A Case Study of the Shaping of a New Party Ideology," *Soviet Studies,* Vol. XL, 1 (1988), 1–20.

Skilling, H. Gordon and Franklyn Griffiths, eds., *Interest Groups in Soviet Politics.* Princeton: Princeton University Press, 1971.

"Supporters and Opponents of Perestroika: The Second Joint Soviet Economy Roundtable," *Soviet Economy,* Vol. 4, 4 (1988), 275–318.

Taylor, Michael. "Structure, Culture and Action in the Explanation of Social Change," *Politics and Society,* Vol. 17, 2 (1989), 115–162.

Triska, J.F. and P.M. Cocks, eds., *Political Development in Eastern Europe.* New York: Praeger, 1977.

Urban, Michael E. "Conceptualizing Political Power in the USSR: Patterns of Binding and Bonding," *Studies in Comparative Communism,* Vol. 18, 4 (Winter 1985), 207–226.

Wallace, Ian. *East Germany.* World Bibliographical Series, Vol. 77. Oxford: Clio Press, 1987.

White, Stephen. "Political Culture in Communist States. Some Problems of Theory and Method," *Comparative Politics,* Vol. 16, 3 (1984).

Ziegler, Charles E. "Issue Creation and Interest Groups in Soviet Environmental Policy. The Applicability of the State Corporatist Model," *Comparative Politics,* Vol. 18, 2 (1986), 171–192.

Zimmermann, Hartmut. "Power Distribution and opportunities for participation: aspects of the socio-political system of the GDR," in: K. von Beyme and H. Zimmermann, eds. *Policymaking in the German Democratic Republic.* Aldershot: Gower, 1984.

Sources on the Private Economy in Other Communist Countries

Alexeev, M., G. Grossman, N. Malyshev, A. Sayer, V. Treml, "Studies on the Soviet Second Economy," *Berkeley-Duke Occasional Papers on the Second Economy in the USSR,* Paper No. 11 (December 1987).

Antal, Endre. "Förderung der Privatinitiative in Ungarn 1981–1982," *Osteuropa,* No. 6 (1983), A313–A324.

Aslund, Anders. *Gorbachev's Struggle for Economic Reform.* Ithaca, N.Y.: Cornell University Press, 1989.

_____. *Private Enterprise in Eastern Europe. The Non-Agricultural Private Sector in Poland and the GDR, 1945-83.* New York: St. Martin's Press, 1985.

_____. "Private Enterprise in Poland, the GDR and Hungary," *Bidrag Till Öststatsforskningen,* Vol. 11, No. 1 (1983), 26-33.

Ball, Alan M. *Russia's Last Capitalists.* Berkeley: University of California Press, 1987.

Belkindas, Misha. "Privatization of the Soviet Economy under Gorbachev II: 1. The Campaign Against Unearned Income; 2. The Development of Private Cooperatives," *Berkeley-Duke Occasional Papers on the Second Economy in the USSR,* Paper No. 14 (April 1989).

Blough, Roger, Jennifer Muratore, and Steve Berk. "Gorbachev's Policy on the Private Sector: Two Steps Forward, One Step Backward," in U.S. Congress Joint Economic Committee, *Gorbachev's Economic Plans,* Vol. 2. Washington, D.C.: U.S. Government Printing Office, 1987, pp. 261-271.

Brezinski, Horst and Paul Petrescu. "The Second Economy in Romania—A Dynamic Sector," *Arbeitspapiere des Fachbereichs Wirtschaftswissenschaft,* Universität-Gesamthochschule Paderborn, Neue Folge No. 6 (1986).

Brezinski, H. "The Second Economy in the Soviet Union and its Implication for Economic Policy," in W. Gaertner, A. Wenig, eds., *The Economics of the Shadow Economy.* West Berlin: Springer, 1985.

Cichy, E. Ulrich. "Parallelwirtschaft und Wirtschaftsreform. Das unorthodoxe Experiment der Ungarischen Volksrepublik," *Osteuropa Wirtschaft,* Vol. 30, No. 4 (1985), 243-261.

Dallago, Bruno. "The Role of the Non-Socialized Sector in Hungary and Poland," in R. Weichhardt, ed., *The Economies of Eastern Europe under Gorbachev's Influence.* Brussels: NATO, 1988.

Elek, Peter S. "Symbiotical Coordination of the Plan and Private Sector in Eastern Europe and China since the 1970s," *East European Quarterly,* Vol. XXII, 4 (1989), 417-440.

Feldbrugge, E.J. "Government and Shadow Economy in the Soviet Union," *Soviet Studies,* Vol. 36, 4 (1984), 528-43.

Gabor, I.R. and T.D. Horvath, "Failure and Retreat in the Hungarian Private Small-Scale Industry (Data for a revision of government policy towards the small industry in the eighties)," *Acta Oeconomica,* Vol. 38, Nos. 1-2 (1987), 133-153.

Galasi, Peter. "Schattenwirtschaft, Staat und Beschäftigung in den sozialistischen Ländern Osteuropas—eine ordnungspolitische Betrachtung," in K. Gretschmann, R.G. Heinze and B. Mettelsiefen, eds., *Schattenwirtschaft. Wirtschafts- und sozialwissenschaftliche Aspekte, internationale Erfahrungen.* Göttingen: Vandenhoeck & Ruprecht, 1984, pp. 230-241.

Globokar, T. "Le secteur privé legal en Europe de l'Est," in T. Schreiber, ed., *L'U.R.S.S. et l'Europe de l'Est en 1983-1984* (Paris: La Documentation Francaise, 1984).

Gold, Thomas B. "Urban Private Business in China," *Studies in Comparative Communism,* Vol. XXII, 2/3 (1989), 187-201.

Grossman, Gregory. "Sub-Rosa Privatization and Marketization in the USSR," *Berkeley-Duke Occasional Papers on the Second Economy in the USSR*, Paper No. 17 (November 1989).

———. "The Second Economy: Boon or Bane for the Reform of the First Economy?" *Berkeley-Duke Occasional Papers on the Second Economy in the USSR*, Paper No. 11 (December 1987).

Hegedüs, A. and M. Markus. "The Small Entrepreneur and Socialism," *Acta Oeconomica*, Vol. 22, 3–4 (1979), 267–289.

Hershkovitz, Linda. "The Fruits of Ambivalence: China's Urban Individual Economy," *Pacific Affairs*, Vol. 58, 3 (1985), 427–450.

Hewitt, Ed A. *Reforming the Soviet Economy. Equality versus Efficiency*. Washington, D.C.: The Brookings Institution, 1988.

Kaschin, W.N. "Zur sozialökonomischen Natur der individuellen Erwerbstätigkeit in der UdSSR," *Wirtschaftswissenschaft*, Vol. 36, 4 (1988), 532–545.

Kästner, Hartmut. "Die Überwindung des Privatkapitals in der Großindustrie Sowjetrußlands bzw. der UdSSR (1917 bis Ende der 20er Jahre)," *Jahrbuch für Wirtschaftsgeschichte*, 3 (1984).

Kovacs, G.J. "Job-Creating Capacity of the Private Sector in Hungary Between 1981–1985," *Acta Oeconomica*, Vol. 37, 3–4 (1986), 341–354.

Kutas, J. "Innovation, Social Environment, Human Factors," *Acta Oeconomica*, Vol. 32, 1–2 (1984), 125–136.

Laky, T. "Small Enterprises in Hungary—Myth and Reality," *Acta Oeconomica*, Vol. 32, 1–2 (1984), 39–63.

Los, Maria. "The double economic structure of communist societies," *Contemporary Crises*, 11 (1987), 25–58.

Lukas, Zdenek. "Der Privatsektor in der tschechoslovakischen Landwirtschaft seit 1970," *Forschungsberichte*, The Vienna Institute for Comparative Economic Studies, No. 121 (Sept. 1986).

Mars, Gerald and Yochanan Altman. "The Cultural Bases of Soviet Georgia's Second Economy," *Soviet Studies*, Vol. 35, 4 (1983), pp. 546–60.

McIntyre, Robert J. "Economic Change in Eastern Europe: Other Paths to Socialist Construction," *Science and Society*, Vol. 53, 1 (1989), 5–28.

———. "The Small Enterprise and Agricultural Initiatives in Bulgaria: Institutional Invention without Reform," *Soviet Studies*, Vol. XL, 4 (1988), 602–615.

———. "Economic Changes without Conventional Reform: Small-scale Industrial and Service Development in Bulgaria and the GDR," in NATO Economics Directorate, *The Economies of Eastern Europe under Gorbachev's Influence*. Brussels: NATO, 1988.

Neuhauser, Kimberly and Clifford Gaddy, "Estimating the Size of the Private Service Economy in the USSR," *Berkeley-Duke Occasional Papers on the Second Economy in the USSR*, Paper No. 15 (July 1989).

Nyers, R. "Small Enterprise in Socialist Hungary," *Acta Oeconomica*, Vol. 25, 1–2 (1980), 147–162.

Oi, Jean C. "Market Reforms and Corruption in Rural China," *Studies in Comparative Communism*, Vol. XXII, 2/3 (1989), 221–233.

Okolicsanyi, Karoly. "HSWP Economic Committee Proposes Selling Off State-owned Enterprises and Land," *Radio Free Europe Research,* Vol. 14, 22 (2 June 1989), 31–36.

Oros, I. "Small-Scale Private Agricultural Production in Hungary," *Acta Oeconomica,* Vol. 32, 1–2 (1984), 65–90.

Pomorski, Stanislaw. "Privatization of the Soviet Economy under Gorbachev I: Notes on the 1986 Law on Individual Enterprise," *Berkeley-Duke Occasional Papers on the Second Economy in the USSR,* Paper No. 13 (October 1988).

Roesler, Jörg. "Die Rolle der Leitung und Planung bei der Zurückdrängung des privatkapitalistischen Sektors in der Industrie der Sowjetunion und einiger europäischer Volksdemokratien (zwanziger und vierziger Jahre)", *Jahrbuch für Geschichte der sozialistischen Länder Europas,* Vol. 22, 1 (1978), 87–95.

Ronnas, Per. "The Role of the 'Second Economy' as a Source of Supplementary Income to Rural Communities in Romania: A Case Study," *Bidrag Till Öststatsforskningen,* Vol. 11, 1 (1983), 34–43.

Rostowski, Jacek. "The Decay of Socialism and the Growth of Private Enterprise in Poland," *Soviet Studies,* Vol. XLI, 2 (April 1989), 194–214.

Roucek, Libor. "Private Enterprise in Soviet Political Debates," *Soviet Studies,* Vol. XL, 1 (1988), 46–63.

Sampson, Stephen L. "The Second Economy of the Soviet Union and Eastern Europe," *Annals of the American Academy of Political and Social Science,* 493 (Sept. 1987), 120–136.

———. "Rich Families and Poor Collectives: An Anthropological Approach to Romania's 'Second Economy'," *Bidrag Till Öststatsforskningen,* Vol. 11, No. 1 (1983), 44–77.

Schöpflin, G. "Corruption/Informalism, Irregularity in Eastern Europe: A Political Analysis," *Südosteuropa,* Vol. 33, 7/8, 1984.

Schroeder, Gertrude E. "Property Rights Issues in Economic Reforms in Socialist Countries," *Studies in Comparative Communism,* Vol. XXI, 2 (1988), 175–188.

Solinger, Dorothy J. "Urban Reform and Relational Contracting in Post-Mao China: An Interpretation of the Transition from Plan to Market," *Studies in Comparative Communism,* Vol. XXII, 2/3 (1989), 171–185.

Squires Meaney, Connie. "Market Reform in Leninist Systems: Some Trends in the Distribution of Power, Status, and Money in Urban China," *Studies in Comparative Communism,* Vol. XXII, 2/3 (1989), 203–220.

Stark, David. "Coexisting Forms in Hungary's Emerging Mixed Economy," in Victor Nee and David Stark, eds., *Remaking the Economic Institutions of Socialism: China and Eastern Europe.* Stanford: Stanford University Press, 1989, pp. 137–168.

Stefanowski, Roman. "Problems with Privatization of Industry," *Radio Free Europe Research,* Vol. 14, 37 (15 September 1989), 25–27.

Tomaszewski, Jerzy. "Die Nationalisierung in den europäischen sozialistischen Ländern—Voraussetzungen und Realisierung," in *Inhaltliche und methodologische Problem einer vergleichenden Wirtschaftsgeschichte des Sozialismus.* Berlin: Humboldt-Universität, 1978, pp. 86–102.

Treml, Vladimir G. "Income from Private Services Recognized by Official Soviet Statistics," *Berkeley-Duke Occasional Papers on the Second Economy in the USSR,* Paper No. 11 (December 1987).

Wädekin, Karl-Eugen. "Private Agriculture in Socialist Countries: Implications for the USSR," *Berkeley-Duke Occasional Papers on the Second Economy,* Paper No. 10 (April 1987).

_____ . *Agrarian Policies in Communist Europe.* The Hague/London: Allanheld, Osmun, 1982.

Index